Moses Hazen and the Canadian Refugees in the American Revolution

A NEW YORK STATE STUDY

Published for the New York State
American Revolution Bicentennial Commission

Moses Hazen
and the Canadian Refugees
in the
American Revolution

ALLAN S. EVEREST

SYRACUSE UNIVERSITY PRESS
1976

Copyright © 1976 by Syracuse University Press
Syracuse, New York 13210

All Rights Reserved

First Edition

Library of Congress Cataloging in Publication Data

Everest, Allan Seymour.
    Moses Hazen and the Canadian refugees in the American
Revolution.

    (A New York State study)
    "Published for the New York State American Revolu-
tion Bicentennial Commission."
    Bibliography: p.
    Includes index.
    1. United States—History—Revolution, 1775–1783—
Canadian participation.   2.   Hazen, Moses, 1733–1803.
3.   United States.   Army.   Continental Army—Biography.
4.   Generals—United States—Biography.   5.   United
States—History—Revolution, 1775–1783—Refugees.

I.   New York State American Revolution Bicentennial Com-
mission.   II.   Title.
E269.C27E9   973.3'46'0924   76–54260
ISBN 0–8156–0129–8

Manufactured in the United States of America

Contents

Foreword   vii
Preface   ix
I   The Start of a Military Career   1
II   Between the Wars   15
III   The Coming of the Revolution   26
IV   The American Revolution, 1776–1778   46
V   The American Revolution, 1779–1781   66
VI   Between War and Peace, 1781–1783   96
VII   The Canadians after the War   113
VIII   Dreams and Nightmares   142
Afterword   171
Appendix: Locations of the Canadian Regiment
During the War   175
Notes   177
Bibliography   197
Index   205

Maps

The Maritimes in the French and Indian War   7
Canada in 1775–1776   35
The Coos Country   72
Canadian and Nova Scotia Refugee Tract   131

Allan S. Everest, Professor of History at the State University College at Plattsburgh, New York, received his Ph.D. from Columbia University. He has taught summer courses for the University of Vermont at the Shelburne Museum and offered joint courses with Plattsburgh and Fort Ticonderoga. He has also held visiting positions at the College of Education in Hull, England, and the Department of American Studies at the University of Hull. Professor Everest's research for this volume has been aided by State University grants and a grant from the New York State Council on the Arts.

Foreword

WHEN THIRTEEN of Great Britain's mainland colonies declared for independence in 1776, the newest British colony in North America—Canada—decided against joining the revolt. But some Canadians refused to accept the decision of the majority in Canada to stay out of the fight for American independence. A large group of these people left their homes and crossed the border to be organized into military units by Moses Hazen. Led by Hazen, who was commissioned a general in the Continental army, these Canadian soldiers fought in many engagements throughout the war. After independence was achieved, Hazen led his followers to the northern reaches of New York to settle on land grants near the border of the country they had left years before. The story of these Canadians who came south to support the cause of American independence thus belongs both to New York and to the people of the United States at large.

This is another in a series of cooperatively produced books which reflect new research and provide new insights into the era of the American Revolution and New York's place in it. While planning its program of publications for the bicentennial commemoration, the New York State American Revolution Bicentennial Commission saw the need to support the work of historians who probe the lessons of the past, and of the educational presses which publish the results of those efforts. It is also a pleasure to help in the production of a book which will have value not only for Americans but for Canadians as well. We hope that this book about North Americans who lived through a period of great turmoil and conflict will help in some small way to rededicate the bonds of friendship and international coopera-

tion which have long characterized the relations between Canada and
the United States.

> John H. G. Pell, *Chairman*
> New York State
> American Revolution
> Bicentennial Commission

Preface

This book is an attempt to offer belated recognition of those residents of Quebec and Nova Scotia who, for a variety of reasons, became refugees in the United States during the American Revolution. Whether motivated by the expectation of profit and adventure, anticipation of life in a freer society, or the desire to help drive the British out of Canada, hundreds of them chose what they thought was temporary exile from their homeland.

The refugees from Quebec were largely French, but they were joined by a significant number of Americans who had gone north to seek, and often to make, their fortunes after the conquest of 1763—Moses Hazen, Edward Antill, James Livingston, Udny Hay, Thomas Walker, and others. From Nova Scotia the refugees were drawn from those transplanted New Englanders who migrated during the 1750s and 1760s but who subsequently caught some of the revolutionary fever that infected Boston in the 1770s. Whoever they were and wherever they came from, they left behind them their property and livelihood, their friends and, for many, their religion.

Most of the men joined the American army, while their families led a long, destitute existence, chiefly in the refugee camps of New York State. The great majority hoped that when the British were driven from Canada they could return to their own country, and they were the most enthusiastic and sometimes troublesome advocates of every new project for an invasion northward.

Although many of the refugees drifted back to Quebec or Nova Scotia after the war and picked up the threads of their prewar life, many more chose to remain permanently in exile. Displaced persons

usually present a tragic aspect, and those of the American Revolution
are no exception. Many sustained battle wounds or suffered physical
breakdowns and the collapse of their prewar standards of living as a
result of their war and postwar experiences. A notable example is
Moses Hazen, an American who had established thriving enterprises
in Canada.

The career of Moses Hazen was so intertwined with the lives
and fortunes of the refugees that it is impossible to tell their story
without including his. And so this book becomes partly a biography
of Hazen and his close associates, from which emerges a stormy and
fascinating character. These pages also give rise to a renewed admira-
tion for the patience and integrity of George Washington in his deal-
ings with the refugees and their quarrelsome champion, Moses Hazen.

The fact that there were refugees *into* the United States is
usually forgotten because the focus of attention has been upon the
American Loyalists who fled the country during and after the Revolution. The American refugees have always received a great deal of
attention, traditionally portrayed as traitors to a great cause. Only
recently have they begun to receive the sympathetic study they deserve. Instead of being branded as traitors, they are being appreciated
for the idealism of their convictions. Canadians are likewise beginning to display more pride than was formerly the case in the lives of
their exiles. In numbers the Canadians were much fewer than the
American refugees, which is one reason why the Canadians have been
generally overlooked. Another is the fact that the peace treaty at the
end of the Revolution made no mention of them although it consid-
erately tried to make possible the return of the American refugees to
their native country. Forgotten or otherwise, the refugees created a
two-way street, and this study deals with the incoming group.

The materials for this study were widely scattered and have
occasioned numerous trips of exploration. My partner on these expeditions has been my wife, Elsie Lewis Everest, who has shared the
excitement of discovery and the fitting of bits and pieces together into
a credible pattern. We found help in the following institutions, where
the staffs were invariably interested and helpful in our pursuit: the
British Museum in London, the Public Archives of Canada in Ottawa,
the New Brunswick Museum in St. John, the National Archives and
the Library of Congress in Washington, the New York State Library
in Albany, the Massachusetts Historical Society in Boston, the Essex
Institute in Salem, the American Antiquarian Society in Worcester,
the New Hampshire State Library in Concord, the Vermont State

Library in Montpelier, the Clements Library at the University of Michigan, and the Library of the College of State University in Plattsburgh. Aside from the latter's important regional collection, its staff has patiently borrowed numerous materials from other institutions.

The most unexpected discovery was the Bailey Collection of manuscripts dealing with northern New York. The Bailey family of Burnt Hills, New York, has preserved a large collection of family papers, without which this book would have been seriously incomplete. Mr. Claude Bailey III generously loaned the entire collection while work was in progress, and has since placed it in a public repository.

Plattsburgh, New York   Allan S. Everest
Spring 1976

Moses Hazen and the Canadian Refugees in the
American Revolution

I

The Start of a Military Career

IN THE 1630S KING CHARLES I was trying to rule England without Parliament, and his Archbishop of Canterbury was prosecuting all who refused to conform to the practices and creeds of the Church of England. As a result, during the short span of two decades some 50,000 Englishmen took part in the Great Migration to America.

Among the emigrants were all the families, about twenty, of the parish of Rowley, East Yorkshire. This was a small village a few miles from Cottingham, the home of the Grant family. When Archbishop Laud ordered the Book of Sports read from every pulpit, the pastor at Rowley refused. The new regulations he would have been obliged to publicize permitted games on Sunday, and to the Puritanical soul of the Reverend Ezekiel Rogers this was unthinkable. Many years later his will read: "For refusing to read that accursed book that allowed sports on God's holy Sabbath, or Lord's day, I was suspended, and, by it and other sad signs of the times, driven, with many of my hearers, into New England." In 1638 he sailed for America, joined by his whole parish. Rowley became and still remains a ghost town. The emigrants, after a first winter in Salem, where they were augmented to about sixty families, founded a new Rowley in Essex County, Massachusetts.[1]

With this little band went Thomas and Jane Grant and their four children. One of them, Hannah, was only seven years old but she was destined to provide the female ancestry of the Hazen family in America. For the settlement of Rowley the Rogers Company was formed which purchased the land for £800. The purchase money was contributed by all those able to pay. In laying out house lots, all who had no money to invest obtained one and a half acres, while those who paid were given lots in proportion to the amount they subscribed. That the Grants were not affluent is seen in the survey of 1643, when the Widow Grant owned the minimum acre and a half.

The earliest English traces of the Hazen family appear in the county of Northumberland. A township near Alnwick is still known as Hazon. In the early records the family name was written Heisende and philologists believe it derived from Hegges ende (softened into Heies Ende), meaning "end of the hedge." The name seems to have worked southward through Yorkshire and into Lincolnshire. In the late 14th century it had become Haysand or Hayzaund. Later variations in its southward migration were Hasande, Hassand, Hasson, and Hassen.[2]

Edward Hassen was baptized at Cadney, Lincolnshire, in 1614. His first wife was named Elizabeth, but when and where he married her is not clear. He found his way to Rowley, Massachusetts, in the mid-1640s and is first mentioned as the owner of land in a survey of about 1647. In subsequent records he is shown to have acquired cows, oxen, and more land. In September 1649 Elizabeth died and in the following March he married Hannah Grant and by her had eleven children. Their ninth child, Richard (born 1669), married Mary Peabody and they also had eleven children. Richard settled at Haverhill, twenty miles northeast of the family homestead. There, on the Merrimack River, a prosperous settlement was developing.[3]

One of the sons of Richard was Moses (born 1701) who married Abigail White and thus brought the White connection into the family. Moses lived and prospered in Haverhill. In 1731 he and Joseph Whittier, grandfather of the poet, John Greenleaf Whittier, petitioned for the right to build a wharf on the Merrimack. For £50 they obtained the privilege provided they kept the two bridges near them in repair "forever," and built a proper wharf at least 100 feet wide from the highway to low-water mark. That Moses was well established is suggested by his ownership of two slaves in the 1750s. In addition to his local enterprises he and his brother William were original proprietors of Pennycook (Concord), New Hampshire.[4]

Moses fathered six children, all of them destined to pioneer in new lands or professions. Abigail married Moses Mooers, and their son Benjamin plays an important part in this book. John obtained the charter for Haverhill, New Hampshire, and settled there. The third child of Moses was also named Moses, with whom this account is chiefly concerned.

Then came Anna, who married Robert Peaslee and pioneered in the settlement of Gilmanton, New Hampshire. William was the fifth child of Moses. He established business connections between Newburyport and St. John, New Brunswick, and moved there before the Revolution. He was joined by his nephew John, son of John of Haverhill. William had sixteen children and John had twelve. Between them they established the Canadian branch of the Hazen family.

The third child of this remarkable family was Moses, Junior, who was born in 1733. As a young man he was independent of his family, having been apprenticed as a tanner, his profession at the time of the French and Indian War. But the outbreak of the war lured him away, and he chose a career that was to remain with him intermittently for the rest of his life.

The war of which he became a part had opened inauspiciously. General Edward Braddock had been defeated and killed in his attempt to take Fort Duquesne in 1755. In the same year Governor William Shirley of Massachusetts failed to take Fort Niagara, and General William Johnson also fell short of capturing Crown Point, his assignment, although he fought a successful battle for possession of the lower end of Lake George.

There is a contradiction in the records concerning Hazen's first enlistment. Francis Parkman maintained that he assisted in the capture of Fort Beauséjour, Nova Scotia, in 1755, whereas the family biographer asserts that his first military service was on the Lakes in 1756. That Colonel Monckton captured the fort in that year is indisputable, and it was followed by the removal from the province of all the Acadians (French settlers) who could be rounded up. Loescher documents the fact that Hazen was also there as a lieutenant in a Massachusetts Provincial Regiment. Nothing is known of his activities except Parkman's brief account of his boldly replacing siege cannon that had been knocked out by enemy fire.[5]

He must have returned home for the winter because he heeded the call for volunteers in the spring of 1756. Colonel Richard Saltonstall raised a provincial regiment for an expedition to the scene of expected action on Lake George. Captain John Hazen, brother of Moses, led one company and was in service through the reduction of Fort Carillon (Ticonderoga) and Fort St. Frédèric in 1759. Captain Edmond Mooers, cordwainer and uncle of Moses, led another. His company needed only fifty men but ninety-five volunteered for action. From them the required number was selected and among them was Moses Hazen, commissioned a lieutenant in his uncle's company.

What these enthusiastic volunteers did not know was that 1756 was not going to offer them the military excitement of the previous year. During the winter the French had started building a strong fortress at Ticonderoga which occupied their energies during the following season. The English were also unprepared to launch any offensive action, so the Massachusetts volunteers spent their time repairing forts and making scouting expeditions. The muster roll at Fort Edward in July included the names of both Mooers and Hazen, still listed as a tanner.

He was also at Fort William Henry in October. He seems to have been with Lieutenant Samuel Kennedy on his famous expedition to the Richelieu, and Parkman adds him to a short list of officers who won distinction in this partisan warfare. It is likely that Hazen met and admired Captain Robert Rogers, who was already proving the deadly effectiveness of guerilla fighting in this war. Evidence of their contact appeared later when Rogers recommended him as an officer in a new Ranger company.[6]

The home town of Haverhill was generous to its servicemen: "This may certify that the Persons Belonging to this Town whose names are as follows were in the Service on the Expedition for Crown Point and were not rated in the Year of 1756." The list included Captain Mooers and Lieutenant Hazen. The poll tax was nine shillings, and the town lost £27 12s 11d. However the company was back home for the winter. In the spring of 1757 Hazen was on the "alarm list," which included all men between the ages of sixteen and sixty, who were exempt from regular military duty. They could be called for duty in their own town during extraordinary emergencies. Apparently his year of voluntary service in 1756 had put him on the exempt list the following year.[7]

During 1757 Moses was engaged in shipping provisions and supplies to Halifax for the British build-up before an attack on Louisbourg. He seems to have been his brother's agent in Halifax. From there he urged William to send livestock, the proceeds of which could be "profitably invested" in the plentiful, cheap English goods there. Already alert to the main chance, he was nevertheless back in Massachusetts for the winter, just in time to be intrigued by a new call to military duty. If it was action he wanted, 1758 held plenty of it in store.[8]

It is apparent that Moses, at twenty-four years of age, had discovered two of the three occupations that would preoccupy him for the rest of his life—soldiering and commerce. Only the acquiring of land remained in the future, and even that was to become an obsession within the next half decade. There is no evidence that he ever again engaged personally in the business of tanning, although he later did establish a tannery on his estate in Canada.

Meanwhile, at Fort Edward, Robert Rogers and his Rangers, temporarily threatened with reduction, obtained a new lease on life. Prime Minister William Pitt directed that 600 Rangers be at Halifax for the summer campaign against Louisbourg. This resulted in the formation of six new companies of Rangers. One company under Captain Joseph Gorham was already on its way to Halifax. So five 100-man companies would be added in order to meet Pitt's requirements. Rogers was to remain the titular commander of all companies, wherever they served, and in April he was promoted to major. He himself was to remain at Fort Edward. A standardized uniform was agreed on, to be paid for by deductions from the men's pay. The uniform of an officer included a green jacket lined with green, a black hat with white lace bindings, buckskin breeches and leggings.[9]

Rogers proposed the names of the officers; the Earl of Loudon, commander-in-chief, shuffled the subalterns but approved the recommended captains. They were: John McCurdy, who had been Rogers' first lieutenant and had been with him since he organized his group in 1755; his brother James Rogers, Jonathan Brewer, William Stark, and Moses Brewer. Moses Hazen was recommended as a first lieutenant, but was commissioned a second lieutenant. He refused the appointment on the grounds that it failed to recognize his previous service. When a later vacancy occurred, he was made first lieutenant in McCurdy's company on April 7.[10]

Back in Albany by late January of 1758, Rogers dispatched his new captains to recruit in New England. The enlistees began to arrive at Rogers' Island for an Albany rendezvous in March. However, the orders were changed and all companies were redirected to Boston. Each of them arrived with more than 100 men, although Moses Brewer was late, thereby holding up embarkation. In the meantime, provincial recruiters tried to entice Rangers with the offer of higher bounty and pay. Rangers were being paid $10 in bounty and told to bring their own clothes, arms, and blankets. In each company one captain was paid ten shillings sterling a day; two lieutenants, four shillings, eightpence sterling; four sergeants four shillings; and 100 privates two shillings, sixpence, the sergeants and privates in New York currency. Officers could advance the cost of the uniform and later deduct it from a soldier's pay.[11]

Since Massachusetts recruiters were able to offer higher financial inducements, Brigadier Charles Lawrence, who was in charge of dispatching, sought some way to hasten the Rangers' departure. Not wanting to wait for a regular convoy, he chartered the provincial vessel *King George* to accompany the transports. The five companies were hurriedly put on board and they sailed on April 2, arriving in Halifax Harbor on the 7th. To avoid a smallpox epidemic in Halifax, the troops were housed across the bay in Dartmouth, where they trained until late May. There, four of the companies plus Gorham's Rangers and 500 Highlanders and Light Infantrymen were organized into a provisional battalion under Captain George Scott of the Fortieth Regiment. Scott led the unit at the landing on Cape Breton, but during the siege and subsequent actions, it was divided up for service on various detached commands. It supplemented the British forces at Louisbourg by 499 rank-and-file Rangers, together with their 49 commissioned and noncommissioned officers.[12]

The Rangers sailed for Louisbourg on May 28 and went ashore on June 8. The landing at Freshwater Cove was a desperate enterprise against stoutly defended shores, and it appeared that General James Wolfe's first effort would fail. But Scott with his battalion saved the day by being the first to land and force an enemy retreat. Wolfe, who had previously formed a low opinion of the Rangers, revised his estimate upward and made good use of them in the next twelve months. They were in the thick of the siege, serving on outpost and raids, taking (and scalping) prisoners, especially Indians, and closing in on Louisbourg. The great fortress capitulated on July 26.

The fall of Louisbourg did not complete the dispersal of the bands of Acadians who roamed the woods or had settlements throughout Nova Scotia, which then included New Brunswick. Several mopping-up operations were consequently conducted. One of them was Colonel Robert Monckton's attack upon Fort St. John at the mouth of the river of the same name. Part of his force included McCurdy's, Brewer's, Stark's, and Gorham's Ranger Companies. The fort was once Boishébert's headquarters but was now abandoned. After its capture the British renamed it Fort Frederic. Raids in the neighborhood netted numerous prisoners and two schooners. In mid-November the army was assigned winter quarters. Gorham's went to Lunenburg, Nova Scotia, Brewer's and Stark's remained to help McCurdy cut wood for the winter, and then embarked for Halifax. McCurdy's remained to man Fort Frederic and to carry out further raids.

In January 1759 McCurdy led his men north on snowshoes to

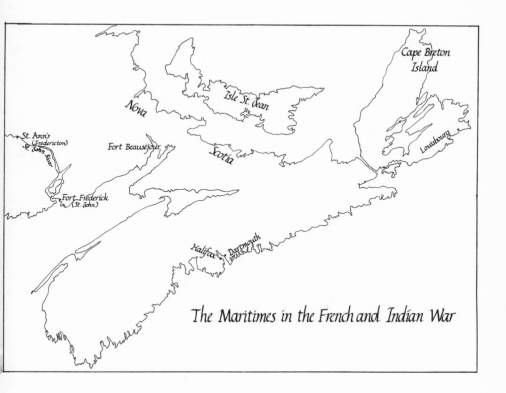

The Maritimes in the French and Indian War

demolish additional French settlements. On their first night out, a birch tree cut by one of his own men fell on the captain and killed him. Lieutenant Hazen succeeded to the command of the company. In February he led a party upriver to St. Anne (Fredericton). He burned the large settlement on the 28th—"147 dwelling houses, two mass-houses, besides all their barns, stables, granaries, etc." The inhabitants had left for Quebec or taken to the woods. But thirty or forty of them organized and forced Hazen to make a hasty retreat. During his return trip he found a small settlement (Grimross) with cattle, horses, and hogs, which he destroyed. He pursued the inhabitants into the woods, killed and scalped six men and brought in four others together with two women and three children. He set a house on fire, threw the cattle into the flames, and departed with his prisoners. By reversing his snowshoes to confuse his pursuers and by making forced marches, he was back in Fort Frederic on March 5 after an absence of sixteen days and a winter trek of 150 miles.[13]

On the recommendation of Major Scott, Commander in Chief General Jeffrey Amherst confirmed the appointment of Hazen to lead McCurdy's company, together with a promotion to captain. However, he later wrote Governor Charles Lawrence of Nova Scotia: "Major Morris sent me the particulars of the scouting party and I gave a commission of Captain to Lieutenant Hazen as I thought he deserved it. I am sorry to say what I have since heard of that affair has sullied his merit with me as I shall always disapprove of killing women and helpless children. Poor McCurdy is a loss he was a good man in his post."[14]

The war against the French and Indians was a brutal affair whether fought on Lake George or in Nova Scotia, and the Rangers in both places were schooled to be ruthless. Amherst was not the only officer who felt that Hazen's raid had exceeded the bounds of even that kind of warfare. But the Reverend W. O. Raymond attempted to exonerate him: "It may well be doubted whether this tragedy of the wilderness was enacted in Lieutenant Hazen's presence or with his consent. It was probably an exemplification of the words of Captain Murray, written at the time of the Expulsion of the Acadians: 'Our soldiers, you know, hate them, and if they can find an occasion to kill them, they will.'" However, it is unlikely that the leader of a small scouting party did not know what was going on, particularly with Hazen's background of partisan warfare and the prolonged siege of Louisbourg.[15]

Captain Hazen remained with his company at Fort Frederic during the rest of the winter and early spring. In May his and three of the other Ranger companies joined the army at Louisbourg. From there they embarked for Quebec early in the following month. The embarkation return of June 5, 1759, showed that Hazen's company contained three officers and eighty-six NCO's and Rangers. They were a small but vital part of Wolfe's grand design to capture Quebec City. In the coming campaign Loescher finds that the two most popular Ranger captains were James Rogers and Moses Hazen, with the latter having the edge and, as Major Scott reported to Amherst, he "met with universal approbation, both on account of his conduct as well as his gallantry."[16]

The strategy of the campaign is not difficult to retrace today, although it lacked coherence to Wolfe, who sometimes despaired of taking Quebec that season. His 9,000-man army landed on the Isle of

Orleans on June 27 and set up its tents. From then until September 13 Quebec held out, but in the end it was in British hands and both the French and British commanders, Montcalm and Wolfe, were dead. At the start, Hazen's company was given the humiliating assignment of herding the army's cattle on the island, and they became known as the "Cowboys." But as soon as the army began to move, all of the Rangers were assigned more active duties. Wolfe's first venture was to occupy Point Lévis, opposite Quebec, from which point the city could be bombarded. He then occupied the east bank of the Montmorency River, seeking a way to attack the city from the east. Finding that approach impossible he hit upon the difficult stratagem of landing at Wolfe's Cove, west of Quebec, climbing the cliffs, and approaching the city across the Plains of Abraham.

As the summer wore on and the situation grew desperate, the importance of raids in the surrounding countryside became more apparent, and in these the Rangers performed their most valuable services. Before the fall of Quebec they served in more than twenty different scouts and actions. The taking of prisoners (and scalps), the destruction of villages and the capture of food supplies helped the British while at the same time denying Quebec any assistance from its hinterland. Prisoners were useful for the information they could give, while scalping, although supposedly limited to Indians and Canadians disguised as Indians, sometimes got out of hand.

One of the worst atrocities in which some of Hazen's men may have been involved occurred at St. Joachim, on the south shore of the St. Lawrence. After a heavy skirmish, the French prisoners were ordered shot in cold blood by the commander of the detachment, Captain Alexander Montgomery. The priest of St. Joachim, Robineau de Portneuf, with thirty parishioners, occupied a stone house in a nearby parish and held off the English for some time. They were finally drawn out, ambushed, and killed; since they were disguised as Indians, the Rangers scalped them all.[17]

Not all the engagements were as savage as this, but the Robert Rogers example of partisan warfare had been transplanted to a new war zone. Indeed, Hazen became known as his Canadian counterpart. He was recognized for his bravery and his boldness in volunteering for one expedition after another. He soon became highly regarded by Wolfe, who frequently referred to him in his journal, and personally dispatched him on intelligence-gathering missions. One of Hazen's men, Daniel Lane, gives some insight in his journal into the almost daily expeditions of his company:

July 24th, this day Captain Hazzen march'd from this Place with
50 men in order to get Prisoners or Scalps and the same day we
returned, and brought 8 with us, and one of our men got wounded.
26th . . . The Same day Captn. Hazzen took 6 Prisoners.
July 31st. Anstruthers Regimt. Coll: How with the Light Infantry and Captn. Hazzens Compy of Rangers march'd up Montmorency River, About one Mile, the Enemy gave us one or two fires
and Run, but doing us no hurt we returned to Camp.[18]

Hazen was on a scouting expedition down the St. Lawrence at
the time of the capitulation. However, he was back in time to take
part in the sharp engagements which followed. The French army had
been allowed to escape, and the Rangers were assigned to patrol the
roads to Ste. Foy and Sillery to guard against their return. A large
body of Rangers was sent out to cut wood for the Quebec garrison.
For that duty they received one gill of rum per day and five shillings
above their regular pay for every cord of wood they could cut and
put aboard their bateaux.

In the second week of October all but Hazen's company, plus
some of his own men whose time had expired, embarked for Boston.
Twenty-five men from Rogers', Brewer's, and Stark's companies were
transferred to Hazen's, giving him a command of 134 rank and file
for the winter. The other Rangers received discharges in Boston in
November.

Meanwhile, Brigadier Murray had established British outposts
at Ste. Foy and Old Lorette. French war parties lurked around them,
ready to attack the unwary and to drive off their cattle. Partisan warfare was on the increase again. Early in April 1760, Hazen was stationed at a house near the Lorette post. Hearing that a French force
was on its way to attack him, he left fourteen Rangers in the house
and started for Lorette to get reinforcements. Meeting a body of the
enemy, he ordered his troops back to the house but they objected,
saying that they "felt spry" and wanted to show the regulars that
they in their green coats could fight as well as their enemy in red
coats. Therefore, they charged their opponents and put them to flight,
but were immediately fired upon by another force between them and
the house. They attacked and routed them.

But the two French forces united and decided to let Hazen go
his way while they attacked the house. Hearing the firing, Hazen
turned and came upon the attackers from the rear, while the Rangers
in the house sallied forth with guns ablaze. The French were driven

off and pursued for two miles, resulting in the killing of six and the capture of seven of them. Knox praised the event in his Journal by recording what Hazen's men said: " 'Sir, lead us on, and rely upon us; the regulars have displayed prodigies of valour this winter on many occasions; we will fight and chace the enemy, as they have done, or die'.—Here is a notable instance of emulation and bravery in our simply honest New-England-Men, who, feeling *quite bold* or *spry*,— that morning (according to their own phrase) were, by their Captain's report, unanimous for fighting." [19]

A few weeks later a much larger engagement took place. The French commander, the Chevalier de Lévis, had brought his entire force up to Ste. Foy, barely on the outskirts of Quebec. Murray, with fewer men but a better position and superior artillery, left his fixed position in order to attack. By doing so he lost his chief advantage and his cannon were mired in mud and melting snow. The British suffered 1,000 casualties, more than a third of their entire force, and retreated into Quebec to make desperate preparations for a siege.

Hazen's company was in the thick of the fighting and he himself was badly wounded in the thigh. Making his way to the gate on the arm of his servant, he saw at a distance a French officer leading a detachment across an open field. Demanding his rifle, he sat on the ground, took careful aim, and brought down his man. Upon being congratulated for his extraordinary marksmanship, he commented: "A chance shot may kill the devil." With the help of his servant he reached the town, where he slowly recovered from his wound.[20]

Both the British and the French forces, unable to dislodge each other without help, anxiously watched the river for reinforcements as the ice went out in the spring. Both sides had requested help, but it was the British ships that arrived first. They were in sufficient strength to destroy the French vessels, with all their supplies and equipment. Lévis had no choice but to raise the siege and retreat toward Montreal.

Most of Murray's army, 2,400 strong including the Rangers, embarked for Montreal on July 15. Hazen was still convalescing from his wound and was forced to remain in the hospital at Quebec. Thus he missed the second great capitulation when Montreal surrendered. By prior arrangement, Murray's force was to link up at Montreal with Haviland's 3,400 from Lake Champlain and Amherst's 10,000 from Lake Ontario. Bypassing Three Rivers, Murray arrived at the rendezvous first and Haviland came next after having subdued the Richelieu Valley. Amherst arrived early in September after destroying several strongpoints en route and then riding the dangerous rapids of the St.

Lawrence. The three armies converged upon the little city of Montreal, whose defense had been left to the 2,200 regulars and 200 colony troops, the Canadian militia having gone home. The city was surrendered on September 8 and with it the French hopes for holding any of Canada.

Four Ranger companies had been kept on service during the winter. Major Rogers' and one other were at Crown Point and were a part of Haviland's expedition. Waite's was at Fort Brewerton on Lake Oneida and joined Amherst's host, while Hazen's was with Murray. All of them arrived at Montreal in 1760. The officers of the disbanded companies had been kept on full pay during the winter until Amherst decided how many Rangers he would need for the Montreal and subsequent campaigns. Ultimately he ordered the raising of four new companies.

Within four days of the capitulation at Montreal Major Rogers received orders to go and receive the surrender of the French posts westward from Detroit. He embarked on September 13, taking with him Waite's company and Jonathan Brewer in command of Hazen's old company, a force of 198 men. On the side Rogers contrived to engage in the fur and supply business on this expedition, through Rogers and Company which he formed at Niagara. But he also made friends with Pontiac and received the surrender of Detroit and other posts. He sent most of his men, including Hazen's, back to Fort Niagara for the winter. In the spring of 1761 they marched to Albany and New York, where those who wished it were mustered out of the service. Others volunteered for duty under Lord Rollo in the West Indies.

Captain Amos Ogden recruited for this campaign among members of Hazen's old company. When Hazen learned this fact, he petitioned Amherst for permission to maintain and recruit his own company. He apparently yearned for the kind of action the Rangers had formerly given him. He was refused and was thus finally severed from any connection with the Rangers who had filled such an exciting chapter of his life.[21]

In the spring of 1761 Hazen and Rogers met, probably for the first time since 1756. It is interesting to speculate what life would have been like in either war or peace if these two buccaneers had been in constant contact. Both were intrepid, sometimes savage, warriors and both had an eye on all the commercial possibilities of a situation. In this particular meeting, they and others formed a land company called "Major Rogers & Associates." In March they petitioned Cadwallader Colden, president of the New York Council and provincial commander in chief, for 25,000 acres of vacant land above Fort Edward, west of the Hudson River. Hazen's associates, aside from Rogers, were colonial leaders involved in other land deals at the time, including Alexander Colden and Goldsbrow Banyer, secretary of the province. They first needed a permit to conclude purchases with the Indian proprietors of the land, so as to be able to obtain His Majesty's patent for it.

The petition was read in Council on May 27 and a license to purchase issued the same day. On June 16 a surveyor for the company visited Sir William Johnson and acquainted him with its intentions. Johnson sent for the Mohawk chiefs, who arrived next day and upon hearing of the proposal they protested that they owned everything west of the Hudson, Lake George, and Lake Champlain, except for what had already been sold. Thereupon Johnson urged Colden to block the transaction "to his Majesty and the Publick good." This ended the project, for without a valid purchase from the Indians a patent was impossible to obtain.[22]

In August 1761 General Murray penned a testimonial, at the command of Acting Governor Cramahé, in fulsome praise of Hazen's war record: "During all that Severe Winter, Capt. Hazzen was from the Circumstances of Affairs ever upon Duty, he was allways Ready and willing to go upon Every Service Even the most hazardous on the least Notice. . . . he Discovered so much still Bravery and good Conduct as would Justly Entitle him to Every military Reward he Could ask or Demand, I wish I could procure him Such a one as I think he Deserves."[23]

His fighting qualities had already been officially recognized. On February 21, 1761, he had been allowed to purchase a lieutenant's commission in the Forty-fourth Regiment. Commissions in the British army were normally purchased at a considerable price, and Hazen paid 800 guineas sterling ($3,600 in 1790 dollars). He thus made a very large investment in his career, partly for prestige but partly for the pension he would get upon retirement. He replaced another officer who transferred, but his appointment was noteworthy because in the spring of 1761 most of the British army was being reduced, following the fall of Montreal. His commissioning suggests that the army was quite happy to take his money, but also willing to assure him a life pension, probably after only a short service.[24]

The Forty-fourth or Essex Regiment was established in 1741 as the Fifty-fifth and renumbered in 1748. Its first years were spent

in the British Isles, but in 1755 it was sent to North America to join
Braddock's expedition against Fort Duquesne. It suffered heavy casualties there as elsewhere in its campaigns on Lake George and Lake
Ontario. When Hazen joined the regiment in 1761, it was therefore a
battle-scarred and highly regarded outfit. Unfortunately for him, perhaps, the war was over and the regiment was assigned to garrison
duties largely in the Montreal area. So when it was reduced to nine
companies in 1763, Hazen chose a retirement which promised him
half pay for life. He was carried in this status on British records until
1781. That this was the result of inefficient bookkeeping is likely,
because there is no evidence of Hazen's collecting his half pay during
the Revolution. The Forty-fourth sailed for home in 1765 but was back
in Boston ten years later, and it fought throughout the Revolution.[25]

There can be no doubt that Hazen's career as a Ranger was
one of the high points of his life and there is every indication that
he reveled in it. It brought out leadership qualities, the ability to gain
the loyalty of his men, and the satisfaction of a restless surge within
him. Whether he felt impelled to prove himself repeatedly cannot be
known. There are hints that his restlessness was a part of his makeup,
and that he was never happy except in action. A combative man, he
adjusted readily to the brutalities of this particular war and just as
readily to the events that followed it—land-grabbing and numerous
court battles. He was courageous, impetuous, and impatient of ob-
stacles, and this latter trait increased with the years. He was more
loyal to Moses Hazen than he was to any cause. For as long as this
kind of loyalty enhanced his self-respect and his ambitions, he was
happy to serve such a cause.

II

Between the Wars

BRIGADIER GENERAL JAMES MURRAY, first Governor of British Canada, once described the postwar British settlers in Quebec as "men of mean education, either young and inexperienced, or older men who had failed elsewhere," and as "licentious fanatics." In another report, published in London in 1766, he called them "in general the most immoral collection of men I ever knew and of course little calculated to make the new subjects [the French] enamoured with our laws, religion and customs." The second governor, Sir Guy Carleton, writing in 1768 to Lord Hillsborough, the colonial secretary, referred to the same group: "The Protestants, who have settled or rather sojourned here since the Conquest are composed only of Traders, disbanded Soldiers, and officers, the latter one or two excepted, below the Rank of Captain. . . . they naturally sought to repair their broken Fortunes at the expense of the People; Hence a variety of Schemes to increase the Business and their own Emoluments. . . . In my last Tour through the Country, the outcry of the People was general." [1]

The quotations express the alarm of two royal governors over the divisive aspects of the new immigration. British and American adventurers from all levels of society moved into Canada to fill the void left by the departure of many of the former French leaders. They occupied legal and political positions, engaged in trade and took over some of the French seigneuries. Ten years after the conquest there were 200 English landowners, 30 of them holding seigneuries. They bought them primarily to exploit them as the French had done by making the most of the rent rolls, the timber rights, and the banalités, or fees the seigneur charged his tenants for the use of his mills and other services.[2]

Yet the governors' protestations do not ring entirely true. In 1765 Murray named twenty-seven justices of the peace. None of them were French Canadian; only five spoke French, and they were Swiss or French Protestants. Moses Hazen was one of the appointees. In the same year, but supporting Murray's contention, a religious oath was subscribed to by Hazen, Thomas Walker, and others with English names, who later joined the American cause in the Revolution. The oath said in part: "I do believe that in the Sacrement of the Lord's Supper, there is not any transubstantiation of the Elements of bread and wine into the body and blood of Christ at or after the consecration thereof by any person whatsoever, and the invocation or adoration of the Virgin Mary, or any other Saint, and the sacrifice of the Mass, as they are now used in the Church of Rome, are superstitious and idolatrous."[3]

Before 1763 the valley of the Richelieu River, sometimes called the best land in Quebec, had been divided into large seigniorial grants to French officers who, as one of the conditions of ownership, were supposed to populate their lands with their soldiers or other settlers. The officers became, in effect, feudal chiefs and the whole settlement a military cantonment. A reminder of this fact is the modern designation of a portion of Chambly as Chambly Canton. Canada benefited by getting new areas settled while at the same time creating a frontier settled by soldiers.[4]

After the Treaty of 1763 the British who began to arrive faced favorable prospects because those French who refused to become subjects of the King of England were given eighteen months in which to dispose of their property. For ex-soldier Hazen, the opportunities looked irresistible. He first met Lieutenant Colonel Gabriel Christie during the siege of Quebec. Christie was already on the way to becoming the biggest British landowner in the province. While in the service he had plenty of opportunity to judge the best areas for development. He focused his attention upon the Richelieu River area, where he acquired the seigniories of Lacolle and Léry, and as a partnership, of Noyan. Christie was deputy quartermaster general and captain in the famed Forty-eighth Regiment of Foot. As a military man he did not hesitate to apply pressure upon the militia captains to impress laborers under the corvée, unpaid labor on the roads, for his personal use. He was sued by two merchants, Knipe and Lequesne, for having illegally conscripted their employees and they received

£3,600 in damages. He also attempted to apply the old seigneurial requirements against his tenants. At La Chenaye, for example, he told them they need not bake their bread in his ovens if they paid a fee. But when they took their wheat elsewhere to be ground, he pursued them and forced them to pay mill dues and a fine in addition.[5]

It was to this man that Hazen was attracted, and with whom he eventually agreed to go into business. Their first opportunity arose when the seigneuries of Sabrevois and Bleury on the Richelieu came on the market. Both seigneuries had first been granted in 1733 and reconfirmed in 1750, although the owners had not lived up to the conditions of the original grant. De Bleury possessed a seigneury about nine miles square fronting on the Richelieu River opposite and below St. John, and it remained a wilderness until he disposed of it. Charles Sabrevois had the land next to it on the south, containing about six square miles. De Bleury was a merchant and commissary during the war. Sabrevois was a military man who left the country at the time of the conquest, deeding his property to his brother, Clement.

De Bleury was not unwilling to become a British subject, but he knew that his lands were vulnerable. Since he had never developed his property, the French government could have revoked his title, and the British reserved the same right. Therefore, one week before the expiration of the eighteen-month period of grace, he also sold his seigneury to Clement Sabrevois. Hazen and Christie jointly purchased both seigneuries from Clement in August 1764. The next day the two completed their obligations by rendering "foi et hommage" to Ralph Burton, governor of Montreal.[6]

Their joint properties, as well as Christie's individual ones, were all on the east bank of the Richelieu River, variously known as the Chambly or Sorel. As if these princely holdings were not enough, they eyed property on the west bank. Some of this was under the control of the Baron of Longueuil. But they recognized what the Baron did not—that the site of Fort St. John, surrounded only by a few farms, had a promising future, located as it was at the beginning of the rapids and therefore at a critical transfer point on the river. They jointly purchased five large farms from James Robertson within the confines of the present St. John and, just to be sure, they rented the ground of the Fort from the Baron of Longueuil, reduced to ten acres in breadth, with the stipulation that the lease would become invalid if the government retook possession. With these acquisitions Hazen and Christie became virtually the masters of the Upper Richelieu.

Since Christie was required in line of duty to be out of the country for long periods of time, he arranged to have Hazen direct the development of their joint properties. This new role Hazen performed in his usual strenuous manner. He cleared land, settled tenants on it and built two mills, one on the rapids of the Richelieu and one on the Hazen River, now known as the Rivière des Indes. He also erected the first manor house, in Iberville opposite St. John. For all this Christie furnished more than half of the capital, Hazen having no reserves to contribute.

In addition to these duties Hazen took on other responsibilities. In 1765 he was appointed a justice of the peace. In the same year he accepted an appointment as assistant surveyor of the king's forests, on the recommendation of Governor Benning Wentworth of New Hampshire, the king's chief surveyor. In view of the high price of ship masts in New England, Wentworth proposed the use of timber from lands above Montreal, and London agreed to give Canadian masts a trial. The King's broad arrow was used to designate trees on private property that were reserved for the navy's use.

The next year Hazen entered into an agreement with Samuel McKay in Canada and John Henniker, a London merchant and contractor for His Majesty's Navy, to supply a large quantity of timber. They prepared a cargo of white pine, apparently from the locality. For yellow pine they went into Lake Champlain, where the French had once cut masts for the French king, and took out 200 logs. These they floated to Quebec to be prepared for England. But claimants of the land on which the yellow pine was cut seized the logs and prepared to auction them for their own benefit. Whether this transaction was as straightforward as it was made to appear, Hazen and McKay were forced to petition Governor Carleton to free the logs for England.[7]

This was not their last trouble with landowners from whom they took timber, but they justified their actions on the basis of their naval contract. However, it is not clear how much of their lumbering was for the navy and how much for commercial channels. Their naval contract alone was of such magnitude that they were unable to fill it. They therefore took in Christie and Francis McKay as partners in an involved agreement that provided for a sharing of all profits and the borrowing of £1,000 to get the enterprise moving. There is no record that any fortunes were made.[8]

The industry was still quite primitive and confined to the shores of rivers and lakes. The demands for timber were so specific that selective cutting was necessary—usually on someone else's land. Adolphus Benzel, a resident of Crown Point and assistant surveyor of the king's woods, visited Lake Champlain in 1772 and reported his findings to Surveyor General Wentworth. What he saw alarmed him. He commented upon the plentiful but fast-dwindling supply of mast timber six feet and more in diameter, and of white oak twenty to thirty inches across when squared. However, much of this was being ruined by the wasteful method of making staves. At the mouth of the Saranac River he found a deserted sawmill and a great quantity of white pine destroyed for the export of masts. The enterprise, he reported, had been operated by de Fredenburgh, McKay, and Hazen. The latter two had apparently been trying to fulfill their London contract; de Fredenburgh was the owner of a large tract at the mouth of the Saranac, so the operation must have been carried out with his cooperation.[9]

That cooperation of the owners was always the case is doubtful. Benzel reported many parts of the western shore of the lake from which the best timber had already been cut, although it was barely beginning to be settled. Hazen probably gave a broad interpretation to the authority given him under his naval contract, and took out more than the occasional white pine. Professor Philip White is convinced that he poached on the Beekman property at Point au Roche and at other points along the western shore.[10]

Hazen also tried to enter the shipbuilding business. In 1766, upon hearing that the government's vessels on Lake Champlain were so old and out of repair that they were about to be replaced, he wrote General Gage in New York to offer his facilities. As the possessor of plenty of good timber and a sawmill, he thought he could construct any size of vessel that was needed. He also proposed that they be dry-docked on his property in winter, where they could be overhauled and thus could occupy the time of his men who "must be kept under pay During the Long winters in this Country." He asked only for a ten-year contract and assurance that the vessels would not be required on the Lake between November 10 and April 10 of any year. But Gage had no intention of building new ships at present, he politely told Hazen; if circumstances changed, he would be happy to give Hazen's application full consideration.[11]

In spite of all this activity, or perhaps because of it, Hazen's affairs did not prosper. Tactics that had proved successful in the Rangers did not necessarily apply to civilian life. He had plenty of schemes and energy but he lacked money and patience to channel them properly. He was in and out of court on a variety of matters such as suing Nathan Wheelwright and being sued by Daniel Desonslavy. Christie began to be concerned about the property they held jointly. In 1766 he granted Hazen a mortgage of £800 on his half of the two undivided seigneuries for a term of 500 years, repurchasable for that amount plus interest before the following January. Upon demand Hazen must pay annually "at or upon the Feast of St. John the Baptist one pepper corn." Before he went to England, Christie laid out instructions for Hazen on the seigneuries. He was to spend no more than £3,000 on improvements of any kind. Since he had already spent or anticipated £2,150, he had a balance of £850. "Reasonable" improvements might include the completion of houses already begun. Christie had already paid his half of the first amount and would pay half of the remainder. Hazen was to keep accounts and make a report once a year.[12]

One would suppose that such stringent guidelines would be sufficient to keep Hazen in check. However, Christie wrote Hazen from England: "That you are here £5500 in Debt Suppose £2000 cash advanced and suppose the vessells to be Sent out would be less than £2500 you therefore see the Situation we may get ahead this year by proper care if not all will be ruin'd. I'm Convinc'd this present Credit with whats to be sent making £2000 will do a great deal to effect the Service your upon." He also complained that Hazen did not put four turrets on the house at St. John: "A less hurry would do things better, at least I'm of opinion a plan should first be Consider'd and then not alter'd—I thought this was fixed."[13]

That Christie was a hard taskmaster there can be no doubt; neither can there be any question that Hazen was imprudent in pursuing his many schemes. Despite Christie's loans and subsidies, Hazen found himself forced to borrow wherever he could find the money— from a tipsy notary at Chambly and from the business partners, Leonard Jarvis and his own brother William in Newburyport, Massachusetts. For £2,000 he gave the latter two a second mortgage on his half of the two seigneuries and a first mortgage on his nine lots in the seigneury of Longueuil.[14]

Christie meanwhile had extended his holdings still further. In 1765 he purchased lands on the west side of the Richelieu and Lake Champlain to a point three miles south of the mouth of the Great Chazy River and nine miles in depth, and for good measure he bought Isle la Motte as well. In view of the fact that the boundary was now fixed at the 45th parallel, he wrote Governor Henry Moore of New

York in 1766 to request that none of his lands in New York province
be disposed of until he could be heard because they had been expensive both to purchase and to improve. In 1771 he issued a caveat
against disposing of these lands but the Revolution postponed any
settlement of his claims. He undoubtedly paid heavily for the purchase of such a large tract, but he exaggerated the extent to which
he had improved his lands below the border with "houses and conveniences." [15]

Christie finally lost confidence in Hazen and in 1770, upon his
return from England, he forced an accounting of his management and
insisted upon a division of their joint properties. Christie kept the
seigneury of Sabrevois and the northern half of Bleury while Hazen
received the area in between which was the southern half of Bleury
(the present village of Iberville), most of the land around St. John, and
a farm at Savanne de St.-Luc. The land within the fort at St. John
was divided between the two. Henceforth Hazen was properly titled
the Seigneur of Bleury-Sud.

But reverses continued to dog his steps. In the fall of 1770 his
debts led to the public sale at St. John of his cattle, stock, farming
utensils, and household furniture by Sheriff Edward Gray. Hazen
probably rescued at least part of his goods by repurchase, and shortly
afterward went to Montreal to get married. His wife was Charlotte
de la Saussaye, a Roman Catholic lady of a respectable family who
was born in 1740. She was thus thirty years of age to his thirty-
seven. [16]

In addition to free-spending proclivities, indebtedness, and
voracious appetite for more lands and offices, Hazen's reputation suffered in other respects during the years before his marriage. He was
involved in at least one highly publicized sexual escapade. In 1766 he
was attacked in the press by Captain Joseph Kelly, whose wife he was
alleged to have seduced. Kelly appealed for assistance because, he
said, when he tried to go to Quebec for redress he was seized in his
"canoo" on Hazen's orders and imprisoned for debt in a Montreal jail.
He professed not to know the basis of the arrest, and to his appeal for
help he appended the names of 100 men who testified to his good
character. Some of them were from Massachusetts and ironically included two of Hazen's relatives in Haverhill. [17]

After his setbacks and his marriage, Hazen seems to have settled down. Some lawsuits pursued him and he almost lost his farm
at the Savanne by a sheriff's sale. But as far as he could he abandoned
his endless litigation and his lumbering and mining operations to

devote himself exclusively to farming. In this he was at last successful, and he owned all his mortgaged Canadian lands at the outbreak of the American Revolution. He had a two-story, twenty-room manor house opposite St. John, he built a second sawmill on his own property, and he also constructed a forge and an ashery for the making of potash. Thus the years passed in the active development of his lands and the attainment of a good reputation in the neighborhood.

Yet even this did not satisfy his ambitions. While Murray was still governor, he petitioned for a large grant of land near St. Regis, and when nothing came of it he asked for 2,000 acres on Mississquoi Bay. This request was apparently on the way to being granted, and the government advertised for rival claimants prior to making a decision. But the claim was disallowed when the land was discovered to lie partly outside the province. After his affairs had settled down somewhat, Hazen in 1773 petitioned for a large grant east of and adjoining his own seigneury. He explained that it was not an excessive request because "a Considerable if not the Greatest part of the land herein Desired is not of the best, but a very Indifferent kind," and he wanted it solely because of its contiguity to his own property. At the same time he petitioned for seigneuries for both his brother William and for the latter's partner, Leonard Jarvis. The tensions leading to the outbreak of the Revolution terminated consideration of any of these applications.[18]

Meanwhile, the activities of two of his brothers at widely separated points had engaged more than his passing interest. One was the settlement and development of the Coos Country astride the Connecticut River in upper New Hampshire and Vermont. After tours of duty in the French war Captain John Hazen, his brother, and Colonel Jacob Bayley of Newbury, Massachusetts, decided to act together to settle the Coos area (pronounced K-o-a-s), which they had seen on their campaigns. John Hazen arrived on the east bank in 1762 and called his settlement Haverhill for his home town in Massachusetts. Bayley settled on the west bank in 1764 and named his settlement Newbury, also for his home town. In the same year Colonel Timothy Bedel, also a veteran of the recent war, arrived in Haverhill. He and Bayley were to play important roles in the Revolution.

Meanwhile, charters for both towns were obtained from the governor of New Hampshire, Benning Wentworth. The Haverhill proprietors were John Hazen, Bayley, and seventy-two associates, including Moses Hazen. The Newbury proprietors were the same except that Bayley's name came first. Moses Hazen thus acquired proprietary shares on both sides of the river. Though isolated and subjected to serious flooding and a plague of worms, the settlements persisted and by the time of the Revolution they had become the granary for that part of the country.[19]

Moses in Canada, hoping to emulate his brother John, had also petitioned Governor Wentworth for a township in Coos. He initiated his request before he became involved with Colonel Christie. For the time being he depended upon John and Colonel Bayley, together with his friend Theodore Atkinson, secretary to Wentworth, to intercede with the governor in his behalf. At first expecting to come and conclude arrangements in person, and even fixing several dates, he was forced by his preoccupation with Christie to make postponements and to acknowledge that his future residence was to be in Canada for, as he wrote Atkinson, "I have lately had so much Encouragement from Governor Murray to Remain for some time in this Country that I thought it would be better for me to stay." [20]

Yet he still wanted the township and hoped his friends would get it for him. They succeeded. Hazen's petition, and others like it, was made easier by the King's proclamation of October 1763, which directed that lands be made available to veterans of the French war. He obtained the grant of a town on the west bank of the Connecticut River, later known as Moortown and still later as Bradford, Vermont. Even before the grant was concluded, he was probably the first to see the value of a road between Coos and St. John. It would give Coos a valuable outlet for its produce and would connect his own holdings. During the Revolution he was able to contribute toward the fulfillment of this dream by building part of the Hazen Road. After the war he set out to expand his Coos holdings.[21]

Brother William Hazen was also involved in large business affairs which peripherally included Moses. In 1764 William formed a partnership with several others at Newburyport, Massachusetts. Their original purpose was to engage in the cod and seine fisheries, the fur trade, and the making of lime. James Simonds had already taken up a veteran's land claim in New Brunswick, and he and James White, both cousins of William Hazen, were commissioned to handle the company's business at the mouth of the St. John River, the later site of the city of St. John. Beaver became the staple of their trade, with more than 4,000 pelts exported from New Brunswick annually. Beginning in 1767, William Hazen and Leonard Jarvis conducted the firm's business in Massachusetts, and it was they who took a mortgage on Moses' Canadian property in 1769. The company expanded, building a sawmill at St. John in 1767 and a grist mill in 1770, as well as acquiring six small vessels for trade with the West Indies. William planned to move to New Brunswick in 1771 but did not finally go until 1775. Only the Revolution slowed his burgeoning enterprises.[22]

William lived until 1814, had sixteen children, and became a wealthy and respected citizen of the growing community. Since he had intended to go in 1771, he can hardly be considered a Tory refugee. Yet he remained loyal to the King, perhaps to protect his large business interests in Canada. Moses bore his brother no ill will; indeed he corresponded with him when he could, and named him executor of his will. It is likely that he hoped until the end of the war that Nova Scotia (New Brunswick was not set off until 1784) might be saved to the United States, and it is possible, as the Hazen genealogist avers, that William's sympathies were really with New England in the conflict.[23]

In 1764 the "Saint John River Society" was organized in Montreal by more than sixty officers and associates who had fought in the French war and were eager to take up the government's offer of land for veterans. Among the high-powered proprietors were Thomas Hutchinson, later governor of Massachusetts, General Thomas Gage, Sir William Johnson, and General Frederick Haldimand, while the associates included Moses and William Hazen and their cousin, James Simonds. The company obtained five large townships of 400,000 acres in 1765, located on or near the St. John River in New Brunswick. Moses Hazen's share lay in the townships of Gage and New Town. The grants required the payment of a small quitrent, and their development in stages over the next thirty years, subject to forfeiture for noncompliance.[24]

In 1783, when the province was filling with refugees, the old grant was given careful scrutiny. For the benefit of the Loyalists, most of the five towns were escheated by the government of Nova Scotia. Thus Moses Hazen lost his claims to New Brunswick property through the defunct "St. John River Society," although by that time he was much preoccupied with land deals in other parts of the continent.[25]

Nevertheless, at the outbreak of the Revolution Moses Hazen was a major landholder in two countries. In modern Quebec he owned a seigneury at Iberville, a farm at Savanne, and substantial holdings on the site of St. John; at Coos he was the proprietor of Moortown (now in Vermont) and had a proprietary share in Newbury and

Haverhill, all in the Coos Country; and in what is now New Brunswick he owned proprietary shares in two townships. He needed time
and a long period of peace to develop and add to his large holdings.
The Revolution disrupted all his plans, and it is against the background of these holdings that his difficulty in sorting out his political
loyalties should be viewed.

III

The Coming of the Revolution

*Notwithstanding this, and their decent and respectful obe-
dience to the King's Government hitherto, I have not the
least doubt of their secret attachments to France, and think
this will continue as long as they are excluded from all em-
ployments under the British Government, and are certain of
being reinstated, at least in their former Commissions under
that of France, by which chiefly they supported themselves,
and families.*

*When I reflect that France naturally, has the affections of all
the people, that to make no mention of fees of office and the
vexations of the Law, we have done nothing to gain one man
in the province, by making it his private interest to remain
the King's subject; and that the interest of many would be
greatly promoted by a revolution.*[1]

THUS WROTE SIR GUY CARLETON, governor of Canada, to Lord Hillsborough in 1768. He was trying to impart his alarm at the apathy
of the French Canadians toward the British government, and his disdain for the new British immigrants, a greedy lot who "sought to
repair their broken Fortunes at the expense of the people." He felt
so strongly that he went to London to work for a change in policy
and, ultimately, to help write the Quebec Act, with which he returned
in 1774 after an absence of four years.

The Anglo-American, Protestant minority in Canada had been
busy for years petitioning the British government for the creation of
a situation more favorable to their own interests, and they maintained
a lobbyist in London. They particularly desired an elected General
Assembly, having in mind the disfranchisement of the French Catholic majority from the electoral process. With such a body they could
run the country in a manner best calculated to foster trade and industry. But Carleton's view prevailed in London and it was supported
by French petitions requesting entry into the armed forces and an en-
larged, appointed Council containing French members, which "would
be a much fitter instrument of government" than a general assembly.[2]

The Quebec Act gave the French, but not the English, much of what they asked for and was thus an act of political and economic justice. It broke the bonds of a restricted Canada by annexing the Great Lakes area south to the Ohio River, taking it out of the hands of the traders and trappers who thrived in an unregulated area. Although maintaining British criminal law, it recognized French civil law, including the prevailing system of land tenure. It recognized the right of the Roman Catholic Church to execute its traditional functions, including the collection of tithes. By abolishing the old oath which barred Catholics from holding office, it was far ahead of the British in their own islands, and altogether was an act of considerable statesmanship.

It was recognized as such by the French-speaking leaders of Canada. The clergy were gratified by the new position of the Church, and became firm adherents of the regime. The nobility were likewise pleased with the confirmation of their land titles and their right to continue their seigneurial practises. Only the habitants failed to see substantial benefits. They realized that they must resume the payment of tithes to the Church and feudal dues to their seigneur. Their loyalty consequently hung in the balance with the invasion of Canada in 1775. On the other hand, the English-speaking minority were aghast at the calamity that had overtaken them. In large numbers they openly opposed the British cause in the Revolution, partly because so many of them were transplanted Americans.

In the colonies to the south the Act was greeted with fear and dismay. Perhaps the reaction would not have been as frenetic if its timing had been different because it became associated generally with the Intolerable Acts, which Parliament purposely intended to be coercive on the heels of the Boston Tea Party. Americans were horrified, enamored as they were of representative assemblies, that Quebec was being denied one. They felt robbed by the annexation of the Ohio Country to Canada. New Englanders particularly professed fear that a papal establishment was being made in North America and that their own religion was somehow threatened.

The first Continental Congress met in Philadelphia in the fall of 1774 to consider the American response to the Intolerable Acts. In respect to the Quebec Act, John Jay wrote an "Address to the People of Great Britain" in which he declared that "the Legislature of Great Britain is not authorized by the Constitution to establish a religion, fraught with sanguinary and impious tenets, or to erect an arbitrary form of government in any quarter of the globe." He expressed as-

tonishment that Parliament should establish a religion that "has del-
uged your island in blood, and dispersed impiety, bigotry, persecution,
murder and rebellion through every part of the world." At the same
time Richard Henry Lee penned a message to the inhabitants of
Quebec. Omitting any reference to their religion, he lectured them
on the blessings of a free government and then asserted that the
French were not receiving them: "The Crown and its Ministers are
impowered, as far as they could be by Parliament, to establish even
the INQUISITION itself among you."[3]

Lee's letter from Congress was translated and copies in both
English and French were sent to Montreal. The recipient was the well-
known disaffected merchant Thomas Walker, who called the other
English-speaking merchants together to hear its contents. They also
met with John Brown, who brought a message from the Massachusetts Committee of Correspondence. It denounced the British acts as
"oppressive and unconstitutional," and urged Canadians to join Americans in a common cause by sending two delegates to the next session
of Congress. Some of the Anglo-Americans, like Walker and James
Price, were ready to choose delegates. Others believed that the country was not yet ripe for revolt, and they particularly feared the effects of the American determination not to import British goods if
they joined the American cause and the French did not, for, they
pointed out, "The French would immediately monopolize the Indian
Trade."[4]

The Congress met for its second session in May 1775. By that
time shooting had occurred at Lexington and Concord. This Congress
therefore had a war on its hands—not yet a war for independence but
a struggle for the "rights of Englishmen" within the Empire. On May
29 it dispatched a letter to the "Oppressed Inhabitants" of Quebec
expressing the hope that they would join in the defense of their mu-
tual liberties. Eight months later it sent still another to its "friends
and countrymen," asserting that "We have also shewn you, that your
Liberty, your Honor, and your Happiness are essentially and necessarily connected with the unhappy Contest, which we have been
forced into for the defence of our dearest Privileges." Congress was
trying to reconcile contradictory emotions. Deeply suspicious of the
Catholic religion, its members nevertheless felt compelled to woo the
French Canadians away from their British allegiance. Overestimating
the importance of annexing Canada, it underestimated the difficulties
in bringing it about.[5]

Meanwhile the war had reached the Champlain Valley. Fort Ticonderoga fell to Colonels Ethan Allen and Benedict Arnold early in May. Shortly afterward Arnold, surmising that the government's lake sloop was being loaded at St. John, sailed for that place. He surprised the garrison, which surrendered without firing a shot. Arnold seized the sloop, a vessel of seventy tons, and several bateaux, destroyed others that were faulty, and within two hours embarked with all the provisions and stores he could find.

Moses Hazen, dismayed at the turn of events south of the border, had visited Carleton in February and the governor, describing him as a brave and experienced officer "greatly distressed in his circumstances," recommended a commission for him. In March Hazen carried dispatches from Carleton to Gage in Boston. In May, after Arnold's incursion to St. John, he carried word of the danger to Carleton at Quebec. Leaving the government in the hands of Cramahé, the governor hurried to Montreal in order to deal with the emergency. Hazen returned to his seigneury to spend the summer brooding over the role he would adopt if war returned to the Richelieu. Economically, his future was linked to that of Canada, but emotionally his heart was with his native land.[6]

Congress, which in May had been shocked by the seizure of the forts at Ticonderoga and Crown Point and had toyed with the idea of turning them back to the British, had had a change of heart by June. Both Allen and Arnold submitted plans for a full-scale invasion of Canada, but Arnold's was more carefully thought out and was adopted. He believed that a force of 2,000 men could conquer the valley of the Richelieu and seize Montreal. Carleton without reinforcements would be helpless and the rest of Canada, including Quebec City, would give up the struggle. Then at last the British would be forced to recognize American claims and accord them a more reasonable place in the Empire.

Congress entrusted the campaign not to Arnold but to General Philip Schuyler, the owner of large estates in New York, whom Congress appointed on June 27. Carleton made his headquarters in Montreal and started organizing a defense. He had no more than 600 regulars along the entire length of the St. Lawrence. As for the militia, Carleton miscalculated by appointing seigneurs to the senior positions rather than promoting the French captains, thinking that the seigneurs could more effectively enlist their tenants. The French habitants, intrigued by the messages from south of the border, were loath to take

up arms and did not feel they owed any military service to the no-
blesse, despite the fact that Bishop Briand of Quebec on May 22 issued
a mandement instructing the people in their duties and threatening to
withhold the sacraments and even burial in consecrated ground.[7]

Looking to his fortifications, Carleton despaired of Montreal
with its weak stone wall and inadequate citadel. But the Richelieu,
gateway to the country, could be strengthened. The old fort at Chambly would suffice as a supply depot. St. John was the pivotal spot,
connected as it was by road to Montreal and situated at the head of
navigation on Lake Champlain. So Carleton's engineers reconstructed
the old fort there, joining the two separate redoubts and preparing
their defense with a palisade and a deep ditch. The land on which this
new fortification stood, including a large stone house, had been leased
to Christie and Hazen, but the lease was voided when the government
repossessed the property for military purposes. Into this fort Carleton
poured all the troops he could spare, a total of 662 from various services, commanded by Major Charles Preston.[8]

Slowly the American force gathered at Ticonderoga and Crown
Point under Major General Schuyler and his second in command, Brigadier General Richard Montgomery. The need for haste was acknowledged by all, and yet unconscionable delays postponed the invasion
until September. But finally the boats were built and the troops gathered, equipped, and supplied, and on August 30 the army moved
northward.

The invasion of Canada in 1775 was actually a pincer movement from two directions. Benedict Arnold, disappointed at not being
chosen the commander on Lake Champlain, devised another project
to which both Washington and Congress gave their blessing. Twelve
days after Schuyler sailed down Lake Champlain with 1,500 men,
Arnold left Massachusetts for Maine with about 1,200 more, intend-
ing to go overland to Quebec City. The strategy called for him to be
joined there by Schuyler after the capture of Montreal. Enormous but
not insuperable difficulties were expected, but the plan's attractiveness
was the possibility of reducing all of Canada in one campaign. And
it almost worked.

The first of the unanticipated difficulties was the severe illness
of General Schuyler at his base at Isle aux Noix. The command de-
volved upon General Montgomery, a younger man and a veteran of
the British army who had settled in New York State and married into
the Livingston family.

The second setback, which disrupted the timetable of a coordinated campaign, was the tenacity with which the British held St. John. The siege which began on September 4 ended weeks later with its capitulation on November 2. But between those two dates important events took place. Montgomery's force was built up to about 2,000 men. James Livingston, an American who had settled in Chambly, began to recruit Canadians. With them he harassed the neighborhood and helped plan for the capture of Chambly, which took place on October 17. This spot, twelve miles below St. John, surrendered after a weak defense and yielded up large quantities of supplies and ammunition, including 124 barrels of gunpowder and 500 hand grenades. Its fall made the defense of St. John, gateway to Canada, more desperate.[9]

Meanwhile Hazen had been authorized to raise troops for the British service and report for duty to Major Preston at St. John. Instead, he seems still to have been hoping that a military confrontation could be avoided and that he would not need to choose sides. He visited Schuyler on September 6 and presented a very gloomy prospect for the Americans. He portrayed St. John as forbiddingly defended and the Canadians not to be counted on for any assistance. On the strength of his report, with the American army at a standstill and Schuyler ill, a council of war decided to withdraw from Canada. But before the decision could be implemented, Schuyler received quite different reports from James Livingston. According to him, assistance and a friendly reception could be expected from the Canadians. He already had a force of 300 men along the river and could raise 3,000 when the American troops approached: "I shall notwithstanding keep up a spirit of faction amongst them, till I hear what advances you are making towards a general attack of St. Johns." Partly on the strength of this encouraging word, Schuyler ordered a renewal of the attack upon St. John.[10]

This decision did not solve Hazen's dilemma, but he continued to follow an equivocal course. According to his wife, he gave secret information to the Americans concerning the fortifications at St. John, but he did not act openly because much of his property lay within range of the guns at the fort. He only succeeded in arousing the suspicions of both sides, and on September 18 an American major, John Brown, captured him while he was at work in his fields. Before they could get away a British detachment appeared. Brown abandoned his prisoner and retreated, while the British took Hazen into custody and

marched him to the fort.* At about the same time Charlotte Hazen
was arrested at Chambly, where she was visiting, and held in the fort
there until freed by the Americans two days later.[11]

At St. John Major Preston was uncertain what to do with his
prisoner because only the week before he had received word from
Carleton about Hazen's commission to raise troops. He confined him
in the fort while he applied to Montreal for instructions, and he was
told to send Hazen there to explain his behavior. Lorimier, the Indian
leader, was designated to accompany him. Lorimier tried to refuse,
fearing some kind of treachery, but was told that Hazen's wife and
his own sons were hostage to their appearance. They went together
as far as Hazen's farm at Savanne de St-Luc, where they stopped to
rest. Fearing his own arrest by Americans, Lorimier left his prisoner
there after receiving Hazen's promise to proceed to Montreal on his
own.[12]

Hazen was unable to give a satisfactory explanation of his
movements to Brigadier General Richard Prescott, commander in the
absence of Carleton, and he was closely confined in a Montreal jail.
According to both of the Hazens he was denied pen, paper, ink, and
even a fire, and he could have no visitors. Upon Carleton's return
these rigors were relaxed somewhat and Charlotte was allowed to visit
him and take him supplies. Hazen was offered the command of a
British regiment or, if he preferred not to fight, he and his wife could
each receive a guinea a day for expenses if they would go to England
and wait out the war. When he spurned both offers he was held in
close confinement, a total of fifty-four days, until he was freed by the
Americans.[13]

During Hazen's incarceration the Americans plundered his estate of livestock, grain, tools, and everything movable that could be
of use to their army. For example, a large potash kettle was brought
from his ash house to brew beer for the troops. His manor house was
used at various times as a hospital and an inn, and his other buildings
were used as barracks or guardhouses for as long as the American
army remained in Canada.[14]

After Carleton failed to send a relief force, St. John fell early
in November and the way to Montreal was at last open. The Ameri-

---

*Years later Mrs. Hazen testified that her husband had been arrested only by
the British. But the recollections of others who were closer to the scene make it
certain that the Americans got to him first and then had to abandon him to the
British.

can forces entered the city on November 13, only two days after Carleton had departed for Quebec. Sailing in the *Gaspé* with Prescott and other officers and his prisoners Moses Hazen and Thomas Walker, his little fleet was becalmed opposite Sorel, where an American force under Major Brown demanded his surrender. Carleton escaped in a whaleboat and arrived in Quebec on the same day (November 19) that his vessels and men, including Prescott and the prisoners, surrendered to Brown at Sorel. Their capture gave Montgomery the transports he needed to reach Quebec.[15]

In Montreal Montgomery faced the advent of cold weather with a melting away of his troops, who were approaching the end of their enlistment and considered the campaign concluded. But not Montgomery. He knew that Arnold might even then be approaching Quebec, and that the campaign was not finished until that city was captured. With a force of about 800 men, he quickly made his dispositions for a further effort. He placed Brigadier General David Wooster in local command and commissioned James Livingston a colonel with authority to raise a regiment of Canadians. He then set sail for Quebec, arriving at Pointe aux Trembles (Neuville) to make a junction with Arnold on December 3. He brought with him no more than 300 men, including Hazen and Livingston, with the latter's growing regiment.

Meanwhile, Arnold had struggled all autumn by way of the Kennebec River, the "height of land," and the Chaudière River to Point Lévis opposite Quebec, which he reached on November 8. The hardships of this incredible journey are fully chronicled in other accounts. He first viewed the city with about 500 emaciated men. He carried with him Washington's address to Canada in which the General proclaimed that the British "instead of finding in you that poverty of spirit and baseness of soul, they see with a chagrin equal to our joy, that you are enlightened, generous and virtuous. . . . Come then, my brethren, unite with us in an indissoluble union, let us run together to the same goal."[16]

Early in November Washington at Cambridge had forbidden his men to take part in the local celebration of Guy Fawkes Day which in Massachusetts had become an occasion for denouncing the Pope. He called the parades "ridiculous and childish" and not to be tolerated, especially when the friendship and help of the Canadians was being sought; and "to be insulting their Religion, is so monstrous, as not to be suffered or excused; indeed instead of offering the most remote insult, it is our duty to address public thanks to these our

Brethren, as to them we are so much indebted for every late happy Success over the common Enemy in Canada." Thus the General put into practice his own convictions, and his letter to the Canadians was more than mere propaganda.[17]

After crossing the St. Lawrence in Indian canoes, Arnold lay before Quebec for six days while he tried by bombast to secure the surrender of the stronghold. His men fatigued, his powder wet, and his fears of an attack from within the walls growing daily, he withdrew his men to Pointe aux Trembles on November 18 to wait for Montgomery. On the same day Carleton's vessel passed the point in his successful attempt to reach his capital. During his absence Acting Governor Hector Cramahé had put his finger upon one of his major problems in a letter to London: "The Enemy without however is not so much to be dreaded, as their numerous Friends within the Town, they endeavour to alarm and threaten to storm Us." After his arrival Carleton purged the city of these "numerous Friends" by giving them four days to depart or be treated as rebels or spies. Their departure, in significant numbers, ended all talk of surrender and stiffened the tight defense of the city. Among those who left at this time was Edward Antill, a New Jersey man of good family who had been practising law in Canada for ten years. When he left Quebec he accepted duty under Montgomery as chief engineer of the army and was with him when he was killed.[18]

On December 3 Montgomery joined Arnold at a point eighteen miles from Quebec, and six days later the first of his batteries opened fire on the city. The combined army of about 1,000 men faced a well-entrenched British force of about 1,250, and his efforts to bluff Carleton into surrender went unheeded: Montgomery to Carleton, "Should you persist in an unwarrantable defence, the consequences be on your own Head!" Finding that he could not induce the British commander to come out for battle, he determined to take the city by assault. After several modifications of plans, he and Arnold put an intricate attack into operation early on the morning of December 31. In deep snow and a blinding snowstorm, and with the temperature below zero, he and Arnold attacked the lower town from opposite directions, expecting to join forces and storm the upper town. But the weather and British alertness threw their plans awry, and the wounding of Arnold and the death of Montgomery ended the project altogether. The Americans suffered 461 casualties, most of them as captives.[19]

Arnold maintained an ineffective siege for the rest of the winter and early spring. Carleton refused to do battle outside the city and

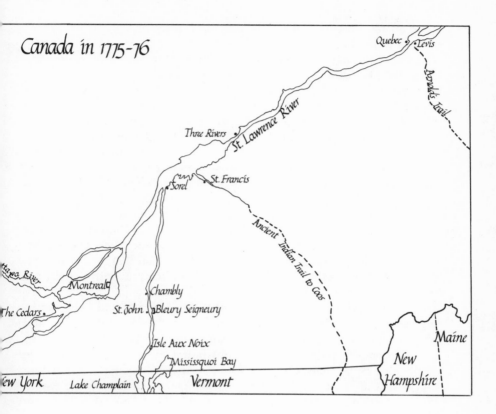

Canada in 1775-76

Arnold, with 800 men of whom probably no more than 350 were fit for duty, was in no position to attack. Besides injuries, his army suffered from a variety of diseases, especially the dreaded smallpox. Yet wounded as he was, he grimly held his position, gambling that American reinforcements would arrive before the spring thaw would allow the British to reach the city by water.

Shortly after the attack on the city, Arnold sent Antill with a report to Wooster in Montreal. Moses Hazen, who had escaped capture during the attack on Quebec, also went to Montreal. On January 13, 1776, Wooster sent both men to Philadelphia to notify Congress of the death of Montgomery and to urge relief for the desperate situation in the north. Fearing the collapse of the campaign Congress, through the states and General Washington, obtained more troops for Canada. To encourage enlistments, bounties of six and two thirds dollars were authorized.[20]

On January 6 Congress confirmed Montgomery's earlier appointment by directing James Livingston to raise a regiment of Canadians, although his rank as colonel was not certified until later. His came to be known as the First Canadian Regiment. Livingston at Quebec had led about 200 men, the recruiting of which had been greatly assisted by a Canadian, Captain John Dugan. This officer, a barber, was very popular among his fellow countrymen. Both Wooster and Arnold commissioned him to raise troops as a colonel. He aspired to lead a regiment like Livingston's, but Hazen and Antill reached Philadelphia first, got control of the new unit, and agreed to prevent Dugan's employment. When Dugan reached Philadelphia he was able to obtain money only to raise three companies of Rangers and pick his own officers. Since Dugan was a successful recruiter, friction developed with agents. After an attack by Hazen on Dugan's character, the latter temporarily withdrew from all military activities until his name was cleared.[21]

Meanwhile in Philadelphia Antill and Hazen had been working closely together. Impressed by their apparent enthusiasm and ability, Congress on January 20 created a Second Canadian Regiment of 1,000 men to be composed of four battalions each containing five companies of 50 men. On the same day it directed the commanding officer in Canada to appoint commissioners whose function it would be to ascertain the losses suffered by Hazen. Two days later Congress named Hazen to command the new regiment and Antill to be second in command as a lieutenant colonel.

At first Hazen tried to refuse the honor, which included appointment as a brigadier general. A committee of Congress was designated to persuade him, "whose Arguments got the better of every Objection which I then made, and I at last consented not without Reluctance to take the Command of the four Canadian Battalions." His reluctance stemmed from two concerns. If the expedition failed, he faced the prospect of the confiscation of his property in Canada; he was also likely to lose his British half pay for life. On the first problem, Congress assured him that failure was impossible, considering the size of the force that would be sent into Canada. On the second, he was promised indemnification for any loss of half pay he sustained by entering the American service. In consequence, he accepted appointment as a colonel.[22]

Briefly his appointment was withdrawn because he was thought to be under parole to General Carleton. When the committee learned that he had been paroled but still kept in close confinement until he had been freed by the Americans, he was reinstated. He and Antill were given £1,000 in specie for the use of their battalion. Antill also received $200 for his expenses and Hazen $533 as an advance on the property losses he had sustained in Canada. They were also authorized to pay the bounty sum of six and two thirds dollars.[23]

On January 24 President of Congress John Hancock penned another letter to the Canadians. As translated, he addressed them as "Amis et Compatriotes" (Friends and Fellow Countrymen), and stated: "Nous ne vous laisserons pas exposé à la fureur des vos ennemis & des nôtres. . . . Si des forces plus considérables sont requis, elles vous feront envoyées" (We will not leave you exposed to the wrath of your enemies and ours. . . . If larger forces are needed, they will be sent to you). In promising additional troops, he was committing Congress to more than it could deliver, but the Canadians were supposed to see the call to arms and the brotherly tone of the letter instead. Hazen probably carried the address to Montreal, where he and Antill arrived in February; Wooster published and disseminated the document.[24]

The Coos country was swept up in the war almost from the beginning. In November 1775 General Bayley had written Congress to urge the total possession of "so Precious a Jewell as Canada." However, he warned against too great a reliance on the French Canadians who might, once Canada was freed from British rule, turn against the Americans. "Our People are Doubtless amongst them, which will ware out Their Papist Bigotry. Untill that Is Ye Case, No Great Trust to the French." Reminiscent of Hazen's proposal eleven years earlier, Bayley urged the building of a road from Coos to St. John, which an army could cover in six days. Besides its military value, it would promote a valuable fur trade (a million pelts a year, he thought) if independence was on the way.[25]

Captain Thomas Johnson of Newbury was directed to mark such a road with blazed trees. He and three others left Newbury on snowshoes on March 26, 1776, and reached St. John a week later, a distance of 92 miles. According to the journal that Johnson kept, the distance from Boston to St. John by way of Charlestown and Crown Point was 310 miles. From Boston to St. John via Newbury measured 237 miles, or 73 miles and ten days shorter than the route by Lake Champlain. In addition, it bypassed the British navy on the lake and some of the enemy forts on the Richelieu.[26]

During the winter of 1775–76 Bayley wrote Washington repeatedly to urge construction of the road, and he enclosed Johnson's report to strengthen his argument. When Congress delayed a decision, Washington himself ordered it built and sent £250 for the purpose in April. Meanwhile, as soon as the snow was gone James Whitelaw, later surveyor general of Vermont, marked out a military highway. Bayley followed with a force of 110 men and teams to cut out the trees and start construction. Congress approved the plan in May, but the work was already under way. Bayley's men were paid $10 a month, board, and a half pint of rum per day for the forty-five days they worked. They completed construction from Wells River to Cabot, six miles above Peacham. About thirty miles of it were completed, most of it no more than a bridle path. Bayley proclaimed that "Cattle may be Easily Drove to St. John if wanted there, by our army. On the Shortest notice I will Proceed on the road to Compleat it." Work was stopped late in June after Washington's letter describing the retreat from Canada and warning against opening a fast invasion route for the British.[27]

The Coos country had been involved in more than road building. From the beginning Colonel Timothy Bedel had had three companies at St. John and elsewhere in the Canadian campaign. In January the New Hampshire legislature decided to raise a regiment consisting of eight companies under Bedel for the use of the "Northern Continental Army."[28]

Upon their return to Canada, Hazen and Antill began recruiting in earnest. Hazen's recruitment warrant announced the terms of enlistment in French and promised the men forty livres (six and two-thirds dollars) "du jour de leur Engagement" (from the day of their enlistment), plus monthly pay. They were to furnish their own clothing and equipment, or have it supplied at their own expense. For a time recruitment went fairly well among the "Congreganistes," as the supporters of Congress were called, and by April 1 he claimed 250 men, although he had to stop temporarily because his recruiting money had run out. During this period he has been described by a Canadian writer as the soul of the Canadian revolutionary movement. He was seen everywhere, had powerful connections and was "obviously the most active and influential man in this part of the country."[29]

He also lost no time in pressing his claims for compensation for his losses at St. John, which he said represented revenue of more than £500 sterling a year and an investment of £4,000. Writing to

Congress in February, he enclosed the report of the commissioners appointed by Wooster, with which he concurred, together with his own comments on each item. The commissioners made their survey before the final destruction of Hazen's buildings, although they had already been badly pillaged. Including livestock, crops, fences, and many other items, they arrived at a total loss of 68,180 livres or, at the rate of six livres to the dollar, some $11,363. Congress was shocked at the size of the estimate—feeling that it was not sufficiently precise and that it claimed questionable items. It therefore required the commissioners it was sending to Canada to look further into the matter.[30]

When it became apparent that Arnold's injury required that he be relieved at Quebec, Wooster departed for that purpose late in March, having first appointed Colonel Hazen to the command in Montreal. Hazen was directed to send his regiment to Quebec, and some of them went. But he declared that it was impossible for them to go until they had been paid, and that nearly half of a company that started deserted on the way.[31]

Writing to Antill, who was recruiting around Quebec, Hazen said he was moving into the Chateau de Ramezay and had offered Antill's wife and children room and meals there until they were better provided for. He urged Antill to try to take over Dugan's enlistees and to "lay aside the Dilicate Gentleman and put on the Recruiting officer." On April 1 and again on April 7 Hazen wrote Schuyler in some detail about the changing attitude of the Canadians. Painting a gloomy picture of future relations, he attributed the difficulty to the excesses of the American soldiers and civilians, whose behavior was making the French turn against the American cause. The faltering at Quebec; the worthless paper money and so, presumably, the bankruptcy of Congress; the impressment of their goods and services, sometimes at the point of a bayonet; pay, if it was forthcoming, in paper or in certificates the quartermaster would not redeem—all this plus the fact that they failed to see enough Americans on hand to protect them made them appear to be "waiting an opportunity to join our enemies." Hazen was later commended by Congress for his concern and his acute portrayal of a dismaying situation.[32]

Schuyler hastened word by courier to Hazen at Montreal and Wooster at Quebec of the approaching reinforcements and the 3,000 to 4,000 more that would follow. He directed the two commanders to spread as widely as possible an account of the hasty British retreat from Boston. Washington, in commenting to Congress on the reports he received from Schuyler, said that he hoped Hazen's distresses would be obviated by the congressional commissioners and more troops: "The security of that Country is of the utmost importance to us. This cannot be done so effectually by Conquest, as by taking strong hold of the affections & confidence of the Inhabitants. It is to be lamented, that any conduct of the continental Troops should tend to alienate their Affections from us."[33]

Among Hazen's other worries while he was commander was the disposition of the Indians. He took great pains to insure the friendship of at least the nearby tribes and he induced them to call a conference. Of the Canadians in general: "Indeed there is nothing but ploting and preparations making against us throughout the whole district," and he believed that the priests were behind most of it. Indeed the only priest who would grant absolution when all others refused was Father Peter Floquet, who was now his chaplain. Arnold when he assumed command at Montreal called Hazen "a sensible, judicious officer, and well acquainted with this country." He told Schuyler that "if we are not immediately supported with eight or ten thousand men, a good train of artillery, well served, and a military chest well furnished, the ministerial troops, if they attempt it will regain the country and we shall be obliged to quit it, the fatal consequences of which are too obvious."[34]

Reinforcements were hurried into Canada in company-size units, but they were too few and too late to help with the siege of Quebec. Many were needed merely as replacements for American deserters and for militiamen who, at the expiration of their enlistments, could not be persuaded to reenlist. They arrived at Quebec just in time to contract the smallpox or to take part in the disorderly retreat from the area. British reinforcements and a fleet began to arrive on May 6, and at last Carleton sallied forth to break the siege. The Americans abandoned the area, leaving all their munitions and supplies behind them in their hurry to reach the relative safety of Montreal.

In their desperation many American leaders were now pinning all their hopes on the congressional commissioners, endowing them in advance with some extraordinary power to reverse the unfavorable trends. Yet the instructions the commissioners received when they were appointed on February 15 made it clear that they were merely agents of persuasion, armed with nothing more than the power of the tongue and pen. The Canadians were to be shown that their interests and those of the Americans were "inseparately united" and that "it is our earnest Desire to adopt them into our Union as a Sister Colony."

The clergy were to be soothed with a promise of "the full, perfect, and peaceable Possession and Enjoyment of all their Estates," yet the people generally were to be promised civil privileges, free exercise of their religion, and exemption from payment of tithes and taxes to support any religion. Despite their contradictory instructions, these commissioners were to represent the authority of the American government, with power over all officers and soldiers.[35]

The commissioners were Benjamin Franklin, Samuel Chase, and Charles Carroll of Carrollton. By a separate resolution Carroll was asked to invite his cousin, Father John Carroll, to accompany the group. This was a happy choice because John, a Jesuit priest, knew the French language well but was a passionate believer in American freedom. In Montreal he became the confidant of many French people, including Mrs. Hazen. The delegates arrived in that city on April 29 after a forced delay while the ice went out of the lakes. At St. John their carriage from Montreal had not arrived and they spent their first night on Canadian soil at the inn at the manor house of Moses Hazen, although he was not present. In Montreal they established a press and did whatever was in their power, but they were soon engulfed in the rout from Quebec and the resulting reversal of neutral or pro-American sentiment in the French countryside. Father Carroll made contact with the sympathetic Father Floquet, for which the latter was severely censured by his bishop, as he also was for admitting to Easter communion Canadians who were serving in the American army. Father Carroll found that he could not even talk with other priests for, satisfied with the assurances contained in the Quebec Act and well informed about the anti-Catholic sentiments of Congress, they would have nothing to do with its emissaries.[36]

While he was in command at Montreal Hazen sent Colonel Bedel and his regiment to hold a small fortified post at The Cedars, about 30 miles above Montreal. Bedel had acquired great influence among some of the Canadian Indians, and Washington had directed him to attend upon them whenever they asked him. In May they held a council at Caughnawaga and Bedel attended by invitation.[37]

After Arnold came to Montreal, but while Bedel was absent from his post, a British and Indian party attacked The Cedars. Major Isaac Butterfield surrendered without a contest and reinforcements under Major Henry Sherburne were waylaid and overpowered. Arnold set out to relieve the place but heavy fire forced him back. He called a council of war at St. Anne on May 25 to explain his plan of getting above The Cedars and surprising the post from the rear.

Colonels de Haas and Hazen opposed the project, Hazen explaining that the Indians were too vigilant to be surpirsed in this manner, and that they would massacre their prisoners if an attack took place. Hazen as a former Ranger carried great weight and Arnold, highly irritated, was outvoted, some "reproachful language" taking place between the two. A truce was finally arranged for the exchange of prisoners at The Cedars, but Bedel and Butterfield later had to stand trial for their part in the event, while Hazen gained a potential enemy in Arnold.[38]

Arnold sent Hazen to take command at St. John and Chambly, and here in his own valley he served out the remainder of the Canadian war. The commissioners were already pointing out that if the enemy's frigate passed the mouth of the Richelieu, the American army would be cut off from their provisions and a retreat by water. Therefore, Hazen set out to repair the forts and supervise the construction of gundelos. Franklin had already started back for the States and by the middle of May, with the British in hot pursuit of the retreating Americans, there was not enough time to do all that was required along the Richelieu. Increasingly, doubts were being expressed of the possibility of holding any of Canada, or at least of Montreal.

The last half of May and the first half of June brought scenes of utter confusion in the Montreal–Richelieu area. Panic seized the American command as it faced the prospect of a strong British force moving on the city. Soldiers were straggling back from the front carrying the smallpox germs, and many were deserting south to the States. It was a demoralized, disease-ridden army. Hazen warned General John Sullivan, who prepared a last-ditch stand at Sorel: "Do not rely on any real assistance from the Canadians whom you are collecting together—I know them well; be assured that, in our present situation, they will leave us in the hour of difficulty. . . . The Congress has promised them what is out of your power to perform. What are we to expect from a handful of such men, against the well-known best troops in the world?" Hazen knew what he was talking about because his own regiment, which at one time he numbered at 477 men, had dwindled until fewer than half followed him out of the country.[39]

In Montreal Arnold, in preparation for abandoning the city, was engaged in a widespread seizure of goods for the use of the army. His new young aide de camp, James Wilkinson, was directed to purchase or seize specific merchandise listed as the property of the inhabitants. Wilkinson says he refused, for which Arnold called him "more nice than wise," but that others were found to do the work. In any case Arnold dispatched Major Scott with a large consignment of goods to the custody of Hazen at Chambly. At first Hazen refused to accept them, recognizing them as the property of his Montreal friends. Eventually he forwarded them to St. John. In the confusion they were broken open and plundered, whereupon Arnold showered Hazen with accusations and wrote Sullivan: "This is not the first or last order Colonel Hazen has disobeyed. I think him a man of too much consequence for the post he is in." Hazen demanded a court of inquiry into Arnold's accusations, which he called an "undeserved reflection," while the latter prepared military charges against Hazen. And there the matter rested until the retreat was completed.[40]

A romantic tradition persists that Hazen set fire to his own manor house before he abandoned it. On June 18, at the height of the retreat, he is supposed to have crossed the river about sunset and fired the house, barns, and other buildings. The facts are that General Sullivan ordered the destruction not only of Hazen's property but of his wife's at St. Thérèse, so as to prevent their use by the British. Antill later admitted that, acting under orders from Sullivan, he personally directed the destruction.[41]

The retreat was hastily improvised. Wagons for the Canadian women and children were added to the baggage train from Chambly to St. John. Confusion was so great that Amable, only son of Captain Paulint, was left behind; he was later discovered being happily entertained by British soldiers. Time was found to strip two and a half tons of lead roofing from the stone house within Fort St. John, and it was later made into ammunition for the American army. From St. John soldiers and families were evacuated by boat, first to Isle aux Noix and ultimately into Lake Champlain. Hazen's unit was originally harbored at Crown Point but in July was moved to Ticonderoga.[42]

Arnold, dismayed but not dispirited by the debacle, was quick to see the importance of repairing Crown Point, which had been a ruin since the great fire three years previously. This was at variance with the decision of the board of officers at Ticonderoga to abandon the post altogether and fall back on Ticonderoga. Washington in New York unsuccessfully tried to head off such a move in a letter to General Gates in which he declared that to give up Crown Point was to give up the lake, "a key to all these Colonies." Arnold also saw the necessity of the quick construction of an American flotilla upon the lake to counter an inevitable British invasion. Before the summer was over, he was in charge of building just such a fleet at Skenesborough.[43]

Meanwhile Congress directed Washington to conduct inquiries into the behavior of all officers accused of "cowardice, plundering, embezzlement of publick moneys, and other misdemeanours." The occupation of Canada followed by the disorderly retreat provided many occasions for irregular behavior, and during the summer a succession of trials was held at Ticonderoga under the direction of General Horatio Gates, the commander of the northern army in the field. One of the first was the court-martial of Colonel Bedel for his part in the fiasco at The Cedars. On the evidence of Arnold the court convicted, cashiered, and dismissed him from the service. Gates approved the findings and referred them to Congress. After the excitement of the retreat had died down, the papers and Bedel's defense were submitted to the new Board of War which reversed the decision, gave him an honorable acquittal, and restored his rank with a new commission.[44]

Another stormy sitting at Ticonderoga was the court-martial of Colonel Hazen, who was under arrest on charges preferred by Colonel Arnold. The court of thirteen field officers was convened on July 19 under Colonel Enoch Poor, while the judge advocate was Major Scott, who had delivered the goods to Hazen in the first place. The court found that Arnold's charges were without foundation, adjudged Hazen not guilty, and unanimously acquitted him with honor. Gates confirmed the findings and ordered him released from arrest. During the trial the court had refused to accept the testimony of Scott as coming from too interested a party. To this Arnold objected, calling it "unprecedented, & I think Unjust." He was already at Skenesborough, harassed by the fear that he would not have his fleet completed in time to meet the British invasion. The court demanded an apology for his objections, which Arnold refused except that, when the war was over, he would give any member of the court "the Satisfaction his Nice honour may require." The court, viewing this as a challenge to its prestige, was determined to punish Arnold for contempt and asked Gates to arrest him. The General, however, cut its duties short by dissolving the court for, as he told Congress, "The United States must not be deprived of that excellent Officer's Service, at this important Moment." Later he wrote Congress concerning Arnold's work at Skenesborough: "With infinite satisfaction I have committed the whole of that department to his care, convinced that he will thereby add to the brilliant reputation he has so deservingly acquired."[45]

Gates's report to Congress of the court-martial proceedings was apparently never acted upon by that body, which twice postponed a conclusive debate on the subject. Gates's friends thought it not worthwhile to pursue the matter. But Arnold's enemies bombarded Congress with additional information and charges against him, which led him in fury and desperation to write Gates: "I cannot but think it extremely cruel, when I have sacrificed my ease, health, and a great part of my private property, in the cause of my country, to be calumniated as a robber and thief." But Arnold was far too preoccupied at Skenesborough to demand another hearing.[46]

However, the prickly Hazen was not, and he demanded a Court of Inquiry into the aspersions against his character. The court was held at Albany on December 2. At issue were thirty kegs of rum, one of brandy, and several bales of tobacco, removed from Montreal at the time of the retreat. Concerning the rum, Arnold had written: "Colonel Hazen can best tell how much he sold." After examining all the evidence and hearing Arnold, the court found these remarks an aspersion against Hazen's character, and therefore his complaint was just. Exonerated by two courts, Hazen was apparently innocent of disobedience or corruption. On the other hand, they specifically did not accuse Arnold of any misbehavior, especially after his heroism at the battle of Valcour Island.[47]

Two other inquiries, both at Arnold's request, totally exonerated him as well, both concluded in May of 1777, almost a year after the retreat from Canada. The unrelenting Hazen accused Arnold of plundering the Montreal merchants for his own gain, but the Board of War in Philadelphia cleared him of the charge. Major John Brown made thirteen accusations of gross irregularities against him, many of them frivolous, and again the Board of War investigated. From the voluminous papers Arnold supplied, plus the testimony of Charles Carroll, formerly a commissioner to Canada and now a member of the board, it was entirely satisfied concerning Arnold's character and conduct, "so cruelly and groundlessly aspersed" by Brown.[48]

And so Arnold was cleared of any misconduct at the time of the retreat from Canada. Hazen succeeded only in clearing his own name, which he achieved during the first trial at Ticonderoga. A less impetuous or vengeful man might have decided to drop the matter at that point. Instead, he sought additional vindication for himself and the ruin of Arnold, in the latter of which he failed. Much of the evidence against Arnold stemmed from Wilkinson, who spread the word, and later recorded it in his memoirs, that Arnold pillaged Montreal and pocketed the proceeds. But Wilkinson's career was soon to be studded with indiscretions and betrayals of his own, and his suspicions demand no more credence than two Board of War inquiries gave them.[49]

IV

The American Revolution 1776—1778

Ticonderoga in the summer of 1776 was many things—the command post of the northern army, a hospital for the diseased mob that had fled from Canada, and the seat of a series of courts-martial. It was also the gathering point of Hazen's soldiers and their families who had left Canada with him. Almost entirely French, they had either seen profit and excitement ahead, gone too far to be able to remain safely in Canada, or absorbed a few ideas about American freedoms. In any case, they gave up all their worldly goods to follow a retreating army. Others—men, women, and children—straggled out of Canada for many months to come.

Two captains of Livingston's regiment arrived at Ticonderoga in August of 1776 and were questioned closely. They told a harrowing story: officers of the Canadian militia who joined the American army were forced to burn their appointments, even if they burned their fingers in the process. Militia officers who accepted congressional commissions as officers went through the same procedure and then were put on warships for transportation to the West Indies. The governor confiscated the effects of all who followed the American army out of the country or who remained concealed inside Canada. This report was somewhat exaggerated because, although the British tried and convicted many Canadians for rebellion, and even executed a few, they applied the penalties unevenly and the families of some of Hazen's soldiers were able to remain safely, if quietly, in Canada. Nevertheless, the treatment of militia officers who supported the Americans was harsh. French subjects had only recently begun to receive militia commissions, which carried status such as special seats in their parish churches. All the more reason, then, to chastise them at the least sign of disloyalty.[1]

In September Hazen and Antill were directed to take their small regiment to Albany, where a beginning was made to provide housing for the families. But in November the men were ordered into winter quarters at Fishkill.* On the edge of this sprawling village of fifty houses, and forming a town by itself, lay the principal depot of the American army. Here were to be found magazines, hospitals, and workshops housed in large barracks at the foot of a mountain. It was a nerve center of the whole army and, after New York City fell to the British, a post that needed constant vigilance to guard against British raids. This was not the last time Hazen's regiment would be stationed there, and it eventually included housing for the families of some of his men.[2]

In September Congress voted to raise eighty-eight battalions, allotted by quota among the states, and it authorized a bounty of $20 and provided for land grants to veterans at the end of the war. On October 23 it decided to maintain Hazen's regiment "on the original establishment" and authorized him to fill it by recruiting in any of the thirteen states. The regiment was not to belong to any particular state, but was to be officered and paid by Congress. This led to the dubbing of both Hazen's and Livingston's regiments as "Congress's Own" or "General Washington's Life Guards" until Congress finally resolved that the term was "improper, and ought not to be kept up." However, the term "Hazen's Infernals" was sometimes used, usually admiringly, in recognition of their fighting qualities. The regiment was one of the best disciplined in the army and was never guilty of mutiny or other disturbance, as were so many other units. Hazen may not necessarily have been loved, but he was respected and obeyed by his men who, as aliens, perhaps realized that they had no other recourse. When called on they fought bravely, sometimes furiously, and they were the unit, together with their commander, which led the clamor for a second invasion of Canada.[3]

Recruiting proved to be more difficult than Hazen had expected. All the states were trying to fill their own quotas, and Massachusetts supplemented the congressional bounty despite the request of Congress that it not be done. At Albany Hazen found New England recruiters outbidding him. At Ticonderoga, where he tried to recruit from southern regiments, he was blocked by commanders who, reasonably

*See Appendix for the approximate calendar of Hazen's regiment during the war.

enough, refused to release their men until they were regularly discharged. He had little luck in New England and finally did his best
work in New York. Even here he created a controversy because the
New York Convention resented what it called his unscrupulous recruiting tactics, which were making inroads upon a small population
which had its own quota to fill. His success at the expense of the
state's recruiters was attributed to his pretense of raising men to be
stationed near Congress for its direct defense.[4]

Antill recruited for the regiment in the middle states and he
had moderately good luck, especially in Pennsylvania and Maryland,
although his total was below the goals Hazen had set for him. Originally he was to raise eight companies of 50 men each, but with Hazen's
faltering recruitment in the North, four or five more companies were
added. Through their combined efforts the regiment numbered 486
men in June 1777, far short of the 1,000 authorized, a fact which
Hazen attributed to a shortage of recruitment money.[5]

Meanwhile Hazen was learning to wield the pen with as much
facility as the sword. Recognizing his special relationship to Congress
and determined to improve upon it whenever possible, he bombarded
that body with memorials and petitions, some of them running to a
dozen pages. They fall into three categories. First, there were numerous suits in behalf of his regiment and its individual members. He
labored indefatigably in their behalf by interceding with the Congress, although he often made his approaches through Washington.
Second, and equally tenaciously, he wrote in behalf of his own rank,
perquisites, and his lost property in Canada. Finally, and gratuitously,
he delivered himself frequently and at length upon the state of the
war, particularly as it impinged upon Canada. Congress must at times
have wished for some way to stem the flow.

An early example of the third type is his plea of November
1776 to rebuild Crown Point and make Ticonderoga an impregnable
fortress so that the northern front might be secure against invasion:
"A moment's time you have not to lose in making the necessary
preparations, or fatal may be the consequences." He explained his
temerity in pressing Congress by saying that "my motive is good."
He was right, of course, and Burgoyne proved it the following year.[6]

In his own behalf he wrote a memorial during the summer of
1776 pertaining to his losses in Canada. On September 24 Congress
voted him $1,095 to cover the loss of his livestock, hay, and other
articles said to have been taken for the use of the Continental Army.
This amount, together with the $533⅓ already voted, was the total

recommended by the commissioners appointed by General Wooster. However, Congress refused to subsidize his other losses unless a general provision was made for compensating all others who suffered similar distress, and that, thought the members, was "a subject worthy to be considered, after the close of the war." [7]

To Hazen's immediate rejoinder that the amount was inadequate, Congress on October 23 added another $966⅔ to cover his tools, anchors, and cables which were appropriated for the use of Montgomery's army. Thus instead of the $11,363 he had documented in his original claim, he received $2,595. Nothing was allowed on his buildings and their contents, fields of grain, and the loss of work from mills, ashery, and forge. To the original claim he now added another $16,333, his estimate of the debts he contracted for the public service in Canada during 1776. Part of this, $7,600, was a private debt to Colonel Christie, which ultimately went to court. The rest was largely sums he advanced to his recruiters and regimental captains. Many years later he was still trying to collect these sums, together with interest.[8]

After the retreat from Canada the people of the Coos country felt dangerously exposed, and their scouts explored new invasion routes and kept contact with neutral or friendly Indians. The Indians felt poorly treated in Canada—Carleton was reported as refusing to allow them to purchase blankets or ammunition unless they took up arms. They would gladly come to Coos if there were any means for their support. Schuyler allowed $150 for the purpose, but rejected the idea of a fort which the inhabitants wanted built at the border.[9]

Referring to his letter to Congress in which he had urged the rebuilding of Crown Point and the strengthening of the entire northern frontier, Hazen suggested to Bayley some steps that would make the Coos front more secure. He advised the creation of a large observation corps to gather intelligence in Canada, and the erection of blockhouses which would deter marauding parties from attacking with small arms, it being "hardly worth the Enemys attention to Clear a Road for Cannon." The blockhouses were not built for another two years, but Bayley and Bedel repeatedly sent scouting parties north to the St. Lawrence. Years later Bayley had still not been paid for his various advances, which added up to $60,000 for the patriot cause. He sacrificed all of his estate to pay his debts, and died a poor man.[10]

In October 1776 Governor Carleton left Canada on his campaign to capture control of Lake Champlain. He departed with a new hope concerning the attitude of Canadians toward the war, yet it was tinged with sober realism: "I think there is nothing to fear from them, while we are in a state of prosperity, and nothing to hope for when in distress . . . the multitude is influenced only by hopes of gain, or fear of punishment." He captured or destroyed Arnold's fleet at the Battle of Valcour Island and during the subsequent pursuit. Yet it was a hollow victory because Carleton, having delayed his invasion until mid-October, reached no farther than Crown Point before cold weather forced him back to Canada. The Americans, having gained a season by his delay, need not have sacrificed their fleet at Valcour, but could with dignity have retired intact to Ticonderoga. During his short stay at Crown Point, Carleton was gratified by the number of local residents who reported for duty with the king's armies or who wanted a pardon for having erroneously joined the American cause. His report provides abundant evidence of the divided loyalties of residents in the Champlain Valley.[11]

During the summer and fall of 1776 Washington had been forced out of Long Island and then Manhattan, but he brought his troops safely into New Jersey by way of White Plains. Pursued by the British, he crossed the Delaware River into Pennsylvania. The British established several garrisons in New Jersey. On December 26 Washington made a surprise attack against a Hessian fort at Trenton and captured most of the garrison. On January 3 he also repelled the British at Princeton and sent them back to their posts nearer New York City. Then he went into winter quarters at Morristown. His victories had cleared the British from most of New Jersey and greatly rejuvenated American morale after his discouraging retreat of the autumn.

Hazen's unit, which was still growing, wintered at Fishkill, and the families of some of his men gravitated there as well. He reported to General Putnam at Peekskill in the following May of 1777 and at first was scheduled to join Muhlenberg's brigade which, added to Weedon's, was to form a division under Major General Nathaniel Greene. However, Brigadier General Sullivan asked Washington to allow Hazen's regiment to remain with him, and an exchange was arranged between Greene and Sullivan.[12]

In the spring Washington broke winter quarters and on May 28 marched twenty miles south to Middlebrook to be nearer Howe's probable line of march, for the British were known to be about to start for Philadelphia. What was not yet known was that they would decide to go by sea. Washington placed several units of Sullivan's command, including Hazen's, at Princeton, where they had arrived by June 1.

Hazen became involved in two difficulties, one of which brought him a rebuke from Washington. Major Chrétien de Colerus, a French volunteer eager for glory under American arms, had been commissioned by Congress in 1776, but when he reported to Hazen's regiment at Princeton he was not welcomed and was apparently treated with disrespect. Washington wrote Hazen that no officer of inferior or equal rank had a right to complain, "nor will such conduct be countenanced, or the like in future pass without being properly noticed. . . . I shall expect to hear no further objections upon this Subject." Washington did not usually write in so peremptory a manner except when the organization and discipline of the army were in question. Nevertheless, Hazen's officers were disturbed at having to make room for a major outside the unit. De Colerus lost his dispute over rank with Major Taylor, and shortly left the regiment in disgust.[13]

Hazen's other tangle with authority was the complaint he and another officer made to Sullivan concerning the behavior on the march of the divisional surgeon, Dr. John Cochran. Before the dispute was concluded, with a finding against Cochran, Washington and Director General of Hospitals Dr. William Shippen, had been involved, and a court of inquiry held. Sullivan declared that he wanted to be relieved "if I forward a complaint against a Surgeon of the General Hospital I must fight all the sons of Esculapius in Course or bear their insults."[14]

At about this time Congress laid down a new regulation concerning communications. It had recently received letters from Major Generals Sullivan and Greene and Brigadier General Knox. It resolved that they were an attempt to influence congressional decisions, an invasion of the liberties of the people, and an indication of a lack of confidence in the justice of Congress. They were called "an interference of so dangerous a tendency," and officers were warned that if they were unwilling to serve under the authority of Congress they were free to resign their commissions and retire. So much for the subordination of the military to the civilian branch of government![15]

Congress's strictures against letter-writing officers apparently did not apply to Hazen, who frequently unburdened himself of his claims and advice. In July he was in Philadelphia to present his bills for 1776. For the time being all he received was $800 which he had advanced to Antill in Canada, the payment of which had to await presentation of Antill's receipt. For the rest, Congress directed the commissioners for auditing accounts to distinguish between sums due Hazen for hard money advanced by him, and those for commodities furnished by him for the use of the army in Canada. The former sums were to be repaid in specie, with interest at six percent from May 1, 1776, and Hazen figured them at about $10,000.[16]

Hazen's regiment, a mixture of French Canadians and Americans, gave him various kinds of difficulties, not the least of which was the occasional hostility between the two nationalities. An effort was made to minimize this problem by putting the French into companies of their own with French officers. As for desertion, a blight on the whole American army, it was the Americans of the regiment who were more likely to offend, because the Canadians had no home to return to. In July James McMullen of Captain O'Harra's company was charged with "Desertion, with a view of getting to Ireland," to which he pleaded guilty. He was sentenced to receive 100 lashes on his bare back and to be sent on board a Continental frigate to serve out the rest of his enlistment. Discipline was severe during the Revolution, for which Washington has sometimes been criticized, but he approved and published this sentence in General Orders.[17]

In June the British raided New Jersey from New York City and did considerable damage. General Sullivan, as a reprisal, mounted a campaign to Staten Island for August 22. He detached several of Hazen's companies and although Hazen himself did not take part, Antill did. Hazen's total regimental strength was then nearly 700 men. As Sullivan later reported, all was going well, many prisoners taken and much military equipment destroyed when, contrary to intelligence, he ran into the British 52nd Regiment. In the scramble to retreat, he could not find enough boats, and the British captured 8 officers and 127 privates, while 10 were killed and 15 wounded.

Among the captured was Captain James Heron of Hazen's regiment "whose bravery could Scarcely be paralleled." Hazen's total casualties were eight officers and forty men. Another captive, whose name did not appear on the list of men desiring to be exchanged, was Antill. Immediately he was suspected of going over to the enemy, Sullivan going so far as to declare that "his Brother officers Say they have Long Since Suspected his Intentions from the whole Tenor of his Conduct." In November Charlotte Antill petitioned Congress and was granted permission to join her husband in New York. When exchanged much later, Antill was able to convince the authorities that he had not changed sides and that his capture was one of the hazards of warfare.[18]

But Major John Taylor of Hazen's regiment charged Sullivan with mismanagement of the Staten Island campaign—poor planning, unnecessarily long marches without rest or provisions, a long route back into New Jersey, and Sullivan's bringing his horses back and allowing plundering to take place. Congress directed Washington to appoint a Court of Inquiry but the battles for control of Philadelphia intervened. At Brandywine Sullivan caused additional questions to be raised about his competence, so that Congress recalled him from his command until the inquiry could be completed. Only with difficulty was Washington able to persuade Congress to allow Sullivan to continue temporarily in service, the reason being that there were so few officers of his rank.[19]

The Court of Inquiry was held in October and despite the testimony against Sullivan by Majors Taylor and Reid and Captain Chambers of Hazen's regiment, the court honorably acquitted him of "any unsoldierlike Conduct" on Staten Island, declaring that "he merits the approbation of his Country and not its censure." Thus, in spite of the grumbling among some of Hazen's officers, Sullivan emerged with a clean bill of health and his alleged mistakes at Brandywine were forgotten in the general rejoicing of both Congress and Washington.[20]

General Howe had decided to invade Pennsylvania by water instead of by land. He avoided the Delaware River because of its heavy fortifications and instead sailed to the upper reaches of Chesapeake Bay, the head of the Elk River. He landed his 15,000 men unopposed late in August. Washington had to assume that Howe's destination was Philadelphia, about thirty miles away, and he intended to harass and obstruct the British army on the march. He did neither effectively despite the advice of Greene and Lafayette, leading the latter to say later, "le général Washington s'exposa très imprudement" (General Washington exposed himself most unwisely).[21]

Instead Washington chose, probably wisely, to try to block the British path at Brandywine Creek. Unfortunately the Creek had many fording places and Washington could not, not did he see the need to, guard all of them. He took his stand on the east bank of Chad's Ford, the one most likely to be used on the road to Philadelphia. He disposed his other units along the Creek, with Sullivan's main force at Brinton's Ford, next above Chad's. Hazen was sent to watch Jones's Ford, the third crossing, while those above Jones's were left more or less unattended.

Hazen's later recollections of the ensuing events led him to the following conclusions: "However Great & good his Exc the Commander in Chief of the late American Army may be—yet it will be found on enquiry into conduct that he is no more than a man and that as such it is possible he may be subject to some errors as well as some others—In the Battle of Brandywine there was a want of information and in that of Germantown of experience—Success in either case might have changed the face of American Affairs."[22]

The British moved up opposite Chad's Ford on September 10, whether in full strength or not Washington did not know, but he was determined to make a stand there. In the middle of the morning of the 11th he received messages from both Hazen and Lieutenant Colonel James Ross that large British units were marching north along the Creek, apparently headed for crossings at the forks of the Brandywine. Although concerned that that could mean a flanking movement, which the British had used so successfully on Long Island, he decided to attack the rest of their force opposite him. Then he received an unevaluated report from Major Spear which Sullivan believed made Hazen's report incorrect, because Spear declared that he had seen no British troop movements along the west bank. What neither Sullivan nor Washington checked was the timing of Spear's appearance at the locations he mentioned. In any case Washington abandoned his plan of attack and changed the troop movements of two of his units.

Early in the afternoon a farmer arrived at Washington's headquarters with the shocking news that a large British force was advancing down the *east* side of the Creek. Ross and Hazen had been correct, Spear misinterpreted. The British had forded the two branches of the Brandywine without hindrance and were now nearly in the rear of the Americans. By late afternoon a savage battle raged near Birmingham Meeting House. Sullivan's units bore the brunt of the fighting but he and the other commanders, having failed to scout the ground in advance, found themselves fighting on strange terrain.

The rout was complete, including the loss of a large part of the artillery, and the British path was almost clear to Philadelphia. The American casualties were between 1,200 and 1,300, the British 583. Hazen's losses were four officers and 73 men. Washington's battered army, at least 1,000 of which were barefoot, could offer little further resistance. A bad storm ruined tens of thousands of rounds of their ammunition, while the British skillfully smashed Brigadier General Anthony Wayne's division. Consequently, the British entered Philadelphia unopposed on September 25.[23]

The British made their main encampment at Germantown, a sprawling town five miles north of Philadelphia. Washington, having regrouped his army and received reinforcements, decided to seize the offensive. He drew up plans for a complicated surprise attack which called for simultaneous advances on several different roads. Sullivan's division, including Hazen's regiment, was assigned and enthusiastically executed a direct march toward the town. But the surprise was lost when British patrols at 3 A.M. on the morning of October 4 discovered the approach of American units, although the Americans did not know that they had been seen. A unit headed for the support of Sullivan was held up for a half hour at a fortified stone house, all units were confused by the terrain in dense fog and smoke, while troops converging upon Germantown by more circuitous routes than Sullivan's were tardy in arriving. Yet a persistent advance was made into the middle of the town and victory seemed within grasp when everything began to go wrong. In the fog American units on the left fired on each other and thought they were being cut off by the enemy. This exchange of fire, the fog, and the delay at the stone house gave the British troops time to rally on the right and attack Sullivan's extended and exhausted line.

A retreat by leading units turned into a rout. Despite all the officers could do, the retreat became general and ended twenty miles away, where the army was finally reformed. But the battle was over by ten o'clock in the morning, the Americans having suffered about 1,100 casualties, the British about half that number. Hazen's casualties were 3 officers and 19 men. The British were secure for the winter in Philadelphia and its environs, while Washington took his twice-defeated army into winter quarters at Valley Forge.[24]

Later in the fall Hazen, who had been confined in a hospital, sent Sullivan 400 pairs of shoes with the information that he knew where several hundred more could be found if they were needed—enough to outfit the whole division. Hazen merely requested that his own regiment be attended first, the remainder to be used as Sullivan saw fit. Since Brandywine the army had experienced a desperate shortage of shoes. Efforts were made to find a substitute for rawhides, and steps were taken to get leather and deerskins in North Carolina. Only Sullivan's division approached the winter reasonably well clad, even Washington's main army often being barefoot at Valley Forge.[25]

The war had progressed far differently on the northern front in 1777. Burgoyne mounted a massive but slow-moving invasion of the Champlain Valley in June and by early July had taken Fort Ticonderoga. On July 30 he reached Fort Edward on the Hudson River. He expected to be met in the Albany area by General Clinton coming north from New York and Colonel Barry St. Leger coming east from

Oswego. But Clinton never approached Albany, while St. Leger was delayed by the American resistance at Fort Stanwix (Rome) and finally routed entirely in a lightning campaign by General Benedict Arnold. Burgoyne's supply line had meanwhile become overextended, and in mid-August he sent 600 men to Bennington to capture the supplies that were stockpiled there. This expedition resulted in a disastrous defeat, and for the first time Burgoyne was aware of his serious predicament. Gates was now his opponent, having taken command of the northern army from Schuyler on August 2, and Arnold rejoined the army after his expedition up the Mohawk.

In mid-September Burgoyne crossed the Hudson at Schuylerville and began his advance down the river. But on the 19th he was checked at the first battle of Freeman's Farm. Meanwhile Arnold complained to Gates that he was being "treated as a Cypher in the Army." He thought Gates's attitude toward him "proceeds from a Spirit of Jealousy." Nevertheless, he begged the commander to make better use of him. After a second battle of Freeman's Farm, Burgoyne surrendered his entire army on October 17. Arnold, although unauthorized to take an active part, was undoubtedly the hero of this engagement. Yet he was generally overlooked in the adulation that was heaped upon Gates's head.[26]

Inevitably, unfavorable comparisons began to be made between Washington's severe losses around Philadelphia and Gates's victory at Saratoga. Latent anti-Washington feelings began to emerge, based on the belief that he was incompetent and that he had needlessly sacrificed both New York and Philadelphia. An accurate evaluation would have revealed, however, that Howe held a three-to-two margin over Washington at Brandywine, plus an ability to land supplies and reinforcements at will, while Burgoyne, who was isolated in the interior and denied the aid he had been promised, was outnumbered by Gates at the time of the surrender by three to one, although many of his men were recently arrived militia of uncertain value.

Nevertheless, Gates received congratulations from all sides, some of them sincere well-wishing such as Hazen's: "The Services You have rendered Your Country, will be handed down in the Annals of American Honour to latest Posterity." He believed the time was ripe for another invasion of undefended Canada and he volunteered his knowledge and his troops for such an expedition: "I have it so much at Heart that I shall not be easy untill I hear an Expedition to Canada is once more undertaken." He also asserted that Mrs. Hazen was eager to lead the victory ball on the arm of Horatio Gates, governor of Canada! [27]

Others were equally sincere, but some brazenly compared Gates and Washington and yearned for Gates's talents in higher places. A small group in Congress, including Lovell and Dr. Benjamin Rush, were convinced that Gates would make a better commander than Washington. They had sympathetic support from Major General Thomas Conway, a French officer of considerable talent but an overweening personal ambition whom Congress had commissioned, and Colonel James Wilkinson, young aide to Gates. Yet the congressional insurgents were too few to risk publicizing their ideas in that body, and the so-called Conway Cabal, although it remained mostly gossip and innuendo, was worrisome to Washington, damaged his reputation and compromised his prosecution of the war. There is no evidence that Gates conspired to get Washington's job, or that he encouraged others to do so. Yet the flattery he received and the criticism of Washington encouraged him to disregard proper channels and report directly to Congress rather than to the commander in chief. But when the "conspiracy" was brought into the open, talk ended of replacing Washington, or even of harassing him to resign. [28]

The defeat of Burgoyne again raised among members of Congress the hope of another "irruption into Canada," and they could count on the concurrence of the Board of War, now headed by General Gates. Anticipating such a development Gates, even before he left Albany, had directed Colonel Bedel in Coos to raise a regiment of 500 men and march to the mouth of the Mississquoi for a junction with the main army. [29]

During January 1778 planning began to take definite shape at York. Time was of the essence because a winter expedition needed the solid ice of Lake Champlain to be successful. Congress chose Lafayette, a major general at twenty, to lead the foray, and General Conway to be his second in command. Both were French, which appeared logical for an invasion of French Canada. Several of the other leaders were also foreign, which led to much criticism among American officers. Washington would have nothing to do with the affair and he doubted the wisdom of entrusting the leadership to Frenchmen, always concerned lest they decide to annex Canada to France. Thus the detailed planning, under the general supervision of Congress, was left to Gates and the Board of War, to Gates's entire satisfaction.

Lafayette occupied an equivocal role throughout this episode. On the one hand he greatly admired Washington, but he also once offered Gates his "perfect esteem." He warned Washington of the invidious comparisons being made between him and Gates, of their infatuation with Gates and of the desire to push Washington into some hopeless enterprise against a superior army. Yet he accepted the call to duty, trusting the assurances he received that all would be in readiness by mid-February.[30]

Hazen was appointed deputy quartermaster general for the expedition and his instructions were enough to make a lesser enthusiast throw up his hands. For a projected army of 2,500 men he was to acquire sleighs, provisions, ammunition, warm clothing, and beef cattle, all in great quantities for a winter campaign. Hazen's regiment was also commandeered as a part of the invasion force. Reluctantly Washington ordered it to march from Wilmington, Delaware, where it was wintering. It traveled to Albany by way of Valley Forge and Bethlehem, a good 200 miles of winter marching before embarking on the real expedition. He advised the officers to take no superfluous baggage and the men to dress warmly but "do not incumber themselves with any more than necessary Clothing."[31]

Hazen rushed to Albany in advance of his troops. In a whirlwind of activity he proceeded to obtain commitments for the vast quantities of supplies he needed. But nothing went smoothly. Governor Chittenden of Vermont promised 300 men, but wanted evidence of "proper encouragement" of the expedition from Congress. Bedel was running out of money to recruit and equip his regiment. Governor Clinton of New York, although ordering out 400 militia, was unable to meet his quota of clothing except for shirts. Hazen obtained authority from the Massachusetts legislature to impress carriages in the eastern part of the state and a similar power in New York. He thought he had collected sufficient provisions, plus cattle, snowshoes, axes, and forage. But the clothing he obtained from Boston was only enough for his own men, and of the 150 sleds he expected, only 13 arrived.[32]

Despite these setbacks Hazen assured Conway on February 17 and Lafayette the next day that his department was prepared to move sufficient provisions, military stores, and baggage immediately to supply an army of 3,000 men for sixty days. Notably absent from his claims was any mention of winter clothing. Indeed, the return of the troops on February 20 revealed a grave lack of every type of clothing. Nevertheless, Hazen was zealous to get under way. His 366 men, he wrote, "are so warm for the expedition that they would consent to go almost naked into Canada. I wish I could see as much forwardness in the other Troops."[33]

The Fates were against him. Lafayette in accepting the command had told Gates, "This project is yours, Sir, therefore you must make it succeed—if I had not depended so much on you I would not have undertaken the operation." But when he reached Albany in mid-February, he found that none of the promises had been kept. Fewer than 1,500 troops were fit for duty, supplies were still arriving, and winter clothing was almost entirely lacking. He received recommendations against the expedition from Arnold, Schuyler, and General Lincoln. He suspected a trick: "I fancy the actual scheme is to have me out of this part of the country, and General Conway as chief, under the immediate command of Gates." Yet as late as February 18 Lafayette demanded from Hazen a report of the exact condition of his department which he received almost immediately accompanied by an optimistic appraisal. On the same day Conway ordered Hazen to assemble all his sleighs and await further orders.[34]

But on February 19 the expedition was finished. Colonel Robert Troup blamed Arnold primarily for its failure. He reported Arnold was so malicious and vindictive that he accused Gates and Hazen ("two ignorant, & designing men") of promoting a foolish project. Arnold did not have a high opinion of either of these men, and he probably made such a comment. Furthermore, he knew the country and although never known to shrink from danger, he realized that an invasion so hastily planned was militarily and logistically unsound. More important, Lafayette was also convinced that the project was out of the question. He told Washington that there were too few men and that they were insufficiently supplied for a winter campaign. Concerning Hazen he wrote that he "était le plus disposé à aller en avant. Je crois qu'on peut attribuer cette ardeur à des motifs particuleurs" (is the most inclined to advance. I believe that this eagerness can be attributed to personal motives). However, he continued, even Hazen confessed that the army was not yet strong enough. To the Board of War he wrote concerning Hazen: "That gentleman has showed the greatest activity and zeal, no exertions from him have been untried," yet he believed that "by want of men and cloathes the expedition is not possible in this time." Congress on March 13 regretfully concurred with the decision, although the hope of acquiring Canada was far from dead.[35]

Lafayette and deKalb were recalled to Washington's army.

Conway, after supervising the dissolution of the force at Albany, and realizing that his usefulness was at an end, resigned his commission and returned to France. The army units at Albany were dispersed by General Washington over the protests of the Albany Committee of Safety, which feared the town would be left exposed to attack. The Committee specifically asked to be allowed to keep Hazen's regiment. On the other hand, General S. H. Parsons in the Hudson Highlands also asked for some of the Albany troops, "but I beg you not to suffer the Congress's own Regt. of infernals to make Part of the Number." He apparently thought that Hazen's warriors were inappropriate for the construction work he had in mind.[36]

On April 7 Hazen's regiment embarked for West Point to take up duty under Major General Alexander McDougall in the Highlands. Meanwhile General Stark, the new commander in Albany, believed that Bedel's regiment could satisfactorily patrol the northern border from Coos to Lake Champlain, although he worried that Bedel did not have the men he claimed and that he had been collecting pay for unenrolled men and for services not rendered. Whether Hazen accompanied his troops south is not known. Before he left Albany he had time to persuade twenty-six Canadian prisoners of war to enlist in his regiment.[37]

The regiment was transferred to General Enoch Poor's brigade in July, with headquarters near White Plains. Meanwhile, the indefatigable Hazen, still hopeful of a Canadian invasion in the following winter, submitted to Gates a plan for a "safe and easey Rout." It would go from the Coos Country to the St. Lawrence at St. Francis, a distance of sixty miles through level country where a good road could be built. Bedel knew the country well and had many friends among the St. Francis Indians.[38]

Shortly thereafter Hazen left Albany for a bold spying mission into Canada. He was in Newbury on July 12 and either just before or just after this date went to St. Francis, guided by Tavernier, a sympathetic French Canadian. There they met adherents to their cause, and Hazen assured them that soon the Americans would appear in sufficient strength to drive the British from the province. British authorities in Montreal had been alerted to his trip by travelers from Albany, and they made strenuous exertions to intercept him at various points as the rumors gave a clue to his whereabouts.[39]

He was back in White Plains by July 25, where he regretfully had to write Bedel that the Canadian expedition must be put off because Congress and the generals were busy shutting up Howe's fleet

"in hopes of Burgoyning Clinton's Army." He blamed the postponement on the "Cestem of Politicks," although he had to admit that the
army had other demands on its manpower. He was one of a small
group that still retained hope of another invasion, although he had a
few influential backers such as Gates at the Board of War and certain
members of Congress. He found the postponement especially frustrating in the light of Bedel's optimistic report to Gates: that three fourths
of the Canadians would have joined the Americans if the previous
winter's expedition had developed, and that St. John had been held
by no more than 200 men.[40]

In White Plains Washington appointed Hazen to preside over
a court-martial on August 15. The court found Lt. John Lewis guilty
of disobedience and sentenced him to be reprimanded in General
Orders, which Washington did with the comment that his conduct
was "an inexcusable breach of military discipline." The court also
found two enlisted men guilty of desertion and they were to receive
100 lashes each. Washington approved the sentence and ordered it
executed at guard mounting before the regiments to which the men
belonged. Hazen also presided over another court-martial near Hartford in November. This time a lieutenant of the Second New Hampshire Regiment was cashiered from the service and required to for-
feit all back pay for appropriating two privately owned horses to his
own use.[41]

Aside from chores such as courts-martial, Hazen was preoccupied during the summer and autumn of 1778 with two overriding
concerns. One was the proposal to reduce or disband his regiment,
which was already small and top-heavy with officers and therefore
an undue burden on the treasury. In refutation he bombarded the
Committee of Arrangement with regimental statistics and a plea to
maintain his original organization intact.

In a twelve-page document entitled "The State of Colonel
Hazen's Regiment," he rehearsed the origins and development of his
unit and its brave actions and heavy losses at Staten Island, Brandywine, and Germantown. He asserted that for his 522 men 33 officers
were not excessive, although he admitted that his strength was down
from the 720 with which he started the season. He pointed out that
his casualties in the three battles of the summer were 15 officers and
132 men. Some of his officers were on detached service with other
units, and his problem all along, he pointedly reminded the committee, had been a lack of money for recruiting the regiment to its full
strength of 1,000 men. Nevertheless, he thought a reduction would

cause great dismay among his Canadians and lose from the service many good Americans as well. He reminded Congress that the Canadians were fighting as volunteers for the United States:

> They are without Friend, without Acquaintance, without Money; drove from their native Country by the active Part they have took, in Consequence of an Invitation by Congress and a Promise of Support; they have no Parent State to reward their meritorious Services, or provide Bread and Shelter for them.[42]

In a separate petition direct to Congress he reviewed the services of the regiment and recalled that it had "no Parent state to protect or provide for it" save Congress itself. Again he requested that it be allowed to keep its original structure, and he pledged the good behavior of his men as well as staffing practices comparable to those of other units. He won this round in the battle for survival. On November 24 Congress resolved to keep the regiment on its original establishment, with the proviso that no new appointments or promotions of officers be made without the express permission of Congress.[43]

This victory was achieved despite the fact that the regiment undoubtedly was overstaffed with officers. The original table of organization called for a regiment of 66 officers and 1,000 men. Yet in January 1778 he had 44 officers for 592 men and one year later he still had 44 officers for only 491 men. Clearly, his persuasiveness and the sensitivity of Congress to its commitments saved the unit. The monthly pay for a colonel in his regiment was $75, lieutenant colonel $60, 4 majors at $50, 18 captains at $40, 8 lieutenants at $26.66½, 12 ensigns at $20, and 491 men at $6⅔.[44]

On September 10, 1778, Hazen, Bayley, and Gates launched a campaign to persuade Washington to undertake a Canadian invasion. If successful, it would assure a permanent peace with the Indians to the north and gain their trade, while securing the American frontiers and reversing the expansion of Quebec into the Ohio Country. They proposed three routes, all based upon Coos: one to St. John, one to St. Denis (both on the Richelieu), and one to St. Francis on the St. Lawrence. A road to any of them could be laid out by 500 men in a month. Hazen had rushed to Coos in July, studied the routes, and obtained Bedel's promise of a survey of each one. The petitioners recommended a winter expedition, January being the best month. They spoke of the generous quantities of provisions that could be stocked at Newbury: 10 to 20,000 bushels of wheat, 2,000 barrels of salt, 300 tons of hay and 5,000 bushels of oats, although the wheat must be purchased immediately in the locality before it was sold elsewhere.

Washington sent Hazen to Congress with this document and his own commentary, so that Hazen would be available for questioning. Washington ordered the storage of provisions and forage in case the campaign was ordered. He reminded Congress that the usual route by Lake Champlain was barred by the British fleet and cautiously remarked that the new plan "though attended with many difficulties affords a reasonable prospect of success." Yet special supplies and equipment would be needed for a winter campaign, and it would be dangerous to send too much of the army away from New York City if the British kept their present footing there. Congress, which for three years had wanted to acquire Canada, eagerly listened to Hazen and overlooked Washington's veiled warnings. On the 16th it endorsed the project and directed Washington to lay up stores of all kinds "if the Motions of the Enemy shall render the measure expedient." [45]

But by November Washington's misgivings had deepened. Schuyler had written him to oppose either the Coos or Oswego routes in favor of a winter expedition on Lake Champlain. Knowing that Congress still favored a campaign, Washington had decided that the Oswego route was the least objectionable, and he requested detailed information from Schuyler about river routes across New York. [46]

Yet Washington had already written Congress a twenty-six-page letter to argue against an invasion under present circumstances. Among his major points were the following: the danger of a joint campaign with the French when the Americans might not be able to fulfill their part; the vulnerability of the French to the British fleet; the need of 12,000 to 15,000 men to guard against the British in New York and Rhode Island; the impossibility of raising another 12,000 for Canada, plus all the others that would be needed for road building and transport; and the impossibility of maintaining secrecy. Washington seemed to be most suspicious of the promises of large quantities of provisions that had been made to him: "It appears on experiment, that their zeal for the expedition had made them much too sanguine in the matter. The purchases fall far, very far, short of what was expected." He did not, however, entirely close the door on the enterprise, but promised to gather further intelligence and govern future decisions by the army's capability at the time. [47]

The project reached a temporary stalemate when, on November 24, Washington wrote Gates that a campaign into Canada that winter was "impracticable." Even if the British reduced their numbers in New York and Rhode Island, "the want of provisions only, in proper time would have been an insuperable bar." He pointed out the vast difference between supplies promised and those actually on hand, but he asked Bayley to keep laying up material against a more opportune time. The Board of War and Congress did not concur with Washington and in their judgment the project was still very much alive.[48]

In October, while hopes were high in Hazen's regiment, Captain Clement Gosselin wrote his wife at St. Anne du Sud, near Quebec. He hoped that he would see her before the winter was over and he reported that the army was ready to march, although he was unsure of the route. He sent his respects to his grandparents, uncles, aunts, and cousins and asked his wife to embrace his children. He reported that his father, who was also in Hazen's regiment, was well but getting too old for military life. This letter and others like it illustrate the strong desire of the Canadian refugees once again to see their native land. They also reveal, contrary to traditional belief, that the families of men who were fighting in the United States could continue to pursue their quiet lives in Canada.[49]

During the autumn a large shipment of clothing and shoes arrived from France. The waistcoats and breeches were all alike but some of the coats were blue while others were brown, and both were faced with red. Since blue was everyone's favorite color, a lottery was held in October and the troops of four states drew the blue while five states and Hazen drew the brown. A second lottery was conducted to determine which of the brown units would get any blue that was left over, and Hazen ranked fourth out of five. Thus Hazen's regiment henceforth wore brown coats faced with red. This was the first time that a uniform dress was available for the Continental Army.[50]

In November Washington announced the disposition of his army for winter quarters. The New Hampshire and Connecticut troops plus Hazen's regiment were ordered to the vicinity of Danbury, Connecticut, "for the protection of the Country lying along the Sound, to cover our Magazines lying on Connecticut River, and to aid the Highlands, on any serious movement of the Enemy that way."[51]

General Israel Putnam was in command. With the onset of cold weather, the men were marched into the woods, where they constructed huts in the sheltered valley formed by the Saugatuck and its tributaries, along the border of what was then Danbury (now Bethel) and Redding. His camp is now designated as Putnam Memorial Park.

There were shortages of clothing, blankets, and shoes, as Hazen testified in appealing to Washington for these items. Only Putnam's tactful intervention prevented one of his Connecticut units from making an armed march on Hartford to present its grievances. The main excitement of the winter was a British attack upon Greenwich. The sixty-one-year-old Putnam dashed to Stamford to get the militia and took his famous ride down a rocky precipice, which is still known as Putnam's Hill. The enemy had done much damage to Greenwich and departed before Putnam could return.[52]

V

The American Revolution, 1779—1781

THE IDEA OF A WINTER CAMPAIGN TO CANADA was by no means dead. Congress pressed Washington to transmit the plans to Versailles in order to form a joint Franco-American expedition. Washington thought the details were too vague and indecisive. Aside from his own certainty that the American army could not be made ready, he held deep reservations about trusting European Frenchmen in French Canada, where the result might be a French rather than an American province. He expressed willingness to cooperate in an expedition against Niagara as a way of relieving the frontiers from Tory–Indian depradations. A deposition by a traveler from Quebec seemed to belie the earlier reports that there were few troops there. Andrew Stephenson itemized the garrisons at various points, adding up to several thousand regulars and volunteers.[1]

Colonel Bedel at Coos did all he could to keep the project alive. He had 200 men on duty all winter. He collected provisions but no clothing or blankets, for which he petitioned repeatedly. He built bake-ovens, a guardhouse, and a barracks, which cost £536. He kept scouts out in Canada, reported enemy concentrations and asserted that the Canadians hoped for an American expedition "and have kept their Horses fat so as to be ready to help us and Ammo Secreted to proceed along with us." He always seemed to have difficulty collecting for his expenditures and, he said, had provided ammunition and other goods for the thirty families of destitute Indians out of his own pocket.[2]

Bedel and Bayley had become politically as well as militarily involved in their section of the country. Between 1776 and 1781 a fascinating drama was enacted in the Connecticut River valley. The towns on the New Hampshire side of the river felt distant from and neglected by the government at Exeter, which they thought favored the seaboard interests. The Vermont towns likewise felt remote from the seat of authority across the Green Mountains in Bennington. The towns were determined to be under the same government, whether that of Vermont, New Hampshire, or a separate state in the valley.[3]

It is against this background of intrigue and uncertainty that the attempts to invade Canada by way of Coos need to be viewed. There was no doubt of the patriotism of Bedel and Bayley, and of their commitment to a Canadian campaign. In their zeal, however, they sometimes promised more than they could deliver and they mixed their military with their political plans for the area. The British considered Bayley so dangerous a stalwart against their plans in the north that they offered a reward for his capture. He was feared for his great influence in the Coos Country and his friendship with numerous Canadian Indians. The British and local Tories laid several plans for his capture. The last effort, in June 1782, almost succeeded, but he was warned by a neighbor on a British parole, and he and his family escaped by going into hiding.[4]

Bedel, although politically involved in his area, never lost sight of his primary mission to assist in the invasion of Canada. He had been ordered to raise a regiment in preparation for the attempt of 1778 and he experienced great difficulty keeping it together and financing it until it was disbanded in the following year. In 1780 he had still not been paid for his outlays, and he wrote Hazen in exasperation that he was thinking of departing from Coos with his grain and children (his wife died in 1779) and "leave it to itself." In an accusatory vein he continued: "I have done more than every body in this Cuntery. But I should not have don so much by my own Judgement But on your Judgement I trusted and I have not so much money as would By a Drink of Grog."[5]

Bedel's letter is only one of many documents to indicate that Hazen was the prime mover of military planning at Coos. He urged that the north unite in demanding aid and protection, and he told Bedel that "I wish my abilities to serve your Quarter were equal to my Inclinations, I would in that case give you relief." His zeal to reenter Canada was reinforced by his interest in Coos land, and the combination made him sensitive to the political future of the area. In June he proposed to Bedel a partnership for land deals in Coos. As a would-be owner of property on both sides of the river he had a clear interest in their being under the same government, as he suggested to Bedel: "If the People on the River will Join and Hang together they may carry almost any Point."[6]

Meanwhile the plan to invade Canada in 1779 was still alive, as Washington revealed in his directive to Schuyler on February 1 to prepare an attack by way of Lake Ontario, presumably without French help. He ruled out Lake Champlain because of the British naval superiority, and Coos because he thought that a large army could not move effectively from there. Upon arrival at Oswego, if the conditions were unfavorable for a movement to the north, Schuyler was to turn on Niagara. But eleven days later Washington cancelled the plan because of his concern over British strength on the seacoast and the shortage of provisions. Instead, he proposed to attack the hostile tribes of the Six Nations. To Schuyler's suggestion of a Mohawk River route, Washington countered with the Susquehanna, which would save time and expense and be less circuitous, but he agreed that the Seneca settlements were a prime objective. This correspondence marks the evolution of the famous Sullivan–Clinton campaign of 1779 in western New York.[7]

But the Coos project refused to die. Gates wrote Washington early in March to express his surprise and regret over the abandonment of the Coos route into Canada and to quote Bayley and Hazen as like-minded. The routes by way of Lake Champlain or Lake Ontario had serious drawbacks, but the route north from Coos could take maximum advantage of the cooperation of the French fleet, which would enter the St. Lawrence.[8]

Washington was already preparing a sweep through western New York. He hit upon the stratagem of silencing Gates and Hazen while at the same time diverting British attention from New York state. Consequently, he directed Hazen to march to Coos and send back all the intelligence that General Bayley had collected in Canada. He could use his regiment to extend the road toward the Richelieu or, if that were too hazardous until a greater force was assembled, to repair the part of the road completed in 1776.[9]

Hazen, glimpsing at last the possibility of an invasion of Canada, responded in glowing terms about the provisions Bayley had stockpiled and the receptivity of the French in Canada. His faith in the Canadians was surprising considering his disparaging remarks at the time of the American retreat in 1776. Nevertheless, he appears to have believed that the French were now ready, with a little help, to oust the British from their country. Or it may be that, strong-willed as he was, he was merely determined to believe what he wanted to accept as the truth. He asked Washington for blankets and summer clothing, to which the General replied that there were not enough blankets for every man and that "this is owing to the scandalous imposition the public sustained in those imported, many of which were so small that it took two and sometimes four to make one of proper size to cover a Man." [10]

Hazen began to order back to duty his officers who were on leave. One of them was his nephew, Ensign Benjamin Mooers of Haverhill. At the age of eighteen, Mooers had served in the militia at Ticonderoga for five months in 1776. He was called into service the following year and reached Saratoga just in time to witness Burgoyne's surrender. He belonged to the militia unit that guarded the prisoners of war on the march to Boston. In the spring of 1778 he was appointed ensign in Hazen's regiment and joined the army at Peekskill. His experience at Danbury he described as "these long dreadfully cold winter and spring months. Congress did nothing for us, our pay was held back," and there were many desertions. In 1779 he was promoted to lieutenant and appointed adjutant to the regiment, a duty he performed until the close of the war. Before he reported for the Coos expedition Hazen allowed him time to get a smallpox inoculation, but Mooers did not choose to do so, to his later regret. In 1780 he was temporarily detached to direct a military hospital in New Jersey where a case of smallpox developed. He immediately got an inoculation and missed only one day's duty. This recovery was remarkable because inoculation still consisted of inserting the smallpox virus into the body and inducing an attack of the disease. Frequently this was so severe as to deter many from getting inoculated.[11]

Hazen's regiment marched from Danbury to Springfield at the end of March. But a magistrate of Litchfield County, Connecticut, complained to Washington about Hazen's refusal to issue an impress warrant for teams to transport his baggage. Washington, from New Jersey, regretting any dispute with an officer of the army, referred the complaint back to the military authorities in Connecticut, who had authority to take action. What decision was made there is not known, Hazen by this time being long gone from the state. From Springfield Hazen marched to Charlestown, New Hampshire, picking up clothing and supplies as he found them available. Warned by Washington to keep his destination secret, he told no one but General William Heath on the Hudson and Colonel Bedel at Coos, adjuring them both to secrecy. Even when ordering his nephew back to duty he told Mooers their destination was either Boston or Albany.[12]

At Charlestown the shortage of flour for his men prompted Hazen to urge the local military authorities to purchase or borrow all they could find. The alternative was the "disagreeable necessity of Quartering my troops on the Inhabitants for their daily subsistance." However, he did not linger long, but before he departed on April 26 he directed the officials of the towns along his route to repair the roads and bridges for the quick passage of his men and a "Large Quantity of Baggage." He came, he reminded them, "for the Protection of this Frontier Country." [13]

From Charlestown Hazen wrote one of his optimistic letters to Washington about the bright prospects and how many troops would be needed. Washington's guarded reply was that "While I wish to have everything in the utmost readiness, to act according to our circumstances yet till my further directions you will confine yourself to the objects of any instructions." In other words, Hazen was not to precipitate events, because the Canadian campaign was by no means certain and all decisions would be "according to our circumstances." He also requested Hazen to explain how his small numbers could have used 1,700 bushels of wheat. There is no record of Hazen's reply. The wheat was not necessarily consumed this early in the season, but it had been peremptorily demanded by Hazen from the disgruntled local authorities in Charlestown.[14]

The regiment arrived at Coos in May and Hazen embarked upon a frenzy of road building, construction at Newbury, and the gathering of intelligence from Canada, acting apparently under the belief that a large army would converge upon Coos later in the summer. In July he sent a scouting party under Major Whitcomb of the New Hampshire regiment and Captain Antoine Paulint of his own. Early in August he sent another party into Canada which included Lieutenant Mooers and Ensign Boileau of his own regiment. Their instructions were to get all the intelligence they could and bring a prisoner back with them. On their way they concealed part of their provisions in the tops of trees with heavy foliage and were lucky enough to find them intact on their return. They scouted several villages along the Richelieu, meeting old friends of Hazen and acquiring information about the British forces and the sentiments of the French Canadians.[15]

Washington was doubtful about the Canadian intelligence which, he feared, was acquired "in several parts upon slender grounds." Then he launched upon the sternest lecture he had so far made to Hazen:

I am to desire in the most explicit terms that you will not put the public to any expence in those points. I have no objection to your building Block Houses and Stores, if it can be done entirely by your own people. Your command was to answer a particular Object, intimately connected with or at least intended to promote and facilitate the execution of a plan which I had in view. There cannot be a full communication of the real objects of every command to the Officer detached, and he should always in such cases make his instructions as nearly as possible the rule of his Action. In the present instance, I wish you may not greatly have exceeded my intentions in many things and incurred an expence that will greatly disatisfy the public.[16]

Washington almost certainly knew that no invasion of Canada would take place, but he was not ready to impart that information to Hazen.

So Hazen's main effort for the summer, a monumental task, was to push the old Bayley road in a northwesterly direction toward St. John. He took half of his own and part of Bedel's regiments to the roadhead near Cabot and left the rest of his men at Haverhill. The road passed through the townships (no towns had yet been settled in this area) of Cabot, Walden, Hardwick, Greensboro, Craftsbury, and Lowell, and ended at a pass in the mountains still known as Hazen's Notch. It nearly reached the Canadian border but was still almost forty miles from St. John. Along the way stout blockhouses were constructed and garrisoned at Peacham, Cabot, Walden, and Greensboro against possible raids from Canada. Swamps were traversed with logs, and bridges were constructed. It was probably the most ambitious road-building project of the entire Revolution and its two terminals, at Wells River and Hazen's Notch, are clearly marked today.[17]

Although the road was never completed or used for an invasion of Canada, it created three important byproducts. It was, as Washington had feared earlier, a potential invasion route from Canada to Coos, and Indian scouting parties appeared even while the construction was in progress. Later it was used by raiders intent upon capturing General Bayley and terminating his great influence in the area. In addition, the road went through unclaimed country that would be open for settlement with the return of peace. Hazen and many of his men eyed their surroundings with this in mind, and after the war petitioned unsuccessfully for large grants of land along the road.

The most enduring use of the road occurred after the war when the area was about to be settled. It served the frontiersmen as a highway into the wilderness and the blockhouses were used as first houses

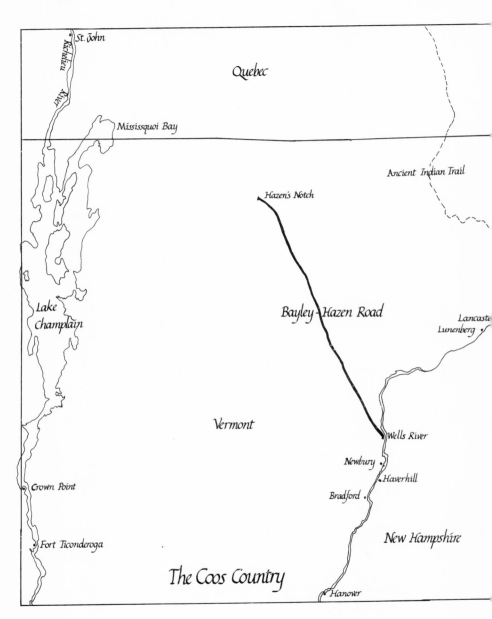

St. John

Richelieu River

Quebec

Mississquoi Bay

Ancient Indian Trail

Hazen's Notch

Bayley-Hazen Road

Lancaster
Lunenberg

Lake
Champlain

Vermont

Wells River

Newbury

Crown Point

Haverhill

Bradford

Fort Ticonderoga

New Hampshire

The Coos Country

Hanover

by the earliest arrivals. So well surveyed had it been that the Boston and Montreal Turnpike Company, chartered in 1805, proposed to follow or parallel it for most of its length. The turnpike was never built, but some of the modern highways still make use of long stretches of the original right of way.[18]

During the Revolution the stubborn fascination with this route as the best way to invade Canada was kept alive by the journal of Thomas Johnson, who had marked out the route in 1776. In it he showed the great savings in time and mileage over any other route into Canada. Its weaknesses were that by 1779 campaigns were not being readily launched from New England, that any campaign requiring a major part of the army in the north invited a British irruption from New York City, and that it placed too much reliance on the men and resources of the newly settled Coos Country, enthusiastic though they might be. It was the eagerness of the inhabitants, sparked by the energy of Hazen's and Bedel's men, that produced the accomplishments of the summer of 1779.

Although Hazen personally supervised the road building, he found time for various other ventures while he was at Coos. He bought two home lots from the estate of his brother John, who had died. He petitioned Washington in behalf of Chief Joseph Louis Gill of the St. Francis Indians, requesting army rank and a command with authority to enlist members of his tribe. Washington thought Gill could be useful in helping to assure the neutrality of his Indian allies in Canada, and he so recommended to Congress. Until a decision was made, he authorized Bayley to provision the Indians at public expense.[19]

Hazen planned to end construction at the Notch late in August and return to Coos. The British were well informed and uneasy about his activities. They learned a great deal from their own scouting parties as well as from travelers from Vermont, much of whose testimony was based upon exaggerated rumors. For example, two travelers from Bennington asserted that 600 men were building a road to Chambly. There they would be joined by 3,000 Canadians whom Hazen had supplied with 2,000 stands of arms. Hazen was aware of the Indian scouting parties around him, and as he approached the border he daily expected an attack from St. John which he felt unable to handle by himself.[20]

But he also found his men so poorly supplied with the necessities of life that he pulled them back to Coos and, as he later said, sent them into the fields to help with the harvest so that they could eat regularly again. Thus, Washington's letter was not the blow it otherwise would have been. He directed Hazen's regiment to rejoin the army. This was necessary, he wrote, because the enemy had been reinforced in New York and the American army must be drawn together. He told Hazen to bring his prisoners with him and to move the magazine away from Coos if it would be in danger after his departure.[21]

What Washington did not tell Hazen was what he told Gates, that Sullivan and Clinton had "fully compleated the destruction of the whole Country of the Six Nations, the Indians of which must be thrown this Winter upon the Magazines of Canada for subsistence, which I imagine will not be a little distressing, as they were unprepared and probably unprovided for such an event."[22]

Washington exaggerated the geographical extent of the damage, which did not include the original goal of Fort Niagara, but the campaign did destroy many Indian villages and crops. Washington later wrote Congress that Hazen's roadbuilding

> was for the purpose of exciting jealousies at Quebec and at the Enemy's posts on the St. Lawrence etc., and of making a diversion in favor of the late expedition under General Sullivan, by preventing Reinforcements being sent into the Upper Country to oppose him. This very happily succeeded, and it was always my intention to recall him, whenever the Object of his command was accomplished. And I would willingly hope, that the cutting of a Road toward Canada, which appeared to me essential to make the feint complete, will not have the least tendency to expose the Country to incursions.[23]

The departure of Hazen's regiment caused consternation on the northern frontier, and the states of Massachusetts and New Hampshire protested to Congress against their exposed condition. They had reason for concern because of the relentless British raids throughout the Champlain Valley in 1778 and 1779. On November 1 Haldimand ordered a campaign along Lake Champlain and another to the Coos country by way of Hazen's road. Major Christopher Carleton told Haldimand of a projected raid into Lake Champlain later in the month, but demurred at attacking Coos. According to his intelligence 200 men were guarding the blockhouses along Hazen's Road, and by the time he could get there the snow would be deep in the Green Mountains.[24]

At some point during the fall, Hazen interrupted the normal transit of prisoners of war. Twenty-eight Canadian and one Scotch prisoner were given a pass for Canada by the British in New York City, with an order on Hazen for provisions. Instead, he took away their pass and sent them to Fishkill. According to their later complaint in Quebec, they were left in prison on a starvation allowance relieved only by the purchase of root vegetables with the money the British had given them. Several of Hazen's officers tried unsuccessfully to persuade them to enlist in their regiment before they were finally allowed to go on their way.[25]

Hazen's summer at Coos led to troubles of another kind. For gross mismanagement of supplies he leveled charges against Isaac Tichenor, deputy commissary of purchases at Coos, General Bayley, deputy quartermaster-general, and Matthew Lyons, deputy commissary of issues. He maintained that his regiment was ill supplied through the neglect of the Purchasing Commissary and on short rations for the whole summer.[26]

The charges were serious enough that Washington ordered courts-martial for January and then postponed them until April. Bayley's trial was held in Charlestown and he was charged with neglect in allowing a quantity of beef to spoil at Coos. No prosecutor appeared to press the charge and Bayley was freed from arrest. Tichenor was tried at Springfield on eight charges brought by Hazen, all having to do with the failure to provide provisions and supplies. The court found evidence of neglect on two of the counts but recommended a reprimand from Washington on only the fifth charge—the lack of proper exertion in getting provisions and rum for troops under Hazen's command, leading to their being on short rations all summer. But Washington overruled the court and exonerated Tichenor by declaring that the commissary had not been provided with the means for purchasing these supplies.[27]

After Hazen's arrival at Peekskill from Coos, twenty-three of his officers complained to him about their desperate shortage of clothing and supplies. Hazen forwarded the document to Washington, at the same time rehearsing his regiments' services and recommending some promotions. The fall of 1779 was one of desperate discontent throughout the country. In Philadelphia a large body of men, under militia leadership, demonstrated against the worthless currency, the high cost of living, and the small group of wealthy men who were adding to the scarcities by their speculations. Several of these individuals took refuge in the home of James Wilson, dubbed "Fort Wilson" during the fracas, and were there besieged by the mob. Captain Robert Campbell of Hazen's regiment, from inside the Wilson house, played a crucial part in deflecting the mob from attacking; it was later dispersed by the arrival of the governor of the state at the head of the City Horse.[28]

Captain Campbell had been wounded, lost an arm and been taken prisoner at Staten Island in August 1777. He escaped one year later, was transferred to the Invalid Regiment in September 1778 and belatedly, in September 1779, was exonerated by Washington of intentionally violating his British parole. Washington considered him still on parole and instructed him to refrain from all military duties until he was regularly exchanged. His action in Philadelphia was thus a technical violation of orders. He was killed later in the same month in some unrecorded incident.[29]

In the fall of 1779 Hazen's regiment was annexed to Major General Edward Hand's brigade, which Hazen joined for winter quarters at Morristown about December 1. Later in the month he was appointed to sit on the general court-martial of Major General Benedict Arnold. However, he was challenged as a known enemy of Arnold, and was replaced on the court. The General had been charged by the Pennsylvania Council with eight counts of misbehavior while he was in command at Philadelphia. Congress reduced the number to the four dealing with Arnold's issuance of a safe-conduct pass for a ship in which he had an interest, his requisition of twelve government wagons to bring the ship's cargo to Philadelphia, his private purchase of goods in Philadelphia shops while they were officially closed for the procurement of supplies needed by the army, and his imposition of menial services on militiamen.

An immediate court-martial was demanded by Arnold, postponed repeatedly and finally held more than a year and a half later. He was found guilty of issuing the pass and of using the public wagons. Washington sent the proceedings to Congress which approved them and ordered Arnold reprimanded in General Orders. This the reluctant Washington did on April 6, 1780.[30]

"Winter quarters" turned out to be a euphemism for what really happened. It brought deep snow and bitterly cold weather, unheard of for its severity. The men lived in huts they built in the woods near Morristown. They lacked suitable clothing and their provisions gave out, sometimes for three or four days at a time. Both the Hudson and East Rivers were frozen solid, as was part of New York Bay.

Consequently, the months of January and early February 1780 degenerated into savage raids across the ice between the New Jersey coast and Staten Island.

The season started with Washington's order to Major General Lord Stirling to attack Staten Island with 2,500 men. It was to be a highly secret operation because it depended completely upon the condition of the ice and because the enemy's 1,000 men should not be alerted to seek reinforcements. The object was to bring away or destroy all public stores of every kind, including livestock. Hazen's regiment was to join the expedition. Washington allotted it two days to make the march from Morristown and was dismayed for the sake of the troops when it was made in one.[31]

The attack was made on the night of January 14. Five hundred sleighs, obtained under the pretense of going into the country for provisions, crossed the ice on what was to have been a secret expedition. But the British received advance intelligence of the operation and retired into their forts. The Americans remained on the island twenty-four hours without shelter and about 500 were slightly frostbitten, for the snow was nearly four feet deep and the weather extremely cold. Nevertheless, they brought away a quantity of blankets and stores including tents, arms, and baggage, together with seventeen prisoners. Apparently some of this was plunder from civilians, which occasioned a heated exchange of correspondence.[32]

Within five days Hazen proposed to Washington a second attempt on Staten Island. Subsequently, almost daily exchanges took place between the two men. Washington at first showed interest if a thorough study revealed its feasibility: "Indeed we ought not to expose ourselves to the hazard of a second disappointment without a very high probability of succeeding." Yet he left Hazen "at full liberty to act as you think proper." But a note of caution began to enter Hazen's communications because of the intelligence he was receiving, on which Washington commented, "I am sorry a better opportunity does not present itself, as I am persuaded you would make a good use of it." The project was not dead, although Hazen heard that British reinforcements had reached the Island. But on January 25 Washington reported a doubling of the British garrison and warned that they might make an attack of their own across the ice. He suggested that Hazen try to intercept British sleds transporting wood across the river from Hoboken.[33]

It was difficult for Washington to obtain vigilance from his scattered, half-frozen army, and in any case his warning of possible attack came too late. On the very night of his letter the British made a rapid two-pronged sortie into New Jersey. The raiders at Elizabeth-town took prisoners, burned several buildings, plundered some of the inhabitants, and retired without loss. Another group duplicated this accomplishment at Newark, the enemy taking in all four officers and about sixty men. Immediately the air was filled with proposals for retaliation from Hazen, Lieutenant Colonel Marinus Willett, and Major General Arthur St. Clair. Washington directed St. Clair to ascertain how the British could have surprised Elizabethtown and Newark, told him to take command of both Hazen's and Willett's units, and invited ideas for new operations, "bearing in mind always, that new disappointments will add discredit to our arms." [34]

Between January 28 and February 2 St. Clair reported almost daily to Washington. He emphasized the high rate of desertion and the lack of sufficient troops to guard against surprise along such an extended coastline. But he also suggested various projects such as a small raid by Hazen's unit and faster ways of calling out the militia. His last proposal, on February 2, called for an attack on Staten Island by both Hazen and Willett. Nothing came of any of these plans, and while the ice lasted both sides maintained a posture of watchful waiting.

Acutely aware that younger colonels than he had been pro-moted to the rank of brigadier general, Hazen petitioned Washington for a similar preferment. In a remarkable memorial he rehearsed his entire military career, his great losses in Canada, and his debts result-ing from the large advances he had made to supply and provision his unit, all of which "shew he served his Country with a fair Character, Reputation and Honour to himself." He realized that promotions to high rank had to be proportioned among the states, but since his unit belonged to no state he asked that he not be denied the same oppor-tunity. He asked for a command commensurate with the new rank unless a Canadian expedition was being planned, in which case he would be content to lead his own regiment and accept the rank that went with it. [35]

A year later he was still petitioning for his promotion. Mean-while the demands of the service continued relentlessly, some of them producing satisfaction and others trouble for him and his regiment. While he was in winter quarters at Morristown, he tried to maintain strict discipline over his troops, as revealed in his Orderly Book. On January 1, 1780, for example, he directed that no soldiers were to be exempt from duty to serve as waiters to officers of different companies.

Next day he ordered that no provisions be issued to any woman whatever, nor any admitted or "harboured" in camp except with the permission of the commanding officer. Security was maintained by daily
passwords, usually of a geographical derivation. Nevertheless his, like
all other units, suffered from desertion during the hard winter
months.[36]

In the spring the regiment received a careful scrutiny by the
demanding Inspector General, Baron von Steuben. He found "The
Regiment in good order, the Arms and Accoutrements, well taken
care of." However, he was unhappy about its size and organization.
He recommended that Livingston's regiment of 103 men, mostly
Canadian, be joined to Hazen's to make a regiment of 504 men. It
should then be divided into eighteen companies of 28 men each. But
before this change could be effected a dispute concerning rank arose
between Colonels Livingston and Hazen. A Board of General Officers
conducted an inquiry beginning on June 23. Livingston's claim to
seniority was based upon his commission by General Montgomery,
dated November 20, 1775, whereas Hazen's from Congress was dated
January 22, 1776. Hazen's response was that Montgomery's was only
a temporary commission to Livingston that Congress did not confirm
until the following August 15. The Board supported Livingston's
claim, thus giving him seniority over Hazen.[37]

Steuben's proposal was eventually carried out. In the fall
Congress reorganized the army, effective the following January 1,
into four regiments of cavalry, four of artillery, one of artificers, and
forty-nine of infantry apportioned among the states. Hazen's was to
be the fiftieth regiment and would include Livingston's and all other
foreigners from the reduced regiments, plus foreign volunteers, present and future. The total number of rank and file would thus be
31,000, a sensible consolidation since only half of the enrolled troops
appeared during the summer, making an excessive number of small
regiments. One of the most important reforms, long advocated by
Washington, was the guarantee that all dismissed officers and all other
officers who served until the end of the war would be entitled to half
pay for life.[38]

In his brigade orders of July 6 General Hand called his regimental commanders to account for failing to equip their men in
accordance with General Orders, and especially on parade the previous day. Hazen took the orders as a personal affront for, as he wrote
Washington, "Insensible of any Neglect of Duty in me, I feel my self
hurt at the Censure." Having several times been denied a court of

inquiry into his conduct by General Hand and also by Lord Stirling, he asked Washington to convene such a court. The commanding general tried to assure Hazen that Hand's order did not apply to him personally or specifically to his regiment, but that Hand was quite properly calling attention to the lack of accoutrements in his brigade. Washington concluded that he could not supersede Hand "without calling in question his right to regulate his own Brigade." Hazen disagreed and again, without result, asked Washington for a court of inquiry.[39]

For the campaign season of 1780 Hazen's regiment was at first transferred to the brigade of Brigadier General Enoch Poor, which also included the New Hampshire Regiment. However, by the time the transfer took place early in August, Hazen was named to replace Poor in command of the brigade. His yearning for more troops was thus satisfied, but still without the promotion he had requested.[40]

In his new command Hazen almost immediately became involved in serious trouble with a high-ranking officer but he came through unscathed for, as he wrote Bedel, "I do not think my self a bad hand in making a Retreat in these matters." On August 23 Hazen was arrested by Baron von Steuben for halting his brigade without orders to do so. The army was on the march from Tappan to the Liberty Pole, a prewar landmark located near Englewood.

He was arrested and brought before a general court-martial on the charges of disobedience of orders and unmilitary conduct; halting his brigade without orders, thereby creating a gap of nearly a half mile in the center of the left column; and "unofficer and ungentlemanlike behavior" in falsely asserting that he had received an order to halt from General Stark. Stark testified that Hazen had sought his permission and that although he gave no orders he thought the halt was necessary to allow the men to get water, and he saw no negligence by Colonel Hazen. Hazen testified that his men were under arms at 6 A.M. and marching by seven o'clock laden with packs on a very hot day. He further said that Steuben had used "insulting language" at the time of his arrest.[41]

Hazen was honorably acquitted of all charges but in his General Orders Washington took the occasion to warn that an officer leading a brigade had no inherent right to order a halt, that it should be done only in cases of extreme fatigue and then only after reporting to his immediate superior so that steps could be taken to keep the column in order.[42]

Immediately upon his acquittal Hazen charged Steuben with

the same "unofficer and ungentlemanlike behavior" of which he had been accused. A board of seven senior officers was appointed to hear the dispute, one from each of the states having troops in the vicinity. Colonel Israel Angell of Rhode Island was a reluctant member and he recorded in his Diary: "a troublesome world this. As Soon as one gits out of trouble them selves, are Called upon to Settle Disturbances with others. . . ." That the dispute was hot is evidenced by the board's sitting on September 19, 21, and 22 before making a settlement "to the Satisfaction of both parties." The apparent solution was that Steuben showed a letter around the group which amounted to an apology, leading Hazen to boast: "On the whole I have not lost but gained Honour by the Trial." [43]

By 1780 the military action in the northern states had settled down to skirmishes and raids by both sides in the vicinity of New York City. After Saratoga the British, viewing the war in the North as stalemated, put all their efforts into the lower South, hoping with the help of the Loyalists to knock several states out of the war. But in the North the British fought a new kind of warfare—the bribery and subversion of leading Patriots. They looked for military men who had a grievance against Washington or Congress, or otherwise showed signs of disillusionment with the Patriot cause.

Major John André, aide to General Clinton in New York, was useful in searching out possibilities. In his "Observations" he commented: "Hazen may be had. He is artful and enterprising. He will be a good creature of [Arnold] whom he knows and to whom he betrayed us in Canada." André apparently knew that Hazen had originally taken the British side in Canada by carrying messages to and from the governor and by accepting a commission from him. Perhaps he also knew that Hazen was unhappy over his lack of promotion. What he apparently did not know was that Hazen was a personal enemy of Arnold. So far as is known, no approach was ever made to Hazen by the British. Other targets of British efforts were General Schuyler, General Sullivan, Ethan Allen, and General Arnold, and indirect approaches were made to all of them. Allen made a whole year's pretense of being interested, but only Arnold participated in a specific plan. [44]

In the subsequent plot to hand West Point over to the British, Arnold escaped capture but Major André, in civilian clothes, was taken on his way back to New York. A hundred men of Hazen's regiment were detailed to be present at his hanging. Lieutenant Mooers, who was there, "witnessed the whole melancholy scene. The prisoner was dressed in his full military regalia except his sword and spurs, and he seemed perfectly composed, speaking to his attendants in a cheerful way. It was the most affecting sight to every man who witnessed it, and can never be forgotten." [45]

In addition to his other involvements during the summer and fall of 1780, Hazen was again agitating for a winter campaign against Canada. This time he was a willing agent of the towns along the Connecticut River which, at a convention at Hanover, broached the idea as a way of improving their own political bargaining power. Hazen was in correspondence with Bayley and Bedel, and he obtained the usual enthusiastic pledges of support from the Coos Country. In May he went to Boston and found enthusiasm for the project. In June he reported from New Jersey that Lafayette was "warm" and Washington "steady to the point." He urged the Coos officials to procure all the grain they could. [46]

He buttonholed various members of Congress whenever he could, but his main approach was to General Sullivan of New Hampshire who, after years of active campaigning, had resumed his seat in Congress. In two vehement letters Hazen promoted the project: "It really appears to me to be the lucky moment; and I wish you to undertake the most arduous task in this enterprise." He promised to open the road to Canada and to be responsible for transporting artillery, ammunition, baggage, and provisions for an army sufficient to conquer the country. If Congress would repay him his cash advances for their service in Canada, he also promised to raise 2,000 Canadian troops within ten days of his arrival. A month later, upon learning of British plans for a raid into the United States, he told Sullivan that the frontiers would be ravaged for as long as they were undefended and that only the conquest of Canada would secure them. He attributed to Congress motives not hitherto suspected—that by continuing his regiment on its original establishment it was acting principally "on some Distant expectation of our Returning to that Country—It is my Hobby Horse I must own It." [47]

Hazen was again doomed to disappointment because insufficient support materialized to begin even the preliminary planning for such an expedition. It is difficult to see why Hazen himself was so enthusiastic after his bad experiences with supplies and provisions the year before. It is possible that he was motivated in part by the hope of leading the next invasion, but chiefly by the burning desire of himself and his men to return to the land of their homes and property. Hazen attributed his failure to the French leaders who declared for an attack upon New York City, the "Centre and Focus of all ye British Forces," as they called it, and so the Canadian invasion, "the wish of everyone," was vanishing from sight once more.[48]

In September Major James Reid and eleven other American officers of Hazen's regiment, having received no satisfaction of their grievances from Hazen, appealed directly to Washington without notifying their own commander. Since they were not formed as a regular state unit, they felt excluded from the prospects of promotion and denied the kinds of supplies and support that the rest of the army units received from their respective states. They admitted that they had been "richly clothed and comfortably Supplied with Resolutions, and necessity has marked their conduct with 'temperance, frugality and perseverance,'" but nothing had come of all the grand promises. They claimed to have suffered great inconveniences by the regiment's being upon the original establishment "in consequence of some unexplained powers which Col. Hazen arrogates to himself and have never had the emoluments arising from the Regimental Staff appointments by their own choice." They asked either to be reduced to the establishment of other regiments and attached to some state line, or else to be dissolved and the officers and men sent to their own states.[49]

This was the first time that Major Reid appeared as a challenger of Hazen's leadership and competence, but he was to turn into a thorn in Hazen's flesh for the next three years. Congress took no action on the officers' memorial, probably because a unit with so many foreign members could not readily be fitted into any single state establishment. Meanwhile, Hazen's regiment was posted for the fall at Nelson's Point (Garrison, New York), opposite West Point.[50]

In October General Heath at West Point received intelligence that an enemy foray to gather cattle in northern Westchester County was being planned in New York. Much of Westchester County was a no man's land between the two armies, with constant raids against the strongholds and farms by both sides. Many of them were destructive, and they created a perilous existence for the inhabitants.

On receipt of his news Heath ordered Hazen to move to Pine's Bridge, a hamlet of Crompound (Amawalk), and Lieutenant Colonel Jameson with the Second Light Dragoons to move from Bedford toward Hazen. The two groups met during the night, and since no enemy seemed to be approaching they sent out scouts toward White Plains. Finding no enemy concentration, Hazen regretfully reported: "I do not expect to be fortunate enough to meet with any of them on this occasion." Heath ordered him back with commendation and stated that he had ordered "a Hogshead of rum to be forwarded to the village for the use of your Command, order so much of it Issued as the Comfort of the men may require."[51]

Beginning in November Hazen was preoccupied with the charges brought against him by Major James Reid of his own regiment. Originally, Reid accused him of making a false return of the regiment by listing Reid's majority as September rather than June 1777. General Heath had no choice but to order a general court-martial for November 7, and it sat intermittently for the rest of the month. Major Reid made three charges against Hazen, which were the subject of the trial:

1. "Fraudulent conduct"—that he drew money for the regiment, appropriating it to other purposes and detaining it so long that depreciation "robbed them of considerable sums."

2. False musters and false returns and the requirement that inferior officers prepare them.

3. "Ungentleman and unofficer-like conduct in exacting advanced prices from the Regiment for private as well as for Articles furnished by the Public."

The first charge concerned the road-building expedition to Coos in 1779. The regimental paymaster, Captain John White, who was also Hazen's nephew, was given four months' pay for the troops, two months of which he disbursed. The other two months covered future pay periods and White asked Hazen to take custody of it, for which he received a receipt. Hazen admitted using some of the money to buy provisions for the men. The supply system was such that he had already charged Tichenor with gross neglect. But it did mean delayed paydays before Hazen could process the vouchers for what he had spent.

The second charge was in two parts. Hazen was accused by lieutenant Colonel Varick, deputy commissary general of musters, of preparing a series of muster rolls which did not account for many men on the regimental roster, although Varick admitted that the last one, of August 1780, coincided with the roster. Hazen was accused of carrying persons on the roster such as a six-year-old boy and a slave. He denied responsibility for muster rolls "which I neither see, certify, sign or swear to." Hazen repeatedly tried during the trial to head off irrelevant questioning of the witnesses or to get their testimony declared inadmissible, but he was invariably overruled. The other part of this charge was the falsifying of the date Reid was appointed major. Reid asserted that it was June 1777 and that he was a replacement for Major de Colerus, who left the regiment after a short time. Hazen produced evidence that he had deliberately not replaced de Colerus and that Reid's preferment to a majority followed upon the capture of Lieutenant Colonel Antill and Major Woodson during the attack on Staten Island. Reid's appointment thus dated from September 1.

On the third charge, he was accused of selling army rum for his own profit, which he was easily able to refute, and of deducting $20 from soldiers' pay for new shoes. He demonstrated that the price in depreciated currency was not exorbitant, and that it applied only to clothing beyond the army's issues (four pair a year), in order to discourage enlisted men from reselling them.

Hazen had answers for all the prosecution's evidence; he made a long and impassioned summary, largely duplicated in a long letter to Washington; and he produced witnesses of his own. He partially destroyed the credibility of Major Reid by showing that Reid could not possibly have known what was going on because of his extended absences on furlough or sick leave, and he similarly disposed of another of his accusers, Captain Duncan. His "Summary" and his letter to Washington rehearsed his military career and the battle record of his regiment, with emphasis upon the fact that "my Purse and Credit has always been open to the Service of this Country, and to the Officers and Soldiers of my Regiment in particular, tho' a Volunteer only in the American Cause; and it is not enough that I say that I have raised a Regiment for its Service at my own Expense, but I have further advanced large Sums to feed and clothe it." The court exonerated him of all charges, partly because of Reid's vindictive presentation and partly as a result of Hazen's own eloquence.[52]

Late in November Hazen's regiment was ordered into winter quarters at Fishkill. This important supply depot needed careful guarding against enemy raids, and it was close enough to the British lines that American offensive and defensive campaigns could be launched from there. But for the regiment it had the additional advantage that the families of some of his Canadian soldiers were housed there. But once again, winter quarters brought several troublesome situations for all units of the army, Hazen's included. On December 27 a court of inquiry assembled at West Point at the request of Lieutenant Colonel Antill, an exchanged prisoner of war, to examine his conduct during the attack on Staten Island. He started off with a friend in court, because Hazen presided. Not surprisingly, the court found that Antill "appears to have been captured while in the execution of his duty and that he is not Censurable in any part of his conduct but is deserving the Approbation of every good officer." Washington approved and proclaimed the results in General Orders. Antill was so completely exonerated that he received $965.75 in ration allowance for the 1,159 days of his captivity (five rations a day at 15/90 dollars per ration). At one stage of Revolutionary finance, the new American dollar, based upon the Spanish dollar, was calculated at ninety cents.[53]

Hazen had not heard the last of Major Reid. Hard on the heels of his own acquittal, he arrested the Major and charged him with: (1) disobedience of orders and unmilitary conduct, (2) defrauding the United States and the regiment by embezzling or misapplying public property and (3) conduct unbecoming an officer and a gentleman. Reid immediately wrote an impassioned appeal to Washington in which he reviewed the injustices of his own court-martial: that the court, containing no lawyers, could not understand some points of law that arose; that Mr. Strong, the judge advocate, lacked the requisite abilities for his job; that the court refused a suspension of the trial until a more competent judge advocate could be found and until Reid could produce additional evidence against Hazen; and that the court thought Hazen "guilty of the charges but the proof was insufficient to convict him."

Having been confined to his quarters by Hazen, Reid asked Washington for a speedy trial ("he intends to mannoeuvre in such a manner as to keep me in arrest all Winter"), and for his intercession to reinforce the army's customary definition of arrest. Reid insisted that Hazen had been robbing his regiment. He never produced hard evidence of this, but some doubts persisted about Hazen's highhanded financing, including the collection of pay for men no longer in his unit. But that he profited personally was untrue; on the contrary, his unit always seemed undersupplied, and he repeatedly advanced his own money in emergencies and then suffered unconscionable delays in his repayment by the government.[54]

The manner of Reid's arrest occasioned a flurry of correspondence. Washington told General Heath, Hazen's superior officer, that Hazen should either prepare for an immediate trial or release Reid while he gathered his evidence. When Hazen was apprised of Washington's warning he replied that he expected to get his evidence quickly and that Reid's conduct had been so gross as to deserve "little Indulgence in his present situation." Heath then commented, "As it probably will be some considerable time before the trial of Major Reid is over, his confinement is not to be more *rigid* than is commonly practiced in Cases of arrest in *our army*." Hazen denied that Reid's confinement was too severe. He recounted his own three arrests, during which he also was confined to quarters. Therefore he asked not to be required to liberalize Reid's confinement because indulging him "will hurt my Pride and Vanity greatly, for should your Honour grant his Request it will in that Case effectually put me in the wrong, which I am not by any means conscious of." [55]

By protracting the correspondence Hazen won his point with Heath, because he was ready for the trial on December 21, although no one could have foreseen that, with adjournments, it would last until February 8, 1781. In preparing his case he discovered that Reid and other officers had petitioned Washington the previous September without his knowledge. Hazen thought this was a "new fangled System of Discipline" and he accused Reid of "Secretly and under the Colour of Friendship compiling what he conceives to be Public Errors or Crimes, until he collects a sufficient Quantity to answer Private Purposes." He petitioned Congress on December 10 and again on the 29th for a copy of Reid's petition, but he had to go into the court-martial without it. [56]

The trial opened with Reid's recital of his own defense. To a large extent it was a vitriolic attack upon Hazen which the Colonel tried to interrupt. The court ruled against him on the ground that it was the prisoner's defense, and Reid was allowed to continue. Hazen told Heath that Reid "charges me with every thing that is base and infamous from my Cradle up to the Present Time; he reiterates and positively Charges me with almost all the Crimes for which I was tried by a General Court-Martial at his Instance, and acquitted." His picture of the regiment, Hazen said, was of "one continual Scene of Fraud, Oppression and robbing of the Soldiers." [57]

Yet this was a trial of Reid, not Hazen, and after a series of long and sometimes stormy sittings the court found Reid guilty of two charges. His "disobedience of orders and unmilitary conduct" was proved by his ordering sergeants to do the duty of officers contrary to regulations. His "unofficer and ungentleman-like conduct" was shown in his disrespectful treatment of Hazen and the indecency of a letter he wrote to a minister of the gospel. The court asked that Reid be reprimanded by Washington.

In General Orders Washington concurred, saying in part:

> The inflammatory expressions used by Major Reid against his commanding officer and other instances of disrespect are highly excep-

tionable, an inferior officer can never be justifiable in attempts to make his commanding officer suspected and odious to his corps. . . . The General cannot forbear remarking with regret that it is too common for officers on trial to indulge themselves in a vein of invective and abuse as inconsistent with decency as with the respect they owe themselves and to others. He is sorry that Major Reid has so far forgot himself as to have erred in a more than ordinary degree in this article.[58]

In his letter to Heath, referred to above, Hazen regretted the lack of rules of procedure for the conduct of general courts-martial. Rehearsing the trials with which he had been involved, he pointed out the wide and ill-defined latitude that judge advocates could exercise in admitting evidence, whether it was opinions, hearsay, or baseless charges. He pleaded for a reform in the system, since he now found himself compromised before his own regiment by Reid's unrefuted remarks. His peroration was: "If no Means whatever can be fallen on to relieve oppressed Innocence and redress the Injured, I have to lament the Period in which I was born, and despise the Country in which I have existed, and for which I have sacrificed so much Blood and Treasure." [59]

This affair left a bitter taste in everyone's mouth and, worse still, left Reid under Hazen's command so that irritations could easily flare up again. But in a small reshuffling during February, Hazen commanded a brigade made up of his own and the New Hampshire regiments. Reid was to command the New Hampshire men at another post and although Major Torrey of Hazen's regiment resented Reid's preferment, Hazen confided to Heath that he was glad Reid was away from the regiment.[60]

Simultaneously with the troubles over Major Reid, other pots were boiling at Fishkill in this winter of discontents. It might have been worse because elsewhere the men of the Pennsylvania Line mutinied and started to march on Philadelphia. Their grievances were eleven months' arrears of pay and shortages of clothing and supplies. The situation at Fishkill was nowhere near as serious, but it centered around the distribution of supplies. A return of clothing and necessaries in December showed the regiment lacking nearly everything. For example, 13 stockings were listed as good, 153 bad, and 803 needed. For shirts the figures were 13, 253, and 803. No "good" hats were counted, but 253 were called bad and 416 needed. The figures were similar for shoes and blankets.[61]

When Hazen went to take command of that post he experienced difficulties in obtaining adequate housing, forage, and rum for his regiment. Upon investigation he discovered what he considered were grave abuses in the issuance of supplies to all the units. Consequently, he issued a Garrison Order on December 20 requiring the heads of every department on the post to submit weekly returns to him. He specifically mentioned the surgeon of the hospital, the acting quartermaster general, the barracks master, the issuing commissary of provisions, and the issuing commissary of forage.[62]

Heath was convinced by Hazen's explanation that abuses existed, and he gave Hazen's course of action his approval. But when Hazen tried to enforce his own directive he found "my orders Trampled upon and your Instructions treated with sovereign Contempt." Quartermaster General Timothy Pickering involved himself in the dispute and directed the quartermaster at Fishkill to disregard Hazen's orders. Other services seem to have done the same. The issue they raised was the authority of Hazen as a subordinate officer to interfere with the functioning of staff departments on his post. Nevertheless, Heath backed Hazen in General Orders by directing that no issues of provisions, forage, or other supplies were to be made without being countersigned by Hazen or, in his absence, the senior officer on the post.[63]

This was too much for Colonel Pickering, a man of some influence who was on leave from the Board of War while he functioned as quartermaster general. To Washington he challenged Heath's orders which, "if carried into execution, will unhinge all public business there, & go near to dissolve my department in the state. They were issued, I am warranted to say, at the instigation of Col. Hazen, whose overbearing disposition aimed at the absolute controul of every transaction at that post." He asked Washington for his "interference to prevent the mischief which otherwise will immediately take place."

Although Washington admitted that he had not had time to examine the situation sufficiently, he wrote Heath to question "how far a colonel has a right to meddle in the business of his general staff at Fishkill, which was not fixed there in consequence of Colonel Hazen's going there, for the conveniences of a particular post, but for general purposes of the army." But after receiving further details from Heath, he concluded that although Hazen lacked the right to require returns of stores and issues, General Heath himself had that right, which he had exercised in his instructions to Hazen, and "the officers concerned were bound to comply with them." [64]

In other words, Hazen had prematurely issued his orders in December, but by obtaining Heath's backing in January, he had carried the day in his attempts to rationalize the system of distribution on his post. Nevertheless, supplies—even when fairly distributed—were seriously lacking. In March Hazen petitioned Heath for 400 pair of woolen overalls which, even if obtained, would leave his regiment behind the other units in proportion of clothing received; for example, his men had had no coats that year.[65]

Despite these frustrating staff disagreements, the military side of the war suffered no interruption. Plans were made to strike a blow at the enemy in Westchester County. Oliver De Lancey, a prestigious leader in colonial New York, had chosen the Loyalist side at the time of the Declaration of Independence. He was commissioned a brigadier general and raised three battalions of Loyalists. His son, Lieutenant Colonel Oliver De Lancey, commanded a brigade at Morrisania. It was against him that an attack was ordered.

In January 1781 Lieutenant Colonel William Hull attacked De Lancey with 350 men. He surrounded the Loyalists, forced a narrow passage to their camp, took more than fifty prisoners, destroyed a bridge and a quantity of stores and retreated, closely pursued. A covering party of 100 men led by Hazen attacked the pursuers who numbered nearly 1,000 men. His men allowed the enemy to pass their place of concealment and, at Hazen's command, fired upon them. They killed or captured about 35 of the enemy and made their own quick retreat. Heath's comment was that the conduct of officers and men "did them much honour." Hazen's orders on January 18 conveyed Washington's "great satisfaction in the enterprise."[66]

The spring of 1781, which brought a lull in military activity, brought in its place a flurry of letters, petitions, and memorials. One of them was initiated by Major Torrey and fourteen other officers of Hazen's regiment to challenge Reid's charges against Hazen. The signers were almost evenly divided between French and English officers. They declined to perform any kind of military duty with or under Reid until his assertions were proved at a public hearing. The letter went to Antill, then to Heath and Washington, but nothing was done for the time being.[67]

On March 1 Hazen renewed his attempts to get a promotion. In a letter to Washington similar to the one of the year before, he reviewed his military career and that of his regiment. He again reminded the General that his returns showed only 418 men when they should show 1,000; that of these, 16 officers and 162 men were volunteers from Canada who, since they belonged to the line of no state, suffered from the lack of supplies and clothing and from arrears of pay and depreciation of wages. He also pointed out that he was now the third-ranking colonel in the army and that others had been promoted over him. Washington forwarded Hazen's memorial to Congress without a specific recommendation except to say that Hazen had "always appeared to me a sensible, spirited & attentive officer." [68]

Hazen was made a brevet (honorary) brigadier general on June 29, but not before Congress had approved and withdrawn the resolution several times. The problems it wrestled with were how to fit a promotion into the table of organization based upon state quotas, and what to do about the two colonels who outranked him, Van Schaick and Greaton. Even Washington was disturbed when he heard of Hazen's promotion because he felt that "Congress would seem to contradict their own Principles." In the middle of the Yorktown campaign Van Schaick made an issue of it in a memorial to Congress, but he received a brevet promotion in October. Hazen was unable to obtain promotions for his men, despite his vigorous recommendations to the Board of War. Furthermore, neither Hazen nor Van Schaick was satisfied with his brevet rank since it carried no increase in pay or authority, and after Yorktown they renewed appeals for something more permanent. [69]

The other matter raised in Hazen's memorial—the condition of his regiment—invoked even more extended debate. Its treatment illustrates the functioning of Congress at its most inefficient. After hearing the memorial Congress referred it to a committee, which duly reported. Before final action was taken the Board of War, the paymaster general, and the Board of Treasury became involved, and they made contradictory recommendations. The differences involved the source of the requisite funds and the choice of a state that could be used as a model for compensating Hazen's unit. The problem was complicated by the fact, as Hazen pointed out, that the members of his regiment who were credited to the states of Massachusetts and Connecticut regularly received their pay, clothing, and depreciation allowance, while those from the other states and the Canadians were compensated only spasmodically if at all. It created, he correctly asserted, serious tensions between the haves and the have-nots of his regiment. A return of a later date shows the scope of his problem. In a regiment of 496 men, 279 were listed as congressional (i.e., foreign) troops. The remainder were spread among the states as follows: Pennsylvania 92, Connecticut 33, Maryland 31, Massachusetts 16,

New Hampshire 15, New York 14, New Jersey and Delaware each 7, and Virginia and Rhode Island 1 each.[70]

The depreciation allowance was the bonus Congress had determined that the states should pay the Continental forces as a partial compensation for the depreciation in the value of the national currency. Congress dealt with it in April. Hazen's men who were not on any state quota were to receive loan-office certificates payable in three years from January 1, 1781, with interest. In June it grappled with the other issues raised in the memorial by directing all states to make the depreciation allowance to their men in Hazen's regiment; ordering the issuance of clothing to the Canadian officers on the same basis as the Massachusetts issue to its officers; paying a bounty of $24 in certificates to each noncommissioned officer and private; and directing that Hazen's regiment be recruited to its full strength as soon as the public finances would allow. These measures alleviated the more pressing inequities in the regiment, although the men had to wait a long time before seeing hard cash in lieu of the certificates, and the public finances never did allow the regiment to be recruited to full strength.[71]

Hazen's other main concern about his regiment was the fact that it rarely functioned as a unit, but was frequently broken up for detached duty under other officers, a company here and a company there. It led, he complained, to the ignominy of a colonel supposed to be leading 1,000 men sometimes left with no more than 100, as was the case in his campaign to Morrisania: "Thus the Means of acquiring Military Fame, the necessary Implements to establish a Soldier's character, gathered at a Personal Expence, and fostered with unremitting Care, are in the necessary Course of Things, taken from me and given to others by which they have opportunities to immortalize their Names." However, no change was made in this situation and the regiment continued to furnish units for duty elsewhere. In this connection it is worth noting that the whole regiment, or parts of it, were sometimes specifically requested by other commanders in recognition of their fighting qualities.[72]

Colonel Hazen also undertook to get his public finances straightened out by a petition early in April. Although Congress had made a tentative calculation of what it owed him in August 1777, he had not received a cent of it. Meanwhile his creditors, who had advanced their own money in order to recruit the regiment, were pressing him for payment. The Board of Treasury reaudited his accounts, verified two large items for which there had not been vouchers in

1777, and concluded that he was owed $10,296 72/90 in specie, which, with interest at six percent from May 1, 1776, made a total obligation on May 1, 1781, of $13,386 2/90. It was to bear the same interest thereafter, and it ought to be paid, or at least the interest "as soon as any other Creditor of the United States." Since there was no specie in the Treasury, Hazen had to be content with small advances in new emission currency.[73]

Although the burden of paper work threatened at times to sap the vitality of the army, yet another campaign season was approaching and the various units were once again brought out of winter quarters. Washington received two intercepted letters from Loyalists in Albany to the British in Canada in which they described the defenseless state of the place and urged a speedy attack. He ordered six companies of Van Schaick's regiment and all of Hazen's to report to General Clinton at Albany, where the General was warned to concentrate his forces so as to repel a raid from Canada. Hazen sailed from Fishkill Landing on June 6, 1781, and upon arrival was detailed to patrol the lower reaches of the Mohawk River. The war scare was soon over and the troops were back at West Point a month later, at about the time the First New York Regiment was mutinying and deserting because of their back pay.[74]

During the summer Washington began to receive word of the movements of Cornwallis in Virginia. When he learned that the British General had unaccountably gone onto the York Peninsula, he decided to cut off his retreat by moving much of the northern army southward. He began to assemble his forces secretly and skillfully. He placed his various units, including Hazen's, in a wide arc around New York City as if he were about to besiege the British stronghold. On August 19 his pickets cleared roads into New York, burning barricades in apparent preparation for an attack. On the same day he sent Hazen and his regiment across the Hudson at Dobbs Ferry to march along the New Jersey shore and appear to threaten Staten Island.[75]

Hoping that he had immobilized the British in New York, in late August he set his whole army in motion southward in three columns, each by a slightly different route. The French army went by way of Philadelphia, but the other troops headed for the Christiana Bridge over the Delaware and then to the Head of Elk (present-day Elkton, Maryland). Hazen was sent to Christiana Bridge to meet the boats coming down the Delaware loaded with ordnance and other stores. He was to hasten the transportation of the goods overland to the Head of Elk, and to have the road in good repair for the passage of the troops.[76]

From Head of Elk the ordnance, stores, and as many troops as could be put aboard sailed down the Chesapeake Bay. Hazen's and several other units traveled in bateaux that had been transported from the Hudson River. The transports sailed to the James River and ascended it to the harbor between Jamestown and Williamsburg. Here they camped about twelve miles from Yorktown. The first of the troops arrived on September 20 and the last on the 30th. They averaged twelve days to traverse Chesapeake Bay and about a month and a half and 350 miles to come from the Hudson River.[77]

On the 24th Washington brigaded his army at Williamsburg. Colonel Scammell's regiment, Lieutenant Colonel Hamilton's battalion of infantry, and Hazen's regiment were organized under Brigadier General Hazen's command. The other American brigades were led by Generals Muhlenberg, Wayne, Gist, Dayton, and Clinton. Together with the French army they numbered 15,000 men; Cornwallis at Yorktown had about half that number but his position was well fortified. Next day Colonel Scammell protested to Washington about being put under Hazen's command and asked for a transfer. Washington gently refused because he was "pressed in point of Time" and because "I had no Idea of giving more, or that you expected more." On the 26th Hazen, anticipating a severe battle ahead, prudently made his will. Next day Washington formed his order for battle. He assigned Muhlenberg's and Hazen's brigades on the right under Lafayette and he created similar divisions on the center and left.[78]

At five o'clock on the morning of the 28th the troops moved out of Williamsburg along the sandy road to Yorktown. Hazen's troops followed Muhlenberg's, his Canadians with their "brown and red rusty and frayed." The officers of the Canadian regiment made their temporary peace with Major Reid by telling him that although they stood by their sentiments of the previous spring, they would act under his orders in the present crisis for the good of the country. The army was soon in a semicircle around Yorktown, but several days were required to bring the artillery overland from the James River. Consequently, the real bombardment did not open until October 9. Meanwhile, the allied forces had barely arrived when Cornwallis abandoned three advance redoubts, which Washington immediately occupied.

The preperation for the siege involved the construction of first one and then a second trench, containing redoubts built as close to the British works as their firing would allow. The two final British outposts were taken by storm, one of them by Lafayette's division which included Hazen's and Muhlenberg's brigades. Hazen's old regiment, under Antill, was in the thick of severe fighting before the redoubt fell and the siege could concentrate on Cornwallis' inner defenses. These were pounded day after day by heavy artillery which at its most numerous consisted of more than 100 guns, the biggest being 24-pounders. The allied forces were apparently prepared to continue this bombardment indefinitely, but Cornwallis opened negotiations for a surrender on October 17. The capitulation was signed on October 18 and on October 19 the British and German forces, numbering 7,240 men, marched out to lay down their arms.[79]

The army remained before Yorktown for some time after the capitulation, arranging for the march back north and the disposition of the prisoners of war, most of whom went to camps in Pennsylvania. On October 31 Hazen gave a dinner to a number of French and American officers. The main work was done, and a brilliantly executed campaign had come to a dramatic end. But would there be other battles? Washington did not know, for he could not guess that the British determination to continue the war would evaporate when word of Yorktown reached London. Yet the French fleet and many of the French troops departed for the West Indies, and by the end of the year Washington was back at White Plains watching the British in New York. To him 1782 was potentially the most dangerous year of the war, which he must face on his own without French allies nearby.

VI

Between War and Peace, 1781—1783

W HILE STILL AT YORKTOWN, Lieutenant Colonel Antill (who had led the Canadian regiment while Hazen commanded a brigade) recommended seven promotions, the most important of which were those of Captains Laurent Olivier and William Satterlee to major. He pointed out that the only promotion during three years of hard service had been Hazen's own, that "the Officers in General are uneasy," and that he wanted to "keep harmony in the Corps and Do justice to Merit." Hazen enthusiastically endorsed the recommendations to Washington. Since the regiment was still overstaffed for its size, little came of this effort. Instead, Congress in January 1782 declared that all supernumerary officers were to be retired at half pay. As a result, a number of Hazen's officers left the service including Captain Antoine Paulint and Lieutenants Pierre Boileau, Francis Guilmat, and Alexander Ferriol. Antill, for reasons of health, requested permission to retire at half pay, which was granted later in the year. Captain Philip Liebert was transferred to the Invalid Regiment in March 1782, and resigned in April 1783.[1]

Neither recruitment nor promotion was yet possible. Indeed, during 1782 the existence of the regiment was again threatened, with Washington doing a curious about-face. In June he recommended to the secretary of war that Hazen's regiment be reduced. "The Canadian part of it may be formed into one or more companies according to their number, and be employed as watermen, or in other services suited to their circumstances; the remainder may be turned over to the States to which they respectively belong." In August he pressed for a decision. In October he ordered Hazen to join his main army and in November: "Hazens Regt is so respectable at present that I should not think a reform expedient at this time. He probably may have more officers than the establishment requires; if so, the supernumeraries may be put upon the footing of those in other Corps." [2]

This charmed existence that the regiment led throughout the war, while other units were being reformed, owed in part to a moral commitment to Hazen's Canadians and in part to their continued good performance. For its winter duty Washington sent the regiment to Lancaster, Pennsylvania, to guard prisoners of war. Heath at West Point had specifically asked for Hazen as a part of the winter force on the northern front, but Washington decided that "Hazen's have already performed a long tour of march and duty; and it may seem hard to send them still so much further." The regiment remained on this duty for eleven months.[3]

Once settled into his new post, Hazen requested a leave in January "upon business that required his personal attendance." He was gone from January 6 to March 24; his wife accompanied him part of the way, Antill much of the way, and his servant Peter throughout the trip. It included visits to important acquaintances, army business, and personal affairs including land deals. He traveled or dined with the near great of his day: Governors Clinton of New York and Chittenden of Vermont, General Lincoln, and Ethan Allen. From Lancaster he went to Philadelphia, then to West Point for a visit with Heath. From there he went to Albany, where his wife turned back. He and Antill crossed Vermont to Charlestown, then north to Coos, where he remained several days looking over the area and hatching land schemes with Colonel Bedel. He returned by way of Boston and Fishkill, where he visited the huts which were the homes of the families of his Canadian soldiers. Back in Philadelphia he pressed Robert Morris for the payment of interest on his loan certificates, and came away partially satisfied. The land deal in Coos was built upon a partnership with Bedel and Colonel Biddle, whom he enlisted in Philadelphia on his return trip. Hazen urged Bedel to "Use all money that comes into your hands to get as much land on Hazen's Rout as possible for the concern." [4]

Hardly was he back in Lancaster before Hazen wrote Washington an eighteen-page letter again proposing an invasion of Canada by way of Coos, advancing all the old arguments and estimating the supplies and men that would be needed. He also expressed his soldiers' dislike of guard duty. Washington at first showed enough interest to pose ten questions concerning the geography of Lake Cham-

plain and Canada, the weather, and British power, and to promise that
Hazen's assignment at Lancaster would last only until the opening of
the campaign season.[5]

These questions prompted a ten-page reply from Hazen detailing routes, the spirit of the Canadians and the fortifications at
Quebec. He had acquired this information during his recent trip to
Coos, and from the scouts that Bedel kept constantly in the field. But
the project expired after Hazen's second letter. Washington was simultaneously exploring the possibility of a siege of New York, but no
campaign at all developed in 1782. The British had ceased aggressive
action and reports of peace negotiations began to arrive. Therefore,
it seemed an unlikely time to talk of costly campaigns and Hazen
consequently stayed in Lancaster all summer and fall.[6]

Guarding the prisoners was more boring than onerous. They
were held at Lancaster, Reading, and York, all a part of Hazen's command. Prior to his arrival the atmosphere had been too relaxed. Paroles
were readily available to officers if they signed this statement:

> I, _____ being a prisoner in the united Colonies of America, do
> upon the honor of a gentleman, promise that I will not go into or
> near any seaport town, nor farther than six miles distant from Lan-
> caster without leave of the Continental Congress or the Committee
> of Safety of Pennsylvania, and that I will carry on no political cor-
> respondence whatever on the subject of the dispute between Great
> Britain and the Colonies so long as I remain a prisoner.[7]

Congress allowed two dollars a week to support each prisoner.
The rations included a pound of meat, with bread and vegetables
daily. The men were allowed, for extra pay, to work at farming nearby,
at casting cannon at Lancaster and Reading, and at making shoes for
the American troops. During the summer and fall of 1781 escapes had
become frequent, often in groups of two or three. The detailing of
Hazen's regiment to guard duty was supposed to bring more discipline
to the situation.

Hazen made his headquarters in the stone Cat Tavern, near
the barracks, where he presided over his scattered command. His
charges included Hessians from Saratoga and some of Cornwallis'
troops. Their numbers were large, for they included wives and children of many of the prisoners. The men were on full ration, women
and children one half, "Whiskey Soap and Candles Withheld." In

early August Camp Security at York listed 474 men, 146 women, and 189 children, including those on bail or pass. Another unit, probably at Reading, showed 286 men, 134 women, and 173 children. Lancaster at about the same period showed 1,322 men and 99 women.[8]

Hazen had difficulty bringing order to the employment of his charges. Tradition decreed that the practice be continued, but he found an alarming rate of escape. He finally reported to the secretary at war that the commissaries of prisoners were lax in giving passes, that they "appear assiduous in supporting an independent, uncontrollable power, at least not subject to his restraint," and that contrary to express orders they were still allowing prisoners to work in "boroughs, towns and country." Congress took decisive action by directing the secretary at war to court-martial the commissaries "for disobedience of orders and neglect of duty," and to appoint others in their stead. That this improved the situation is evidenced by the fact that when Hazen's regiment was ordered away in October the borough council at Lancaster presented him with an address in which the residents "returned him their warmest thanks for the many proofs of regard and attention paid the inhabitants."[9]

But all did not go smoothly at Lancaster, and Hazen committed one of the biggest blunders of his life. The affair started in the spring with an action by former Royal Governor William Franklin of New Jersey, now head of the board of directors of the Associated Loyalists. He caused the arrest of Captain Joshua Huddy of the New Jersey Line, who was subsequently hanged in a cruel and insulting manner in retaliation for a prisoner whom the Americans shot while running away from his guard. Washington immediately decided upon retaliation of his own and Congress unanimously backed him up. But from the start the project was distasteful to him and he requested that the British would make it unnecessary by punishing their own guilty party. They set out to do so on May 3 with a court-martial of Captain Richard Lippincott, who was in local command when Huddy's hanging took place.

Meanwhile Washington directed Hazen to choose by lot a British captain "who is an unconditional Prisoner," or a lieutenant if there was no captain: "I need not mention to you that every possible tenderness, that is consistent with the Security of him, should be shewn to the person whose unfortunate Lot it may be to suffer." Then he appealed again to the British authorities "that the War may be carried on agreeable to the Rules which humanity formed and the example of the politest Nations recommends."[10]

On May 27 the drawing of lots took place at Lancaster in the presence of several officers including Hazen, Captain Moses White, British Major Gordon, and the thirteen British captains in the area. Twelve blank pieces of paper were prepared, plus one with the word "Unfortunate" written on it. These were placed in a hat. Then the names of each of the captains were written on separate pieces of paper and placed in a second hat. The officers were asked to do their own drawing, which they refused, having already objected to the proceedings since they were all covered by the terms of a capitulation. Lieutenant Benjamin Mooers, who was present, described the subsequent events: "Two or three small drummers were called in, and were ordered, one to draw from the hat with names, the other from that with numbers. The names which were drawn were handed to the Commissary of Prisoners, each paper from the other hat given to Captain White. If a blank, so declared. Thus the drawing continued until the eleventh name came out, when against that was drawn 'Unfortunate.'" [11]

The unlucky draw fell to Captain Charles Asgill, nineteen years of age and only son of Sir Charles Asgill. The British officers were outraged at the behavior of General Clinton and obtained Hazen's permission for one of their own number, Captain Ludlow, to go to New York and accuse him of abandoning them in a crisis. Major Gordon, in reporting the results of the drawing to General Carleton, said that "The delicate manner, in which General Hazen communicated his orders to the British officers, shows him to be a man of real feeling, and the mild treatment the prisoners have met with since we came to this place deserves the warmest acknowledgements of every British officer." [12]

It did not take long to discover that Captain Asgill was protected under the capitulation at Yorktown, a fact that Washington said "has distressed me exceedingly." He asked the secretary at war's opinion of the propriety of carrying out the execution of Asgill, if need be, since the Americans held no other unconditional prisoner. Obviously Hazen had stumbled, whether from a misunderstanding of orders or carelessness does not appear. The limited ardor that Washington had ever had for the enterprise waned from this date, although he was still capable of blustering: "The enemy ought to have learned before this that my resolutions are not to be trifled with." Yet he repeatedly cautioned his officers to treat Asgill with every possible respect and tenderness.[13]

In August word arrived that Captain Lippincott's lengthy trial had ended with his acquittal. The report suggested that Governor Franklin was the real culprit and that further inquiry would be made. Whether this was British procrastination or not, Washington thought it unseemly to hang Asgill while the investigation continued. Furthermore, Carleton reported that Clinton had forbidden Franklin to remove or exchange any more prisoners in his custody without permission of Clinton himself.[14]

Washington chose to look upon this as achieving the purpose of the proposed retaliation and he wished there was a way to end the whole matter quietly. But Congress was still adamant that the retaliation be carried out. Indecision lasted until late October, when Washington received a communication from French Foreign Minister the Count de Vergennes, who interceded for Asgill's life. He enclosed Lady Asgill's letter to him which, he said, had deeply affected the King and Queen. Since Asgill was captured at Yorktown, where French arms played a part, Vergennes asked as an ally that a complete pardon be granted the captain. Washington forwarded the correspondence to Congress on October 25 and on November 7 that body, at last able to climb off a shaky limb, directed Washington to set Asgill free. In a touching letter Washington sent the prisoner a passport for New York and assured him of his profound relief that the blood of an innocent person did not have to be spilled.[15]

Late in October Hazen's regiment was ordered to join the main army for winter quarters in New Jersey, which Hazen assumed meant Morristown. However, he was halted at Pompton, in the northern part of the state, and told to make his headquarters there. He was to send one company to Dobbs Ferry on the Hudson, another to Sidman's Clove (a blockhouse near Suffern, New York), and keep the rest of his unit at Pompton. Hazen regretted the scattering of his command. Suffern was a dozen miles to the north and its blockhouse needed major repairs. Dobbs Ferry was even farther away. He also found on his arrival in mid-November that there were insufficient huts and a lack of everything else—blankets, clothing, tents, and tools— and the conditions at Suffern were even worse. Washington tried to alleviate the most pressing shortages by telling Hazen where to apply for the various items.

Hazen's assignment for the winter was "to stop all straglers and suspicious persons" and to watch for deserters at Dobbs Ferry. But especially he was to stop "this pernicious intercourse" of the cattle drives along the west bank of the Hudson, obviously headed for New York. In this work he had some success. He despatched Lieutenant

William Stuart to patrol the shores, watch for deserters and disrupt illegal traffic, but not to approach the enemy lines or stay too long in one place. Washington praised these efforts, remarking that they "appear to have been very alert, and they have succeeded in several instances." [16]

But commendations of Stuart turned out to be premature, because by May he had been arrested three times. In his zeal to intercept the illicit trade with the enemy in New York he had run afoul of the civil authorities of New Jersey. One of his arrests had been instigated by Lieutenant Abraham Kinney, who had himself been arrested through Hazen's efforts but subsequently acquitted by court-martial of illicit trade with the enemy. On the occasion of his third arrest Stuart appealed to Hazen, who turned to both Washington and Governor William Livingston of New Jersey. The Governor was convinced that Stuart acted in line of duty in making the seizures and praised his vigilance in "suppressing that villainous trade and intercourse then carried on with the Enemy." Stuart had been scandalously treated by those who wanted to avoid any interruption of "their iniquitous commerce with New York." Yet Livingston professed that he could not intervene in the judicial process; Stuart must apply to the courts and get himself a good attorney. Stuart was eventually exonerated, but not until the pursuit of the "iniquitous" traders had been slowed down by the long interruption.[17]

Other assignments came the way of the regiment. A group of some 120 prisoners of war who had chosen to enlist in the American army were being marched from Philadelphia. Hazen was required to send a detachment to meet them and bring them to Morristown. The secretary of war also ordered the collecting of all the German prisoners of war scattered among the states. Hazen was authorized to give discharges to those who wished to purchase their redemption for £30 and become American citizens; he could also recruit any of the others who were willing to enter the American army at a bounty of eight dollars per man. He was to secure all the rest for the duration.[18]

The move was a canny one because a considerable number of German soldiers, if they had not already deserted, were eager to remain in the country as citizens. For one of the missions Hazen sent Captain Selin, a native of Germany, and Lieutenant Mooers, both of his regiment, to meet a group of German prisoners at Mt. Hope, where they were employed by a civilian, Mr. Faesch. At first the prisoners were loath to accept any of the options open to them and they tried to escape to New York. They were incarcerated in a Newark jail but their employer paid for their release, for which he billed them and for both of which acts the prisoners instituted an official grievance. Still refusing redemption or enlistment they were, according to instructions, marched off to jail in Philadelphia. On the second day of the march they had a change of heart, sent for their employer and reached an agreement whereby he advanced their redemption money of £30 a head. How they settled their accounts with Mr. Faesch is not clear, but they were released from imprisonment into his custody.

For most of the men the winter dragged on in dull routine and occasional hardships from scarcities of clothing and provisions, punctuated by the running battle of Hazen and his officers with Major Reid. Captain James Duncan, heading fifty men at remote Suffern, complained bitterly all winter about the conditions there and his demotion from the usual duties of a captain at the head of a company. He ultimately asked Washington for a court of inquiry to investigate Hazen's persecution of him. The most he obtained was a relief from his irritating assignment at Suffern.

Hazen and his wife occupied a small Dutch house of one room which was used for lodging, dining, dressing, and Hazen's office. Mrs. Hazen probably suffered the more because there was not a family she could wish to visit within fourteen miles. The other officers found whatever quarters they could. Lieutenant Mooers lived as a member of the family with a Dutchman named Bartolf, to whom he turned over his rations. Even then, the officers fared better than the men, who lived in rude huts. Despite all the difficulties, the army's quartermaster department performed prodigies of enterprise in transporting provisions and stores to its widely separated posts throughout the north. In November, for example, when Hazen's command totaled 35 officers and 464 noncoms and privates, it received 26,000 pounds of beef plus commensurate amounts of other foodstuffs. Equally important for morale was the arrival of 56 gallons, one quart and 1,812 gills of whiskey, and two tierces (casks containing 42 gallons) of taffia rum plus quantities of other varieties of rum.[19]

Another chapter in the Hazen–Reid affair was written during the winter. Hazen's officers, incensed at the aspersions Reid made against them at his previous trial, had refused to serve with him except during the emergency of Yorktown. Apparently at their insistence, but probably without any reluctance on his part, Hazen arrested him at Lancaster in May 1782 and charged him with "disobedience of orders, unmilitary conduct and ungentleman and unofficer-like behavior." Hazen told him the officers would withdraw their charges if he would either resign his commission or transfer out of the regiment. Reid refused both options. It is to be wondered that neither side suggested a simple apology or Reid's withdrawal of his derogatory charges against the regiment. Instead, Reid complained bitterly about his arrest and appealed to Washington for a speedy trial at headquarters. Although Hazen protested that his officers could not be spared at the time, he explored ways by which their testimony could be taken before a civil magistrate and forwarded to the court-martial. Nevertheless Washington, in replying to Reid, decided that the trial must be deferred until there was a better opportunity to form a court, i.e., until the season when the army was gathered in winter quarters and not so preoccupied with other duties.[20]

And so the trial was put off until December 30 when it was held at army headquarters at New Windsor. Hazen's officers chose Captains Moses White and Richard Lloyd to represent them and to require proof of Reid's charges that they robbed and cheated their men and wantonly embezzled public property. But the trial miscarried, or at least Hazen and his officers felt that it did. Hazen in a memorial to Washington accused the judge advocate—the same Lt. Thomas Edwards who had directed the previous proceedings—of bias in not pressing the charges against Reid, of leniency to him while he stated his case, and of severity in rejecting evidence the captains tried to submit. Hazen complained, as he had before, that there were no rules to guide a court or define the role of the judge advocate, and he bulwarked his argument by reviewing the inconsistencies in previous courts-martial. He asked Washington to set aside the proceedings, direct an inquiry into the proper conduct of a trial, and then hold a retrial on the charges brought against Reid.[21]

Washington asked his general officers for their opinion concerning the appropriateness of investigating the conduct of the judge advocate. The officers approved such a move unless Hazen's officers wanted to bring Edwards to trial, in which case they should reduce their allegations to specific charges. Hazen and his officers preferred the latter course and presented Washington with an outline of the testimony they would use, at the same time drawing up three charges against Edwards. Washington named the general officers as a Board of Inquiry to look into the proceedings of courts-martial, the duties of a judge advocate and the conduct of Lieutenant Edwards.[22]

The Board dealt with each of the charges against Edwards. They decided that the lack of a judicial system governing the office and duties of a judge advocate was not a military offense cognizable by a court-martial. They agreed unanimously that Edwards displayed no lack of candor and impartiality in conducting prosecutions, or neglect of duty in his position as judge advocate. Washington approved their report and next day he published and confirmed the results of Reid's court-martial. The court found that Reid had no fraudulent intent in handling public money. He was also acquitted of all other charges although he once signed as major of a nonexistent unit, a matter so trifling that, said Washington, "it so strongly marks the nature of the whole prosecution against him." Reid was immediately released.[23]

The findings were not calculated to soothe the feelings of Hazen or his officers, who still felt their honor impugned and their worthiness for their jobs brought into question. After his trial Reid had been granted a leave of absence, but the regimental officers demanded his return and a public hearing of his charges against them. The long-suffering Washington consequently ordered a Court of Inquiry to convene at West Point on May 15 to examine the conduct of Hazen and his officers in the light of Reid's assertions against them. At the opening of the court Reid challenged its right to inquire into his defense of 1780 and when pressed, refused to supply the requested information. In its quandary the court asked directions from Washington. The commander in chief gave orders to proceed without delay, and if the court's findings were approved they would be considered the end of the matter.[24]

Reid apologized to Washington for all the trouble he was causing, but asked leave to remain in quarters. Washington told him the inquiry would proceed and that his remaining in camp was his own decision. The court finished its work on May 27 without Reid in attendance, and reported to Washington that "they cannot find Reason to justify the Assertions mentioned in the said Orders," i.e., Reid's charges which Washington referred to in creating the court. Washington accepted the report as final. The two courts that had sat at Hazen's insistence seem to have been reluctant to convict Reid of intemperate statements he made as part of his own defense two and a half years previously.[25]

But this lukewarm endorsement of their position gave no satisfaction to Hazen and his officers, who still felt that the charges against them had gone unrefuted. So they sent Washington an impassioned appeal for justice, which the General answered in firm but moderate tones. In their next petition they reported that Reid still refused to prosecute his charges against them and that Hazen had ordered his

arrest, which Reid ignored. Hazen appealed to Washington to enforce
the arrest.[26]

Washington then requested the opinion of his general officers
on three points: (1) whether all "practicable and proper" measures
had been taken to give Hazen and his officers satisfaction; (2) if not,
what further steps should be taken; and (3) whether Reid should be
arrested and brought to trial. He received an affirmative answer to the
first question and a negative to the third, whereupon he brought the
situation to a close with a letter to Hazen in which he expressed
the opinion that the new charges against Reid "appeared to me to arise
rather from a spirit of persecution, than a desire to promote Service."
He further hoped that "you will consider this as finishing an affair
that has given so much trouble to the Army." Thus the regiment
never got the satisfaction it had demanded for so long, but its grievance was soon forgotten in the confusion of the army's demobilization.[27]

During the waning months of the war Hazen renewed his suit
on a matter which had been in suspension for nearly two years—his
pay and emoluments as a general officer. One of the anomalies was
that a brigadier general, which he had been by brevet since 1781, was
not supposed to lead a regiment. But at the time of his promotion he
was not given a brigade from New Jersey, the state to which his promotion was credited. Therefore, in the weeks before Yorktown he had
been without any command. Only in Virginia was he assigned a
brigade of his own, and that was of brief duration. While it lasted he
received a colonel's pay and subsistence, but some of the emoluments
of a brigadier general. The complete emoluments of a brigadier general were considerable: extra rations, forage, and servants.

Beginning in June 1782 he appealed to the War Office for the
usual perquisites of a general, and he asked why he had received a
brevet promotion instead of a regular one. To make his case, he interpreted the congressional resolution of April 30, 1778, as not
applicable to him. In it, Congress had defined the rank and duties of
a brevetted officer, which Hazen believed referred only to regimental
and company grades. The War Office forwarded his petition to Congress with the comment that "to exclude him from the emoluments of
a Brigadier would be peculiarly hard, as he has for some considerable
time done the duty of a Brigadier, and been exposed to the expenses of
that rank."[28]

Having heard nothing on the matter for nine months, Hazen
renewed his appeal in March 1783, and when he learned that it had

been referred to a committee he addressed its members with several additional pages of arguments. Congress in September made an oblique decision by resolving that brevet commissions did not carry additional pay or emoluments unless provision was explicitly made for them in the original commission.[29]

Although Hazen's commission was not couched in these terms, and although he was on the point of leaving the army, he refused to accept the resolution of Congress as final. He renewed his appeal the following February to both Congress and committee. Again he reviewed his military career and all that it had cost him out of his own pocket. He brought up the unique establishment of the Canadian regiment which had been a barrier to promotions for himself or his officers, and he recalled that nearly twenty junior colonels had been promoted over his head, some of whom were now major generals. Since his promotion, four other colonels had been promoted and they were receiving all the emoluments of office.[30]

But all to no avail. The committee recommended that Hazen receive the "pay and subsistence" of a brigadier general and pointed to the precedent of a brevet major once being allowed the pay and subsistence of a major. The motion was amended to read "pay and emoluments" and to be dated from the day of his promotion, but the amendments were lost in a tie vote. The original resolution was then also defeated on Aprli 16, 1784. This by no means discouraged Hazen. Early in 1785 he asked again for the pay and emoluments of a brigadier general, indemnification for his British lieutenant's half pay which he had been promised, principal and interest on the $13,386 calculated by Congress in 1781, and the final settlement of his other accounts. He asserted that he was entitled to the perquisites not just of a brigadier general, but of a major general "by the Common Rules of Justice and regulations of the army."[31]

The committee which considered his petition submitted a negative report. It referred to the resolution of 1783 barring brevet pay unless the promotion specifically mandated it. On his loss of half pay for which he had been promised compensation in 1776, the committee quibbled: that the promise had not included half pay as an American officer and, since he now had half pay as a retired colonel, he had no further claim for the much smaller amount of half pay as a British lieutenant. Part of this report was referred to the secretary at war and the rest to the Treasury Board.[32]

Some idea of the urgency with which Hazen's financial problems were treated is seen in the fact that the secretary at war waited for three years, until 1788, to report. Hazen was undoubtedly wronged by this delay. He was understandably disturbed by his own brevet promotion when so many officers junior to him were getting full promotions. And he had reason to be puzzled by the off-and-on quality of his service as a brigadier general. It is likely that he irritated some members of Congress by his repeated memorials on a variety of subjects. Yet throughout the war he and his unit maintained the respect of Washington and most of the other senior officers for their fighting abilities.

The real explanation seems to lie much deeper. Congress had to approve all promotions in the army but, politics aside, the members of that body operated under their own quota system whereby each state was allocated certain numbers of officers. The Canadian regiment did not fit into the quota of any state. Indeed, its demands made only one more pressure upon the general treasury, which was usually without funds. Congress was undoubtedly niggardly in the matter of promotions in its "own" regiment, but in pay, provisions, and clothing the regiment received approximately the same treatment as other army units, which were always in arrears and occasionally mutinous as a result.

In extenuation of Congress' decisions, it needs to be remembered that Hazen's regiment, through no fault of its commander and indeed to his great anguish, was never built up to its full complement of enlisted men and was consequently always considered overstaffed with officers. Hazen and his regiment were the unwitting victims of the conditions surrounding its creation, and Congress never found a durable solution except to maintain the regiment "on its original establishment."

Hazen had one final brush with authority in April 1783, during the final weeks of his regiment's existence, when he resumed the two-year effort to obtain promotions for his men. At the final muster of the regiment in June, some changes in rank appeared which caused his superiors great concern. Before the matter was settled, Washington, Adjutant General Edward Hand, the War Office, and Congress all became involved. Hand challenged the returns, which showed the promotion of "several officers, five rank and file and several sergeants." But Hazen asserted that the secretary at war had filled out and signed the commissions for the officers and that Hazen himself had delivered them to the president of Congress; the other promotions, he asserted, stemmed from his authority as commanding officer of the regiment.[33]

30438 E269.C27E9 EVEREST MOSES HAZEN AND THE CANADIAN

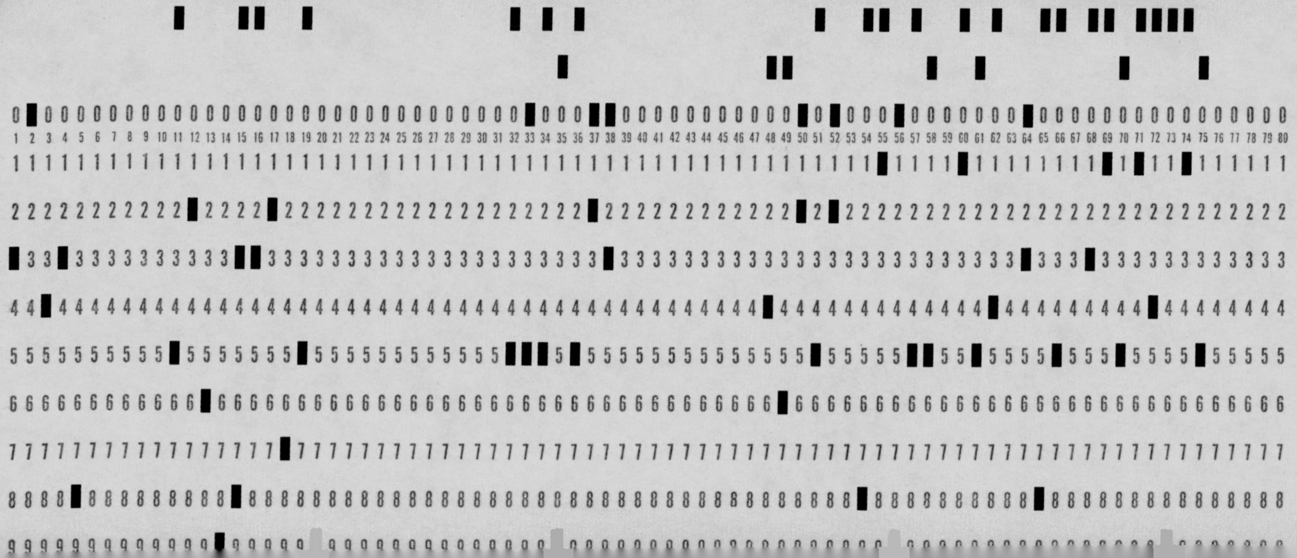

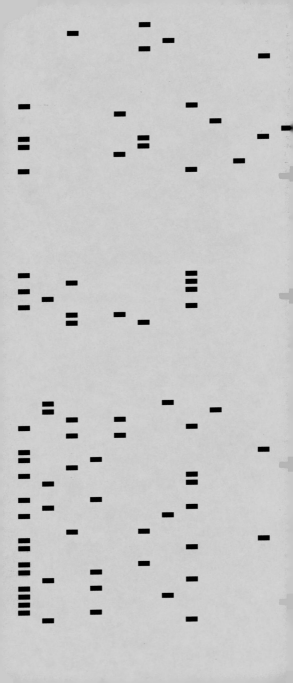

Washington asked the War Office for information and learned that there was no record of the promotions there "and, as all commissions are sealed and registered previous to their delivery, it would seem that the said promotions were not finally concurred in—as in that case, the commissions would have been regularly issued." But according to the president, Hazen brought him the commissions to sign, probably after the War Office had routinely passed on them but had not officially recorded them. The president decided not to sign them before consulting Congress, which directed him not to do so pending further orders. The matter was referred to a committee which conferred with Hazen and reported back to Congress, at which point the subject was allowed to die. Except for zeal for his men, Hazen's actions are difficult to interpret. It is possible that he actually thought he had the authority of the War Office to proceed, and that only subsequently the promotions were "not finally concurred in." On the other hand, Hazen may have relied upon the confusion of demobilization to conceal his efforts. Certainly he felt that promotions for his officers were long overdue.[34]

However, the subsequent action of Congress in September 1783 applied to Hazen's regiment as much as to the rest of the army: the secretary at war was instructed to give honorary (brevet) promotions by one rank to all officers below major generals if they had held their current grade since 1777. The act did not apply to Hazen personally because he had had his brevet promotion two years earlier, but a number of his officers received promotions. For example Captains Laurent Olivier and Clement Gosselin became brevet majors. Most of them enjoyed their new rank as a matter of prestige after the war, but otherwise they gained nothing tangible as a reward.[35]

In military terms the war was over at Yorktown, but at the time Washington and Congress could not know whether it would break out again. Therefore the army was kept intact though largely inactive throughout the campaigning season of 1782 and the dismal winter which followed. In winter quarters Hazen's chief duties concerned stragglers, deserters (of whom there were many), and the illegal traffic into New York City. Washington established his headquarters near Newburgh and gathered his main army around him so as to keep watch over the British in New York. Meanwhile the peace negotiations in Paris consumed much of 1782. It was not until the following March that Congress received word of a definitive treaty.

As the war dragged to a close, army officers grew more desperate at the prospect that when the need for them vanished, their chances of receiving a settlement of their accounts would disappear as well. Congress in 1780 had resolved to grant them half pay for life, and those who left the army before 1783 were retired on that basis. But many states were beginning to express opposition to the measure, and during the last winter of the war members of Congress began to think they had been too generous. Furthermore, all army pay was hopelessly in arrears.

Consequently, in December the officers at Newburgh drew up a memorial to Congress in which they respectfully presented their grievances: their back pay and the depreciation of paper money, short rations, and the lack of proper clothing. They tried to convey the growing discontent in the army, but expressed a willingness to compromise in favor of a flat sum instead of half pay for life. It was signed by fourteen colonels and generals, including Brigadier General Hazen. The memorial was delivered to Congress by a committee of officers who, when they reached Philadelphia, walked into the middle of an exhaustive debate over finances and the payment of the war debt.[36]

Congress had long been divided between the believers in state authority, whose ideas had been imbedded in the Articles of Confederation, and the nationalists such as Alexander Hamilton, James Madison, and Robert and Gouverneur Morris, who wanted a more centralized government. The latter, since the adoption of the Articles in 1781, had been planning ways of amending them so as to allow Congress to collect its own revenues. The former group preferred matters as they were, i.e., Congress should requisition its financial needs from the states. They had been able so far to block the efforts of Congress to raise money by collecting import duties. Such a change in the Articles required the unanimous consent of all the states, and there had always been at least one state to oppose it.

The arrival of the army memorial coincided with a concerted effort by the civilian creditors of the government to obtain a settlement of their accounts. They were all nationalists in favoring the enhancement of the powers of Congress, especially the power to raise its own revenue. Some were authentic creditors who had personally assisted the government during the war. Others were pseudocreditors who had been busily buying up others' certificates of indebtedness at bargain prices. Both groups shouted their conviction that the government should be forced to redeem its obligations.[37]

Some of their leaders glimpsed the feasibility of linking the civilian and military creditors into a pressure group that, through the threat of armed force, might intimidate the states into yielding to the demands of Congress. What originated as a political move in Philadelphia soon infected a few of the army officers at Newburgh. Even Hazen at Pompton, like most of his fellow officers, was a nationalist in political outlook. He viewed the approaching peace with anticipation but also "with not a little gall when we survey our present unfortunate situation, which is like a barrell of thirteen staves without a hoop to keep it together." He believed that the soldiers would not lay down their arms "without seeing a disposition in the people to do justice to them and other public creditors."[38]

At first Washington was unwilling to believe that serious disaffection existed in the army, but upon learning of the secret circulation of anonymous, inflammatory petitions at headquarters, he called his officers together. He made a moving appeal to their moderation and patriotism, and he managed to channel their frustrations into a willingness to give Congress another chance. In their subsequent memorial they rejected with disdain "the infamous propositions contained in a late anonymous address," and they hoped that Congress would not disband the army "until their accounts are liquidated, the balances accurately ascertained, and adequate funds established for payment." This marked the climax of any military effort to seize control of the situation, but the problems remained and Congress grappled with them during the rest of the spring.[39]

The nationalists insisted that all money due the army was a federal obligation that should be paid out of revenues collected by Congress, and they prepared a new revenue amendment to the Articles of Confederation. At the very least they wanted the army to remain intact until its financial claims had been met. Their opponents were determined to apportion the national debt, including the military, among the states. They preferred to see the army disbanded and its members sent home to settle accounts in their respective states. Each side won a partial victory. The states-righters ultimately saw the army demobilized and the states settle most of its accounts. The nationalists, however, managed to keep the army intact for several more months. They also prevailed when Congress on March 22 offered a choice between half pay for life and five years of full pay in money or securities at six percent, "as Congress shall find most convenient." The act specifically applied to Hazen's regiment; each army corps was given two months in which to make its preference known.[40]

Officers overwhelmingly voted for five years of full pay because the money was more urgently needed upon demobilization and because they thought it was more likely to be paid in a lump sum than in payments over the next fifty years. Hazen's officers voted unanimously for it on April 25. Yet the solution of the army's other grievances remained to be found. The nationalists still wanted the army to remain intact, and many of the officers also objected to its dissolution until their back pay and other accounts were settled. The enlisted men, on the other hand, were ready to go home as soon as they could be released. Even Washington was insistent that all accounts be settled before the army was disbanded. After that was done, he thought that three months' pay should be provided, or else the soldiers would be dismissed like a "Sett of Beggars" and the worst might be expected.[41]

A copy of the peace treaty arrived during this debate, and it was published on April 11. Its very existence made a large standing army superfluous. Military unrest increased, resulting in rioting and insubordination in the ranks. Washington received an increasing number of petitions form various units with grievances, and some of them demanded five years' pay for enlisted men as well as officers. Under such pressures he felt compelled to recommend that all men be discharged who were not going to be maintained in the postwar establishment; otherwise, he saw the situation getting out of hand.[42]

Congress finally took action. It directed Superintendent of Finance Robert Morris to provide the soldiers with three months' pay. On May 26 it authorized Washington to grant furloughs to the noncommissioned officers and soldiers, together with a proportionate number of commissioned officers. Full discharges would follow upon the conclusion of a definitive treaty of peace, i.e., ratification of the treaty.[43]

Hazen, who had missed most of the excitement at headquarters by being stationed at Pompton, was ordered to march his unit to Newburgh in June. His officers, like those of the rest of the army, objected to furloughs without their arrears of pay and they protested to Washington, who defended Congress as having done all it could and refused to keep the soldiers in camp. And so in June most of Hazen's soldiers and many of his officers were furloughed, with little more than the promise of Congress to settle their accounts later. A number of his officers remained in Newburgh during the summer to press their special claims, but the unit was finally disbanded at White Plains in November.

VII

The Canadians After the War

At the end of the war the American members of the Second
Canadian Regiment, who formed the majority, were free to return to their homes and pick up the threads of civilian life. But this
was not true of the Canadians (most of whom were French from
Quebec) or the Nova Scotians. They had no state or country to return
to and they were actually the wards of Congress, which had too many
other pressing demands upon it to formulate a consistent policy for
this relatively small group.

The soldiers were furloughed with certificates for three
months' pay in their pockets. Most of them joined families or friends
in the refugee camps at Albany and Fishkill. They went with large
arrears of pay and only the promise of Congress to settle their accounts later. However, Congress fulfilled its obligation on November
3, 1783, by directing the paymaster general to deposit with each regimental agent the arrears of pay due both the officers and soldiers of
his unit. Richard Lloyd was the agent for Hazen's Canadians, and he
received certificates with a face value of $226,544 3/90 for that pur-
pose. He was authorized to charge a commission or keep all the
certificates that he could not deliver. Therefore, he was upset when
Congress, on September 6, 1786, allowed a commission of only one
percent which, he said, gave him only about £93 for all his trouble.
There is no record that he ever received more. At least the soldiers
had their back pay, but it was good for cash only if they waited
several years until Congress could redeem the certificates or, as most
of them did, sold them at large discounts to eager speculators.[1]

The draft of the peace treaty, which arrived in the spring of

1783, created consternation among the foreign members of the Canadian regiment, and Hazen quickly registered their dismay. The peace treaty committed Congress to "earnestly recommend" that the states provide for the restitution of the property of American Loyalists, who should be uninhibited in their efforts to regain their confiscated possessions. Yet it contained no reciprocal provision for Canadian and Nova Scotian refugees to go home and repossess their property. So far as is known, the subject did not arise during the writing of the treaty. Probably their relatively small numbers made them easy to overlook in the face of the more divisive issues that faced the peacemakers.[2]

At this point the idea of compensatory lands in the United States began to take root. The project was not new, for Congress had made such a commitment in September 1776. It had directed the states to take care of their own veterans, the lands to be provided by the United States but the expense of procuring them to be borne by the states. Allotments were to be according to rank, from 500 acres for a colonel down to 100 for a private. Congress later amended the provision to include 1,100 acres for a major general and 850 acres for a brigadier general. But this covered only troops of the Continental Army who were credited to a specific state, which the Canadians were not.[3]

The anxieties of the Canadians were increased by the action of New York State, which most of them, for want of any other, considered their domicile. In March 1783 the state legislature far exceeded the grants that Congress had proposed. It voted 5,500 acres for a major general prorated down through the ranks to 500 acres for a private—five times the amount proposed by Congress for each grade. But the grants were to New Yorkers only, and thus again excluded the Canadians.[4]

Among the many petitions from Hazen or his officers, the first to mention lands for the Canadians was Hazen's memorial of April 8, 1783. He asked for a grant for members of his regiment, their dependents, and all other Canadians who might wish to join them in a land of liberty. Although his geography was somewhat confused, he proposed a tract near Detroit, starting at the mouth of the Huron River and running along the shores of Lake Erie to a point six miles east of the mouth of the Maumee. It would have included the area now occupied by the cities of Monroe, Michigan, and Toledo, Ohio. He chose this location because the Quebec Act had once made it a part of Canada, but the peace treaty returned it to American ownership and it might "draw out of the present Limits of Canada such other Sufferers by this contest as still remain in that Country." Since there was already a "Pickering Plan" under discussion whereby the quartermaster general was proposing a new state in the area for other veterans of the war, Hazen wrote Pickering to suggest a slight modification in its boundaries so as not to interfere with his request. The details are academic, since neither plan went any farther.[5]

Congress' reply to Hazen stated that it "retains a lively Sense of the Services the Canadian Officers and Men have rendered the united States & that they are seriously disposed to reward them for their virtuous sufferings in the Cause of Liberty." It promised grants of land when it could "consistently" do so, meaning when it had taken account of all its other commitments. Hazen tried to prod Congress once more on the subject in January 1784. He reminded the members of their pledges of land and he repeated his request for the area near Detroit.[6]

General Washington also added his voice to the request for refugee lands. In forwarding yet another memorial from officers of Hazen's regiment, he recommended that if Congress could not provide for the refugees in other ways it might consider granting lands in the interior which "would enable them to form a Settlement which may be beneficial to themselves and useful to the United States." Ultimately it was New York State, not Congress, that would provide lands for most of the refugees.[7]

The families of Hazen's French servicemen suffered great hardships during the war. After the retreat of 1776 they spent a month at Crown Point, two months at Ticonderoga, and finally, in September, were sent to Albany in the train of the Canadian Regiment. Many of them remained there, more or less wards of the government, for ten years. Yet when the regiment was ordered to Fishkill in November, some of the families managed to follow, and so two distinct refugee camps developed for the duration—the larger one at Albany, the smaller at Fishkill.

Some of these families were mobile enough to follow fathers, husbands, or brothers into winter quarters, wherever they might be. They had to live on the fringes of the camp, but even then a certain amount of gaiety flourished. There was at least the congeniality of tea drinking from hut to hut, and family dinners and parties. Babies were born in camp, children died also and were buried there. Captain Paulint and his wife, for example, lost twins and other children during the war, of whom there is no official record. Their first child to live after they left Canada was a daughter, born in Albany in the "year of peace," 1783.[8]

It is possible that the families which followed the regiment into winter quarters fared better than the majority who remained at Albany and Fishkill. At any rate, a stream of complaints emanated from those two centers on the subject of rations. Congress originally put all the Canadian volunteers under the care of General Schuyler and instructed him to "enquire into their services and characters, and to order such rewards and wages as shall appear to have been merited." Schuyler interpreted his charge broadly enough to include the distribution of rations to the dependents of the servicemen. But the rations were at best irregular, depending upon the availability of supplies (even the army did not eat regularly or well) and the zeal of the post commanders.[9]

Army rationing for the families seemed to go fairly smoothly during the first few years. But changes of commanders produced uncertainties over the intent of their instructions and a certain degree of negligence. In November 1780 Lafayette brought to Washington a memorial from the Canadian families at Albany who had not been receiving the provisions they previously had been able to collect. Washington took it upon himself to order General James Clinton to furnish a ration per individual (food for one day) until further orders. He then transmitted the memorial to Congress with his comment that "both justice and humnaity make it infinitely to be desired, it were in our power to make some better provision for persons who have left their country, and involved themselves in every kind of distress in compliance with our invitation." Congress immediately approved Washington's order to Clinton of one ration per individual. It also asked Governor George Clinton of New York "to cause an inquiry to be made into their circumstance, at the expence of the United States, as he shall judge necessary."[10]

While the war ravaged his state, there was little that Governor Clinton could or would do for the refugees, so their fate continued to rest with Congress. In October 1781 that body unaccountably repealed its actions of 1776, which had entrusted them to the custody of General Schuyler. Its resolution directed that "all persons, of what character soever, who now draw pay or rations in consequence of the said resolution be not entitled to draw pay or rations after the 1st day of December next." Since this act did not repeal its later directive to General Clinton, issuing commissaries were understandably confused and stopped rationing the refugees. This led to petitions in their behalf, usually channeled to General Washington. He could only reply that "hard as it may appear, that those poor Refugees, who have been driven from their Country for their Adherence to our Cause, should be denied the pittance of provisions for their Subsistence, yet it is not in my power to contravene direct Resolutions of Congress."[11]

By leaving its resolution of 1780 intact, Congress probably did not intend to cut off rations for the refugees. But months were required to untangle the situation and resume the issues. Meanwhile the refugee families existed as best they could by following the regiment to winter quarters or by receiving help from their neighbors. For many of them this precarious existence, which began in 1776, was to last until 1786. Yet there was sentiment in Congress, which Secretary of Finance Robert Morris unsuccessfully tried to exploit, to cut them off from public help altogether after the war. He objected to subsidies for both Indians and Canadians, most if not all of which were to him an unnecessary expense, and he asked Congress to be governed by the "principles of public Economy."[12]

Paralleling the hardships of the dependents were those of some of Hazen's officers, who instituted petitions in their own behalf. As early as 1780, supported by a memorial from Hazen, they had asked a committee of Congress for help—they were nearly destitute of clothes and their families were suffering. They asked for an advance on the money they had disbursed in Canada for recruiting the regiment. Hazen calculated the amount at about £500 sterling, which he had included in his own accounts as guarantees to his officers, and which Congress had verified but not paid. The committee recommended some advances to the officers "without delay." At least three factors prevented Congress from acting on the recommendation. The officers' debts were included in Hazen's claims, which had received preliminary consideration. Congress was perpetually short of specie, which helps to explain its delay in paying Hazen's accounts. And finally, it censured its own committee for accepting petitions which were not first addressed to Congress.[13]

In 1780 a Nova Scotian added his voice to the clamor for attention. Josiah Throop memorialized the governor of New York for either a forfeited farm or assistance in purchasing one, so that he could move his family to the state. At the outbreak of the Revolution he and other like-minded Nova Scotians had espoused the Patriot cause and tried to promote it in their province. For his trouble he was forced to flee to Boston without his family, with a price on his head. In New England he tried to organize an expedition to Nova Scotia, joined several military campaigns, and supported himself by teaching school.[14]

Although large numbers of New Englanders in the 1760s settled in Nova Scotia, which included modern New Brunswick, they subsequently missed the crucial decade of social and political development that Americans experienced prior to the Revolution. They failed in their efforts to obtain concessions from the government in Halifax and resigned themselves to firm British control of the province. At the outbreak of the Revolution only a few ringleaders in widely scattered areas identified with the American struggle, and even they discounted the possibility of organizing any kind of local resistance. Instead, they were obsessed with the necessity of getting Massachusetts troops to come and rescue them by force.[15]

There were two principal areas of disaffection. One was at Maugerville, Sunbury County, near modern Fredericton, New Brunswick. The other and larger one was Cumberland County, that part of Nova Scotia at the Chignecto Isthmus where Nova Scotia and New Brunswick come together. Two of its citizens, Jonathan Eddy and John Allan, were the leaders of revolutionary activity. Eddy, although warned to wait, gathered a liberating army of twenty-eight men in Maine, collected a few more volunteers around Maugerville, and descended upon the Isthmus late in 1776. They made a brief, half-hearted siege of Fort Cumberland but were driven off in November by British troops. Throop was among Eddy's followers.

This ineffectual and premature action stunted the development of any further revolutionary activity in Nova Scotia. Almost seventy families preferred to leave in its wake rather than face the inevitable repression that would follow. Those who remained formally submitted to British authority. They relapsed into a state of apathy and confusion over the issues of the war. Many of them found an outlet for their frustrations in a major religious revival led by Henry Alline. The Yankees of Nova Scotia "turned to a religious rather than a political figure in their search for guidance on the many distressing problems produced by the war." [16]

Throop served in the American army and at the end of the war had attained the rank of lieutenant colonel. As a refugee, he qualified for a land grant in New York State, as did others from his province, hence the term "Canadian and Nova Scotia Refugee Tract" in northern New York. Some returned to their homeland after the initial passions had died down, while still others remained in exile and later qualified for congressional grants of land in Ohio.

During the spring and summer of 1783 a steady stream of petitions emanated from Hazen's regiment and its sympathizers. Hazen led off in April with his reasoned appeal for a grant of land in the west, together with compensation for their losses in Canada and the payment of interest due on their certificates. Congress could only promise lands when it could "consistently" be done. Four of his officers separately asked Congress for relief from their "distressed condition." They pointedly quoted its own words back to Congress: " 'We will never abandon you to the unrelenting fury of yours and our enemies.' " [17]

When the regiment was furloughed in June, the full implications of their stateless condition struck its officers more forcibly. Their pay was in arrears, they had dependents to support but no employment, and they had received no compensation for their losses in Canada or their outlays in raising their companies. In July three of the regimental officers, including Hazen, reminded Washington of their services and sufferings and the neglect they had experienced, and asked for his influence in their behalf. In forwarding their memorial to Congress, Washington argued their case as "unhappy persons, who placed confidence in those proclamations."

The next petition went direct to Congress. Captain Clement Gosselin wrote in behalf of the refugees at Fishkill (eighty men and women and six children) to press for relief from their unresolved difficulties. The committee of Congress, to which it was referred, acknowledged that the petitioners "deserve the attention of Congress . . . your Committee are only withheld, by the present exhausted State of the publick Finances, from recommending such a provision to be made for these unfortunate People as would afford them immediate Relief, and would lay a Foundation for the comfortable Establishment of their Families in future." [18]

Congress took three steps to alleviate the situation. It asked the State of New York to accept the refugees as citizens. It directed a continuation of a ration per day until further order. And it instructed the commissioner appointed to handle the public accounts of the state to settle the claims for advances of money and supplies made by the officers for the good of the army. A halfway measure at best, Congress at least saw to it that the refugees would continue to eat.

This action was taken in August, but it was the following January before Governor Clinton responded. He promised to place the congressional resolution before the next session of the legislature, where he expected no difficulty over citizenship (it was not granted for several years). However, he believed that the refugees needed massive assistance if they were not to become public charges, and it was a job that New York was unable to undertake after its own vast losses. Instead, he recommended that Congress assume the burden and that the commissioners reexamine the war services and the Canadian backgrounds of each refugee.[19]

Food and shelter seemed temporarily assured, although they were subject to the "further order" of Congress. The long-range issues persisted: lands of their own, repayment of money advanced by the officers, and compensation for their losses in Canada. As for the first, a solution in the form of land grants was just around the corner, but no one knew it in the dark winter of 1784. Concerning money and supplies advanced by the officers, the commissioner for New York was grappling with the problem and trying to separate them from Hazen's accounts. Captains Gosselin, Olivier, and Liebert, who made separate petitions on this subject, were referred by Congress to the New York Commissioner, who was told to "give dispatch" to the claims of these officers. Congress also voted each of them $100 on their accounts.[20]

On the third issue—compensation for lost property in Canada —Congress took a less than enthusiastic view. The committee which considered Clinton's letter and accompanying documents found the refugees "meritorious people" but costly to maintain, and the support they were receiving too feeble for their sufferings and the demands of "humanity and justice." Seizing upon Clinton's time-consuming proposal, it recommended that three commissioners study the refugees' status in Canada and their services in the United States, and that they report on each individual to Congress.

This recommendation was referred to still another committee, which came to grips with the main issue. It found that the messages to Canada of 1775 and 1776 were "invitations" only, the acceptance of which did not entitle Canadians to any compensation for their property losses because it was "not authorized by the usage of nations in similar circumstances." However, it believed they were entitled to gratitude, attention, and compensation to relieve their distresses. This put an end to officers' claims for their losses and included Hazen, who was precluded for the time being from further suits to recover the loss of his estate.[21]

In spite of the machinery in New York for settling claims based upon money advanced for the cause, some of the officers were impatient with the slow-moving process and petitioned individually. Captain Olivier reminded Congress that he had been promised a majority and had received it only in brevet form, and that all he had to show for the advances he had made in raising his company was a note from Hazen. He queried whether Congress or Hazen was supposed to pay him. Antill petitioned for the loss of pay he suffered through the depreciation of the currency. Residents of Canada submitted at least a score of claims for compensation for the goods and services they had furnished to the American army.

As might be expected, Hazen was again one of the petitioners. He adopted a direct, sharp tone with Paymaster General John Pierce, but was slapped down by both Pierce and Congress. He pointed out to Congress that his many financial commitments to his officers remained unpaid, and he asserted that he was threatened with jail and was "without bread for my self and family." In a renewal of his request for refugee lands in the west, he offered his services in a civil or military command at Detroit as a "Temporary Subsistence, as well as a Personal protection, untill it may be in the Power of Congress to grant me a substantial relief, by refunding the monies which I have advanced for their service." He expounded to General Gates upon the public service he could perform on such an assignment—he could form a militia unit among the Canadian settlers in Detroit, strengthen that part of the country by encouraging emigration from Canada, and settle the soldiers of his regiment on their own land. Nothing came of his proposals, partly because in the absence of an Indian treaty Congress had no clear authority to make land grants in the area.[22]

Antill's petition served to remind Congress that interest was overdue on the loan-office certificates issued to Hazen's regiment in 1781 for depreciation of pay. Steps had already been taken to pay two years' interest on them (January 1, 1781, to January 1, 1783). Congress in March 1785 resolved to pay one more year's interest (to January 1, 1784) to the officers only, who would cease to draw rations and subsistence when they received their money. The officers and men were told to obtain the remaining interest and the redemption of the certificates themselves from the states in which they resided (mainly New York). The states were directed to settle these accounts and charge them to the United States. This merely continued the practice of a nearly penniless Congress—to distribute its financial obligations among the states, subject to a later balancing of accounts between state and federal governments.[23]

Congress also sought to anticipate the problem of rations in July 1785 by directing that they be discontinued for all grades above captain in Hazen's former regiment, but that they be maintained for officers below that grade who were inhabitants of Canada at the start of the war, and for all other Canadian refugees, until June 1, 1786, "and no longer."

Although Hazen fought doggedly for the rights and prerogatives of his regiment, he seems not to have formed a high estimate of the quality of his French officers. After the war he told Congress that he never pretended that every man in his regiment was fit for the commission he held. Even in 1776, when the formation of the regiment was being considered, he was asked by a committee of Congress if there were sufficient Canadians attached to the Patriot cause who merited appointment as officers, to which he replied in the negative. The committee's reaction was, "We must make use of such people as we can get." [24]

Hazen probably retained these sentiments in 1788. Not only was he a semi-invalid (he suffered a stroke in 1786) but he had just been arrested and brought to court by Captain Liebert and Major Olivier, who were trying to force him to settle their accounts. Although his irritation is understandable, a closer look at some of his officers reveals unexpected competence and striking personalities. Most of them were young, could read and write—especially the captains— and were sufficiently imbued with a spirit of liberty to follow Hazen into exile.

Clement Gosselin, brevetted major at the end of the war, was one of the most dependable. Born in 1747 on the Isle of Orleans, he was a farmer at Sainte-Anne de la Pocatière on the south shore of the St. Lawrence when the Revolution broke out. He joined the American forces before Quebec in December 1775 and was commissioned captain in Hazen's regiment in the following March. He raised his own company but instead of following the Americans out of Canada immediately, he remained in the vicinity of Sainte-Anne to promote the American cause. Since he was wanted by the British he had to be ready to hide whenever an alarm was sounded. He was captured late in 1777, but released during the winter.

Leaving his family behind, he traveled on foot down the Connecticut River to rejoin his regiment at White Plains in the following March. He served in the American army until the end of the war, and was wounded at the siege of Yorktown. In 1778 and again in 1780 he was sent back into Canada on missions preparatory to a possible invasion. During the war he signed various petitions for his fellow officers, and at the close of the war he was a charter member of the Society of the Cincinnati. Subsequently he brought his family out of Canada and settled in Champlain, the New York town bordering on both Canada and Lake Champlain. He was married again in 1791 to the daughter of Francis Monty of Livingston's regiment. The marriage took place before Justice of the Peace Murdoch McPherson in Chazy. But in the following spring the couple went to St. Hyacinthe, Quebec, for a blessing by a priest. Others followed the same procedure after secular marriages in New York.

With minor variations, this is the story of other officers. Germain Dionne, whose daughter was the first wife of Clement Gosselin, was born in 1731 and was a well-to-do farmer at Sainte-Anne before the Revolution. He supplied the American army with foodstuffs at Quebec, joined it in December 1775 and was commissioned a lieutenant in Hazen's regiment in the following March. Like Gosselin, he remained behind at the time of the retreat but accompanied him to White Plains in 1778 and served for the rest of the war. He too was a charter member of the Society of the Cincinnati and received lands in the Refugee Tract, but he returned to Sainte-Anne, where he died in 1788.[25]

Louis Gosselin was three years older than his brother Clement, but he obtained only a lieutenant's commission in Hazen's regiment. He was captured during the retreat from Quebec and held a prisoner in Canada for about two years, but he escaped in 1778 and rejoined his regiment at White Plains in July. He returned to Canada on special service for eleven months but was back with his regiment for the battles of Elizabethtown, Morrisania, and Yorktown. He also joined the Society of the Cincinnati and settled in Champlain, where he was the first mason and perhaps the builder of the first house in town. The two Gosselins and Dionne received back pay totaling $2,512 when they rejoined the regiment. The payment was made under the caption "Returned from Captivity, from Mar 4, 1776 to June 1, 1778," and was unusually generous since they had not spent all that time in "captivity." Presumably they promoted the American cause in Canada during the time they were not incarcerated.[26]

Antoine Paulint was born in 1737 in Grenoble, France. As the second son he was destined for the priesthood, for which he prepared in his youth. But he preferred a military career and enlisted under Montcalm for service in New France. He took part in the major battles of the French and Indian War and then settled at St. Denis in the Richelieu Valley. He was a captain of local militia but he was among the first to take up arms against the British in the fall of 1775. His company was annexed to Hazen's regiment early in 1776, and he and his family retreated with the American army in June. In the confusion of the retreat their young son was left behind, but friends helped him on his way. He served in Livingston's regiment until it was disbanded, when he was transferred to Hazen's, from which he was retired on half pay in 1782 as a supernumerary officer. After the war he settled on the land granted him in Corbeau, now called Coopersville, at the mouth of the Great Chazy River. This was his first permanent home in ten years.[27]

Two of Hazen's French captains served honorably during the war but gave him a great deal of trouble afterward. Captain Philip Liebert and Brevet Major Laurent Olivier had raised companies in Canada, partly at their own expense. After the war both tried to collect for their advances, which were inextricably linked with Hazen's own accounts. In 1785 Olivier reminded Congress that he had raised a company of sixty-four men and had paid their costs and wages for four months "at the influence of Hazen and Wooster," who promised a quick reimbursement. He had nothing but a note from Hazen to show for his efforts. He had also raised a company at Albany in 1776 and delivered it to Washington at Morristown, all at his own expense and under Hazen's orders. He complained that he had long since been promised a majority, but all that had been forthcoming was a brevet commission, which carried no benefits with it. Liebert's situation was similar.[28]

Congress referred Olivier to the Commissioner of Accounts for New York State. Receiving no satisfaction, Liebert and Olivier caused Hazen's arrest in Albany in 1788 and detained him while Olivier sued him for £1,000, which Hazen called "avowedly a public debt." Hazen fought the suit until 1790. Both Olivier and Liebert insisted on being paid in specie. Hazen asserted that he never agreed to pay in money other than the kind he received (paper) and that his doing so would expose all other colonels to similar suits by their men. Complicating the difficulty with Olivier was Hazen's loan of $266 in 1782, for which Hazen's lawyer instituted legal proceedings in 1790. However, a compromise settlement out of court ended a painful affair.[29]

Liebert won a judgment against Hazen in the Supreme Court in October 1789 for about £350. Mooers bought out the claim at a discount, made his final settlement with Liebert in July 1790, and added the costs to his already tangled accounts with Hazen. The latter suspected that Mooers had somehow betrayed him and he chided him for it. He told Mooers that Liebert was a poor mortal who did not dare come out of Canada: "If you expect Beaver off of a Hoggs back you may probably be disappointed."[30]

After the long search for refugee lands, a solution to their problem was finally reached that promised them lands of their own. On May 11, 1784, the legislature of New York enacted a law which provided land bounties for its servicemen. A conspicuous provision included refugees. Nudged by Congress, and fearful that they would become public charges, the state had decided to treat them as its own. Eligibility lists were to be prepared by Hazen and Livingston for their former regiments and by Colonel Throop for the Nova Scotians.

Residence was required in New York for two years after November 1, 1782; at least one settler must occupy each 600 acres within three years or the lands would revert to the state; and claims must be submitted before May 1, 1785. This date had to be extended, and claims were still being processed six years later. The legislators placed the lands "at such place in the northern part of this state as they shall think proper," which was defined to mean "unappropriated and unoccupied lands." Officers were to receive 1,000 acres, enlisted men 500. As the details were later worked out, the lands were to be surveyed into 420-acre and 80-acre lots. Officers were to receive two of each, enlisted men one of each, by the drawing of lots.[31]

In addition to the action of New York, Congress also took a first step in the celebrated Land Ordinance of 1785 toward providing federal lands for the Canadian and Nova Scotian refugees. It set aside three townships, a total of 69,920 acres bordering Lake Erie, specifically for land grants to refugees who could qualify under acts of Congress. As later interpreted, it provided lands only to those who were not already beneficiaries from other sources, which excluded most of the French Canadians who had been associated with Hazen and had received grants from New York State; but it included refugees from Quebec and Nova Scotia who were not residents of New York or who had not joined the American army. However, the Land Ordinance proved abortive because settlement on Lake Erie was impossible before Indian titles were extinguished, and because the townships fell within the lands claimed by Connecticut. Substitute lands in Ohio were not finally made available by Congress until 1798.[32]

Until the commissioners of the Land Office in New York determined the precise location of the tract, several people offered suggestions. Throop, considered the agent for the Nova Scotians, asked for Burk's Island in Lake Ontario and the south side of the mouth of the Black River. In his initial return of Nova Scotian refugees, he submitted sixty-six names, which were returned to him for further information. He had not, declared the commissioners, included evidence that the refugees had actually left Nova Scotia before November 1, 1782, and had resided in the state for two years. Ten of the men were labeled "Dead chiefly in the service" and eight others "Gone back to Nova Scotia." Throop was finally able to prove that three officers and five privates met all the New York requirements.[33]

Hazen urged the commissioners to consider the lands along Lake Champlain as the most feasible location. He had already planted a colony there, as will be described later, and he was naturally predisposed to an area he knew well. But he worried that the lands were being settled by others, and he asked that the state postpone the issuance of further patents. He was particularly concerned over the prewar purchase by Gabriel Christie and Francis and Samuel McKay of several miles of coastal lands south of the border, together with Isle la Motte. In October 1783 he had encouraged the sheriff of Albany County to attach some of the shore property and the island to New York State. He had also instigated a suit against Christie in the Supreme Court, and until it was decided he asked that Christie's lands not be disposed of.

Through an American lawyer, Brockholst Livingston, Christie issued caveats on November 29, 1784, and May 9, 1785, against the issuance of any New York patents to his lands until his claims could be heard. The uncertainty of ownership plus the state's propensity to make large land grants prompted Hazen and Livingston to issue a caveat of their own against further grants of "waste or unappropriated" lands on Lake Champlain until the refugee tract had been located. However, the New York courts ruled against Christie and the state assumed control of his properties. On the other hand, the state's commitment to make numerous private grants in the area had gone too far to be affected by Hazen's caveat.[34]

The precise location of the tract consumed many months of deliberations, although sentiment seemed increasingly to favor the shores of Lake Champlain in what is now Clinton County. But even in that frontier country there were problems in designating "unoccupied" lands. The act of 1784 had specifically exempted Point au Fer from consideration because it was still occupied by the British in contravention of the peace treaty. Furthermore, would-be landowners were petitioning the state for large tracts in this part of the state. Since some of the petitioners were veterans or prominent citizens downstate, their requests received sympathetic consideration. Consequently a number of tracts were issued or under consideration by the time the refugee act was passed. A large grant was made to Smith and Graves in what is now the town of Champlain. In Chazy, William Gilliland and Matthew Watson received lands which are referred to as the Bell Tract, after James Bell, who bought them out. Also in Chazy, patents were issued to Wheeler Douglass, Elkanah Dean, Zephaniah Platt, and William Duer. The whole of Beekmantown was included in the Beekman Patent, issued to Dr. William Beekman in 1769.[35]

In January 1785 the commissioners of the Land Office defined the tract and directed the surveyor general to start surveying it. While this was going on, lists of the eligible refugees were also being prepared. Throop's truncated list of Nova Scotians was finally approved. Determining the Canadian (i.e., Quebec) list was a far more complicated task. Marriages, remarriages, deaths, and times of entry into New York all had to be checked. By January 1785 Hazen's list contained 187 names, and Livingston's 94. But after further checking, Hazen's numbered 102 and Livingston's 49, which were attested to by Governor Clinton. Both men subsequently certified additional names. Ultimately, 227 names appeared in the Balloting Book, including 39 officers.[36]

Impatient with all the delays, a few of the refugees began to gravitate toward northern New York immediately after the war. In the summer of 1783, eleven of them accompanied Lieutenant Benjamin Mooers to Point au Roche in the Beekman Patent. Here they made a small settlement, sometimes known as Hazenburgh after its sponsor, Moses Hazen, for whom Mooers served as agent. Among their number were Jean La Framboise and two Montys, eager to reclaim the farms they had established before the Revolution and had to abandon in 1776. Over the next two years others squatted on sites along the shore north from Point au Roche, mostly on Dean's Patent, so as to be nearby when their own lands were available, and perhaps to exchange them for their squatters' claims.

The main body of refugees, both servicemen and dependents, remained at their camps in Albany and Fishkill, expecting every season to hear that their lands were at last ready for them. In this respect they were worse off than the bolder ones who went north because although both groups were battling for survival, the ones who remained in the refugee camps were idle as well. Almost the only bright spot in their lives was their continuing ability to collect rations—until June 1, 1786, according to a congressional deadline.

Hazen asked Lieutenant Murdock McPherson to help the refugees in Albany draw their provisions, "who for the want of Language are unable to Transact their own business." The Issuing Commissary was Bethuel Washburn, with whom McPherson apparently worked harmoniously and conscientiously. In September 1784 there were 135 men, 36 women, and 57 children being rationed there, but this number included those who had gone to Lake Champlain. There were 59 of them, including families, and they gave Hazen a power of attorney to collect their rations or allowances after their departure. Through McPherson he purchased certificates from Washburn for the rations of the absentees. McPherson apparently advanced the costs and then collected from Hazen. The bill for September and October was more than £145, and similarly high for months to come. But in 1784 Hazen was already short of money to meet his many commitments and he sought a loan from Washburn. Hazen's debt to McPherson was not finally settled until 1792.[37]

Hazen cashed in the certificates with the government contractor, William Duer in New York City, and then made an accounting of them to the refugees on Lake Champlain. Whether the arrangement ever proved profitable to Hazen is doubtful; but it added to his financial involvement with many people, some of whom were still trying to collect their ration allowance from him years later.

The number being rationed at Fishkill was eighty adults and six children. The procedure was directed from West Point. On an inspection tour Joseph Carleton, secretary in the War Office, found that the lack of consistent regulations had produced frauds. He struck off those whose only claim resulted from marrying the widow or daughter of a veteran. He also ordered only one ration a day for officers who were also receiving them as heads of families. But Carleton found that despite the petty frauds the refugees *were* destitute. They had been turned out of their houses in Fishkill in cold weather, and took refuge in the barracks at West Point. He provided them with wood and tried to furnish a modicum of comfort for the winter.[38]

At about the same time Lafayette again interceded for Canadian families. He divided them into three classes: (1) officers and soldiers who had no particular state to support them, (2) people who freely gave their money and services and were expelled from Canada, and (3) others who stayed in Canada but whose certificates entitled them to payment for the goods and services they had provided. He suggested a full-scale inquiry to find out which ones needed immediate relief, and he urged the payment of public debts which would help the refugees become more useful citizens. This was one of Lafayette's last official actions in the United States. Only the day before, Congress had taken formal farewell of him before his return to France.[39]

The long-suffering refugees at Albany and Fishkill were still waiting for their lands in 1786. But with the arrival of June 1, Congress' authorization of rations expired. Washburn did not dare to continue the issues and the governor agreed with his decision. The month of June was therefore chaotic in the refugee camps. But on the 30th Congress extended the rations for fifteen months and also voted to subsidize the removal of the refugees to Lake Champlain.

The surveying of the lands had been going on for some time based upon the lists of refugees prepared in 1785. But in June 1786 Hazen certified fifty more names, which the land commissioners accepted as qualified persons. They then issued further instructions to the surveyor general about how to accommodate the additional claimants. The 80-acre lots, ultimately numbering 250, were to border Lake Champlain or the Great Chazy River. The 480-acre plots, of which there were also to be 250, were farther inland and many of them were in terrain too hilly or rocky for settlement. Much later, errors were discovered in the surveys along the border, resulting in the creation of eighteen additional lots of 333⅓ acres and two of 500 acres. The Canadian and Nova Scotia Refugee Tract started on the lake shore at Rouses Point and extended south to Dean's Patent and west along the Canadian border to include almost all of the town of Mooers, large parts of Champlain and Altona, and about half of Chazy. A narrow projection extended south to include small sections of Dannemora, Saranac, Plattsburgh, and Schuyler Falls. The resulting gerrymander reflected the necessity of veering around the other patents.[40]

The commissioners laid down two further requirements that were to give much trouble later: that no patent would be issued to any person until he produced a certificate from the surveyor general designating the lot balloted to him, and until he paid his proportion of the cost of the survey. The tract ultimately included 131,500 acres and was divided as follows:

39 officers	—	1,000 acres each	39,000 acres
2 officers	—	666⅔ acres each	1,333⅓ acres
1 widow	—	666⅔ acres	666⅔ acres
173 men	—	500 acres each	86,500 acres
12 men	—	333⅓ acres each	4,000 acres
Total 227 persons	—		131,500 acres [41]

By August 1786 the surveying of the small lots was sufficiently far advanced that at last the refugees could be transported to Lake Champlain. The task was under the direction of Udny Hay, an American who, like Hazen, was a refugee from Canada. He originally was in Hazen's regiment but left it to join the Quartermaster Department, where he obtained a colonelcy. After the war he served the interests of the refugees and himself in a variety of ways. He advertised the impending movement of the refugees in the *New York Packet* in July, and the moving of perhaps 250 men, women, and children was accomplished in August.

Beginning on August 28 all of the refugees, squatters and newcomers or their agents, congregated on the Little Chazy River and agreed to priorities for the balloting: first, all officers; second, all soldiers who presented themselves; third, all Canadian refugees who had not served in the army but were still eligible under New York law; and fourth, purchasers of rights of soldiers "who have been so unhappy as to sell them." [42]

Balloting was then conducted by the use of two separate boxes, one containing names and the other the lot numbers. The refugees were dismayed at being required to pay forty shillings for each survey, with the result, they later complained, that "Many of Us were obliged to pledge one half of our land for the Survey of the other half, which to secure a property and procure a home we submitted to." When the balloting was finished, the settlers had very little time in which to prepare shelters against the approaching cold weather.[43]

The fifteen months of rations voted by Congress lasted until September 1, 1787, during which time about 170 a day were provided, according to Congress. There can be no suspicion that the returns were padded because in their petition to Congress the refugees appended an itemized list, certified by eight officers, of 169 settlers residing on Lake Champlain. But as the expiration date approached, forty families were still without lands because their lots fell within

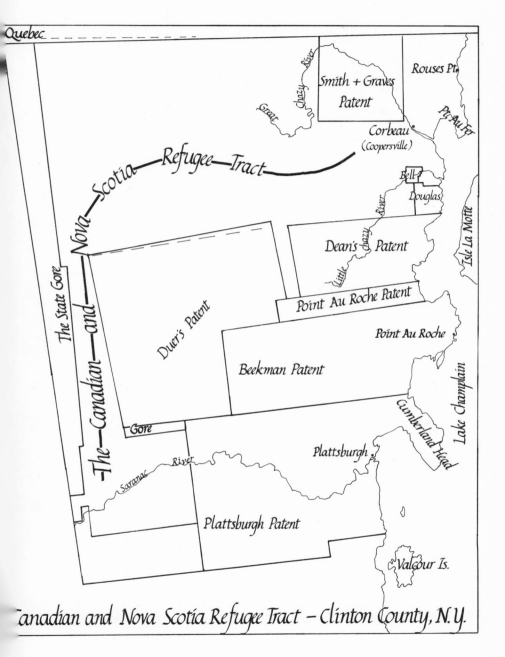

The Canadian and Nova Scotia Refugee Tract – Clinton County, N.Y.

the Douglass Patent or the British reserved lands at Point au Fer. Their leaders asked Zephaniah Platt to intercede in their behalf which he did by suggesting locations to Governor Clinton which could be used to make up the deficit.[44]

They also petitioned Congress in behalf of the forty families who had waited two seasons for their lands. They asked for land and an extension of rations for the landless or "any other Mark of favour or Goodness." In reporting on their petition, Secretary at War Henry Knox believed their circumstances, "sufficient in themselves to embarrass and discourage an industrious and enterprising people in forming a new settlement, have operated with peculiar force on a class of men habituated for a long period to be supported by the government." He asked Governor Clinton to correct their landless condition, and in reference to their continued need for subsistence he subtly reminded Congress that Great Britain had provisioned many refugees from the United States.[45]

Congress subsequently extended for one year the supply of rations for the aged and infirm only—all, that is, except for rum, soap, and candles, leading one commentator to remark that it left them "dark, dirty, and dry." Rations provided under this resolution averaged forty-five a day.[46]

Additional balloting was required to settle the forty families on lands of their own, and as late as 1790 lots were being distributed to a few additional heads of families who had not previously known of their rights. The early squatters either moved on to their own lots or else tried to negotiate exchanges with the owners of the Dean and Douglass Patents. Some refugees drifted back into Canada, others found homes elsewhere in New York. But actual refugee settlements were made at Chazy Landing, Corbeau (now Coopersville), and Rouses Point, on or near the lake.

Life was as difficult as it always was on an untamed frontier, but those who remained could at last toil on lands of their own. Their first homes were log cabins, but the second generation was able to move into frame or brick houses. Nearly a lifetime was required to clear a family-size farm, but the land was good and they had transportation on the lake for their produce. Many persevered in this undertaking. The last certified census of the settlers, almost entirely French, was made in 1787 and showed 169 men, women, and children. Later government censuses can be used only with caution because of anglicized spellings, misspellings, and changes of name when the daughters married. For example, the census of 1790 for the town of

Champlain, which then included Chazy, showed 126 men, women, and children of apparent French extraction. Already Amlane had become Amlong, Boileau was Buylo, Paulint was Poling, and so on. Yet the descendants of the original settlers are still numerous in northern New York—for example, the Bilows (originally Boileau), Montys, Ayottes, and Ashlines (Ausline).[47]

Probably the greatest deprivation suffered by the settlers was their inability to practice the Roman Catholic religion of their homeland. As refugees they were excommunicated in Canada, although the rigors of the ban began to be relaxed after the war. Congress had appointed the Récollet priest, François-Louis Chartier de Lotbinière, as chaplain to Livingston's regiment. He does not seem to have followed the army, "et les interêts spirituels de nos Canadiens furent tristement négligés" (and the spiritual interests of our Canadians were sadly neglected). A very old priest, François Vallée, visited Hazen's regiment on the Hudson and administered the sacraments to the soldiers and their refugee families. But for the most part, during and after the war, they were entirely cut off from "des secours de la religion" (the succor of religion). After the war de Lotbinière apparently tried to return to Canada but was expelled by Governor Haldimand for his American sympathies.[48]

At their settlements on Lake Champlain, however, they were long without priests of their own and, according to Shea, "though they assembled to say mass prayers and sing their old hymns, many in time were lost to the faith." Occasionally a military chaplain or a missionary stopped for a service at Corbeau. But not until 1818 did Father Pierre Mignault of Chambly, Quebec, take the French of northern New York under his charge. Shortly afterward St. Joseph's parish was established. Corbeau, as the most concentrated of the French settlements, became its headquarters. St. Joseph's was the first Catholic parish in northern Clinton County, and for many years it served a wide area.[49]

Not all of the refugees remained on Lake Champlain, or if they did they had no personal use for their large lots in the interior. Even before the drawings of 1786, some had already sold their rights to others. After the allocation a refugee frequently granted some trusted person a power of attorney to dispose of his land. The power often included the right to act as agent in receiving rations, arrears of pay, or anything else due from the government. Several of these agents appeared early on the scene. Pliny Moore, the founder of the village of Champlain, settled on his holdings in 1787 and was subse-

quently entrusted with the rights of refugees such as Clement Gosselin, Murdock McPherson, and Jacques Rouse. Udny Hay and William Torrey, refugees themselves, invested in lands in the Refugee
Tract, as did many others who speculated in lands they never saw.

The largest recipient of the refugees' trust was Benjamin
Mooers, nephew of Moses Hazen and his former adjutant. Mooers
was already settled on Point au Roche. He seemed to have business
ability and money to spend. Most important, he was land hungry.
Probably if Hazen's health had held up, he instead of Mooers would
have become the leading investor in refugee lands. However, he suffered a stroke in 1786, a few months before the drawing of lots, and
his bad health—complicated by his financial problems and his many
other speculative ventures—forced him to adopt a relatively passive
role in helping the members of his regiment occupy or dispose of
their lands.

Into the breach stepped Benjamin Mooers. In 1785 he explored
much of the proposed tract, making careful notes of the kinds of trees,
quality of the soil, and potential millsites on the streams, and he liked
what he saw. As early as September 1786 he began to receive powers
of attorney from some of the refugees. He obtained many more during
the next several years. In addition to disposing of their lands, he was
asked by some to obtain their loan-office certificates and interest,
which Hazen still held, as well as to perform a variety of other chores
like collecting their rations. A climax was reached in 1792 when
twenty-three refugees conferred a mass power of attorney upon
Mooers to seek and receive from the national treasury "pay, arrears
of pay, Gratuity, or Bounty of every Denomination Principle and
Interest for Each and every of our services in the Army of the United
States" in either Hazen's or Livingston's regiments.

Many of the powers of attorney authorized him to dispose of
their lands in the Refugee Tract. He actively sought this authority
by sending agents into Canada to track down refugees and obtain
their signatures. In 1792 Mooers himself traveled to Quebec, looking
up former refugees along the way. He bought 5,160 acres on the spot
and received power to act in a variety of capacities.

As a consequence, Mooers himself became the chief purchaser
of refugee lands. Between 1786 and 1790 he bought 20,126 acres at
a cost of £598. For 500 acres he paid between £12 and £20, the average being about £13. These were bargain prices, depending upon the
location of the land, because the British pound was then valued at
about $2.50 in New York currency, which meant that Mooers ob-

tained his large holdings for an average of a little more than seven cents an acre. By 1808, when he made a complete listing, his holdings of refugee lands included 30,236 acres. As of that date he owned about 23 percent of the entire Refugee Tract. He had bought so lavishly in certain areas that when a new town was set off from Champlain in 1804, it selected the name of its chief landowner for its name.[50]

Mooers bought additional lands after 1808, selling whenever he could. He was also asked by other speculators like himself to dispose of their properties. He was willing to subdivide lots into family-size farms. But on numerous occasions his buyers defaulted on their payments, often after having cut off all the good timber, so that in repossessing them he found himself with less valuable lands or lawsuits on his hands. Sales were slow, partly owing to the long period of uncertainty before and during the War of 1812. By 1817 his holdings amounted to 49,415 acres, of which 2,450 acres were owned in partnership with John Palmer. The taxes on the whole were $461.70. In 1818 the state comptroller billed him for the taxes for 1815 and 1816 together with interest and fees, which he was able to pay.[51]

By 1827, when a tax bill of $242.19 arrived, and the following year another for $278.95, he was unable to meet his obligations. He appealed to John Jacob Astor, offering him 12,000 to 14,000 acres of 420-acre lots at a dollar an acre. He explained that "my sole reason of offering the lands for sale is to enable me to discharge some debts that one of my sons by his misfortune has led me into," and he asked that if Astor did not want the lands, would he "oblige me with a loan." Astor did not have any interest in either proposal. Mooers was able to make a partial redemption of his lands which the comptroller advertised for public sale.[52]

In 1830 at the age of seventy-two, he conveyed to his son-in-law, Amasa Moore, 11,481 acres in the Refugee Tract, to which he added another 1,430 acres somewhat later. Amasa was to sell at not less than $1.25 per acre, pay the taxes on the land and turn over to his father-in-law five-sixths of the proceeds. Sales were still not fast enough to save many of the lands. In 1833 the comptroller advertised all or parts of eight 80-acre lots, seventy-six of the 420-acre lots (almost 32,000 acres), and parts of a 333⅓-acre lot to meet the unpaid taxes for 1827–30 inclusive. Some of these were redeemed but others were permanently lost to him. Mooers made a final contract with Amasa in 1834. He deeded over most of his remaining property

in return for Amasa's settling his debts of $9,675 and caring for him
during the rest of his life. He lived until 1838.[53]

Mooers' speculations in refugee lands thus produced a land-
poor gentleman in his last years. Yet he is also remembered as the
first permanent settler in Clinton County, its first sheriff, and its representative in both the State Assembly and Senate. He lived well, had
a fine home in Plattsburgh, where he spent the last two decades of
his life, and bequeathed a considerable estate to his children. His
financial difficulties, aside from his sterile landholdings, were com-
pounded by his heavy losses when the Plattsburgh Bank collapsed, a
costly business adventure of one of his sons, and his failure to receive
a settlement from the estate of Moses Hazen.

For several years after the initial balloting, the refugees were
still insecure on their lands because they had not received their patents
from the state. In 1783 the refugees chose Udny Hay, Francis Cazeau,
and Moses Hazen as agents to obtain their lands. But Cazeau never
participated and Hazen, because of his illness, was unable to, so the
burden fell upon Hay alone. The legislation creating the Refugee Tract
had required that each refugee pay his share of the cost of the survey.
Beginning in 1785 two surveyors surveyed part of the tract and four
years later had not been fully compensated. The land commissioners
held up the issue of patents until all the costs had been paid.

In 1789 Hay petitioned the legislature for help for the landowners, and he included his own bill as agent at one dollar per 500
acres. The petition was referred to the Land Office whose secretary
expressed embarrassment that the matter had dragged on so long, but
who threatened to issue the patents after the deadline for filing on
November 1, regardless of whether the accounts had been settled. Hay
gave Mooers a full power of attorney to visit the commissioners in
New York and try to reach some kind of an accommodation. Mooers
succeeded in his mission, although it is not clear who paid the initial
costs of the surveys. Patents began to be received by the owners in
1790.[54]

The refugees and the buyers of their lands now wanted their
holdings properly laid out. Apparently none of the 420-acre lots and
only part of the 80-acre ones had been surveyed, the buying and selling that had occurred having been based solely on lot numbers. Various groups of owners began to ask Benjamin Mooers to complete their
surveys. In 1791 sixteen owners of 420-acre lots contracted with him
to survey their lands at a fixed price. In 1793 a group of speculative

owners petitioned him to undertake the survey of some 52,000 acres, and in 1794 fourteen French owners asked the same thing. On the strength of their appeals Mooers commissioned William Beaumont, a professional surveyor of Champlain, to start work in September 1793.

Mooers then petitioned the legislature for assistance. He explained how desirable it was to have the county settled along the border, but he had discovered no claimants for some of the lands; he was thus faced with considerable loss unless the legislature contributed to the cost of the surveys. At about the same time a petition signed by ninety-four owners of land also went to the legislature. They proposed that the whole tract be surveyed and that owners who failed to pay their share of the cost should lose a portion of their land by sale at public auction.[55]

A relief bill cleared the Assembly in March 1794 but it was not until the following February that the Senate acted. The bill authorized Mooers to conduct the survey for no more than six dollars per 420 acres and three dollars for 80 acres. In case any of the fees were not paid, he was authorized to advertise the indebtedness of each owner and after a period of eight months to sell at public auction sufficient acreage from each lot to satisfy the debt. The law restricted sales to no more than 40 acres from a 420-acre lot and 18 from an 80-acre lot. Since there is no evidence of public sales, it is safe to assume that Mooers himself took over the lands he was legally allowed for his services.[56]

In the course of the survey some substantial errors were found in the original plotting of the tract. Beaumont discovered a deficiency of 2,210 acres in the lots along the international boundary.* He also found a shortage of 2,809 acres in the lots on the three sides of Duer's Patent which adjoined the Refugee Tract. All of these deficiencies were in the large lots, with the result that some owners found themselves in possession of somewhat less than 420 acres. The shortages ranged from 22 to 197 acres per lot, as Mooers, a chief owner, revealed in his petition for compensatory lands. His total claim was for more than 1,000 acres. Ultimately he and the other owners received additional lands in the State Gore adjoining the Refugee Tract on the west.[57]

---

*The reason for this was revealed when the boundary was resurveyed in 1818. Because of an error in the original survey of 1774, the boundary did not follow the 45th parrallel, as all the treaties provided, but went somewhat to the north of it. The Webster–Ashburton Treaty of 1842 restored the boundary to its 1774 line, but the owners of lands in the 1790s could not anticipate this development.

Meanwhile, numerous refugees either thought their land grants were insufficient to compensate them for their losses or were unable to qualify under New York law. This was particularly true of refugees from Nova Scotia. Congress lacked a clear title to the lands it had promised along Lake Erie in the Ordinance of 1785. Its next effort was the recommendation of a committee of the House to create refugee lands along the Ohio River, beginning at the mouth of the Miami River and west of modern Cincinnati. Nothing came of the report, and it was not until 1798 that a definite provision was made. The act of that year directed the secretary of war to advertise in the newspapers of the Northeast, requiring refugees to file their claims for lands within two years. The secretary of war, the secretary of the treasury and the comptroller were named as a board to administer the law. Claimants were divided into three classes, depending upon their needs and desserts. They had to be people who had left Canada or Nova Scotia with a desire to aid the colonies in the Revolution, but widows and heirs were also included.[58]

The commissioners made their first reports to Congress in 1800. They listed forty-nine claimants qualified to share 33,500 acres, although seventy-three claims in all had been examined. Their reports went to a House committee which argued for a greater liberality in the granting of land. The claimants had already waited twenty years for Congress to act, many of them were destitute, and Congress could afford to be generous because the total claims had fallen far short of expectation. Consequently, the committee recommended an addition to each class of claimant, an increase of 4,740 acres over the recommendation of the commissioners.[59]

In 1801 Congress legislated the Canadian Refugee Tract into existence. It adopted the committee's recommendation for larger grants and directed the surveyor general to lay out the lots. The tract was a strip of land about four and a half miles wide and forty-eight miles long, running east from the Scioto River and including most of modern Columbus, Ohio. Allocations were to be made by lot after the completion of the survey, and the exact locations assigned in January 1802. According to the procedures established for the Old Northwest in the Land Ordinance of 1785, a designation 21-12-25 meant Range 21, Township 12, Lot 25, which was one of the grants to the heirs of Lieutenant Colonel Edward Antill. Congress had intended the lots to contain 250 acres but as surveyed they all contained more than 300 acres, some being nearly 370 acres. Consequently, lands actually received by claimants were larger than originally authorized.[60]

When the deadline for submitting claims arrived in 1800, Congress was made aware that more time was needed. In 1804 it revived the act of 1798 with a two-year extension, and repeated the process in 1810. In 1812 Congress awarded nearly 17,000 acres to seventeen claimants whose claims had been submitted under the acts of 1804 and 1810. At this time Charlotte Hazen, widow of Moses, obtained three lots. In all, according to Carl Wittke, 58,080 acres were granted in the Ohio Refugee Tract to sixty-seven refugees or their heirs, and their grants ranged from 160 to 2,240 acres. He calculates that seven claimants received the maximum of 2,240 acres; four obtained 1,280 acre grants; twenty-two received 960 acres each; seventeen were given 640 acres; sixteen got 320 acres; and one received 160 acres.[61]

That Congress had overestimated the number of qualified refugees is made clear by the fact that much of the tract remained unclaimed. In 1816 Congress authorized the sale of the surplus lands at public auction for no less than two dollars an acre. Nevertheless, belated claims by heirs of refugees were honored in 1827, 1831, and 1834. Their grants were not in the tract, but elsewhere on public lands.[62]

By 1801, when the Ohio Tract was definitely established, many of the original refugees had died, as is evident from the number of heirs who submitted claims. Either those who were still living were too old, or their heirs too unwilling to move to a raw frontier. Consequently, most of the lands were sold to speculators, although a few were actually occupied by the original recipients. Among the claimants whose suits were dismissed were some familiar names. For example, Louis Gosselin, Philip Liebert, Laurent Olivier, Josiah Throop, and William Torrey obtained no lands because they were considered to have been adequately compensated with 1,000 acres by New York State.

The commissioners appear, however, to have exercised extraordinarily good judgment. Many of their awards went to Nova Scotians who had been unable to qualify for help anywhere else. Among them were Jonathan Eddy, who spearheaded the attack on Fort Cumberland and subsequently led a group of refugees out of Nova Scotia; John Allan, who paralleled Eddy's exploits; and Seth Harding, who fled from the province and took part in American naval warfare. Rewarded also were two Montreal residents, James Price and the widow of Thomas Walker, both of whom had sacrificed their businesses to help during the American invasion of 1775–76. Since Price had already received 500 acres in New York, he was granted only another

500 acres in Ohio. Mrs. Walker obtained 2,000 acres in Ohio because her husband "lost property in the amount of £2,500 sterling, besides abandoning a lucrative business."

More surprising were the grants made to the leaders of the First and Second (Hazen's) Canadian Regiments. All had received 1,000 acres from New York, were Americans residing in Canada at the start of the Revolution, and had abandoned their business or profession to play leading roles in the war. Lieutenant Colonel Antill obtained 500 acres; Colonel James Livingston was granted 1,000 acres, and Charlotte Hazen received about the same.[63]

Forty-five years after the end of the Revolution, on May 15, 1828, Congress enacted a measure termed "An act for the relief of certain surviving Officers and Soldiers of the Army of the Revolution." A pension of full pay according to rank was provided for life, and it was back-dated to March 3, 1826. It did not cover noncommissioned officers or privates already on the pension lists, and it limited officers' pensions to no more than the full pay of a captain. Officers' pensions currently being paid, including half pay for life to those who left the army before the end of the war, were to be replaced by this more generous provision. The estimated payment to a captain was $3,000, to an ensign $2,000.[64]

A special form was printed for the use of the veterans, whose applications went to Secretary of the Treasury Samuel Ingham. He appointed as commissioners for northern New York Benjamin Mooers and D. B. McNeil. As early as June 1828, applicants began turning to C. K. Averill, a lawyer of Rouses Point, as their legal adviser. Averill witnessed and certified numerous applications for the final approval of Mooers and McNeil. These two officials held a series of hearings at Rouses Point, dealing chiefly with disputed claims. At this point the validity of some of the applications was challenged. Averill was convinced that the challenger was Mooers himself and he pointed out to the commissioners the "manifest impropriety in their being tried by their accuser."[65]

Averill was not dissuaded from his belief even when Secretary Ingham wrote to assure him that the suspension of payments to some of the claimants did not originate with the commissioners. Instead, Averill launched a bitter attack against Mooers. He wrote Ingham that the new pension law had drawn veterans back from Canada, to the detriment of Mooers' interest because he had either defrauded them of their lands or had taken over unclaimed lands. He expostulated: "General Mooers was a land speculator in those days, and employed worthless men to go in search of and purchase in their land claims, and in that way derived title to a very great proportion of the land which now composes the County of Clinton. And it is also well known here that the agents employed in this business, committed many frauds on the ignorant Canadians, which has furnished a fruitful source of litigation more or less every year for more than thirty years past." He appended seven charges of malpractices by the commissioners in their conduct of the hearings.[66]

Ingham, who had previously asked Mooers for a complete roster of Hazen's regiment, acknowledged it as "satisfactory" and noncommittally sent him a copy of Averill's letter, which Mooers called a "tissue of falsehoods." He accused Averill of having a pecuniary interest in processing as many claims as possible. He denied that his land acquisitions had been obtained through fraud and he asserted that in the half dozen old suits against him "my titles have been triumphantly sustained." Calling him an "unprincipled man," he declared that "my motives are above the comprehension of a man so depraved as Averill." [67]

Technically, Mooers was probably correct, but he had had some harrowing experiences in proving his claims. One source of trouble was the proclivity of various heirs of the same lot to sell it more than once. For example, Thomas Schieffelin of New York City asserted that he had purchased in Montreal twelve of the 420-acre and nine of the 80-acre lots, only to find that Mooers also claimed them and was able to provide proof. Another type of dispute was the suit in Supreme Court of Joseph Martin, son of the refugee of the same name. His suit was based on the claim that when he sold his father's land to Mooers he was a minor and could not legally transfer land. But the court found that because of the ensuing forty-four years the statute of limitations barred him from recovery.[68]

Nevertheless, there is probably an element of the pot calling the kettle black in the Mooers–Averill exchange. Mooers almost certainly did engage in persuasive if not sharp practices in amassing his vast estate, but fraud was never proved. Averill's charges were extreme, but he apparently believed in the validity of his clients' claims without the military background of the regiment to make him properly skeptical. In any case, the secretary of war had appointed the commissioners and he was therefore obligated to accept their findings.

VIII

Dreams and Nightmares

F OR THE FIRST YEARS after the peace treaty Moses Hazen lived
strenuously, engaging in a multiplicity of projects. He traveled
incessantly in connection with his many enterprises. From his headquarters in New York City he went repeatedly to Philadelphia, Boston,
Coos, Lake Champlain, and Albany. He launched a colonizing venture at Point au Roche, started the process of reclaiming his Canadian
property, pushed his claims against the government, and began to
buy lands in Coos. In 1785 he suffered the first in a series of civilian
arrests (during the war he had been arrested and tried at Ticonderoga,
Teaneck, and West Point) in two suits for £4,000 instituted by his
former Canadian partner, Gabriel Christie. He spent a great deal of
time verifying the lists of his men who qualified for refugees lands.
But he was already borrowing from Peter to pay Paul, and in 1785
he wrote to his brother William that he could no longer contribute to
the support of his mother and sister, Anna Peaslee, as he had during
the war.

His nephew, Benjamin Mooers, was destined to play an important role in Hazen's postwar affairs. Both during the war, when
Mooers served as adjutant of Hazen's regiment, and subsequently,
their relationship remained militarily formal. Yet Hazen obviously
trusted him more than he revealed. Evidence of this is seen in his
assigning Mooers the task of executing his most cherished project at
the end of the war, the establishment of a settlement at Point au Roche
on Lake Champlain.

This settlement was originally planned by Hazen as a syste-
matic colonial venture, which he intended to direct from a distance.

Mooers left the Hudson Valley in the summer of 1783, taking with him ten French Canadian refugees and a cousin, Lieutenant Zaccheus Peaslee, as a labor force at wages of eight dollars a month. They came from Albany to Lake Champlain via Lake George, dragging their bateaux plus all their baggage fourteen miles from Fort Edward to Fort George. They were sixteen days on the road from Poughkeepsie, July 26 to August 10, 1783, but the very day after their arrival they started clearing the land.[1]

There followed weeks of hard work, the building of a log house, and trips of exploration along the lake. Mooers is credited with making the first permanent settlement in Clinton County, New York, although farms had been started, then abandoned, at the time of the Revolution, by the Monty and LaFramboise families on the shoreline of Chazy. Likewise the settlement at the mouth of the Saranac River, started in 1765 by Captain Charles deFredenburgh, had also been abandoned and destroyed during the war. So at the time Hazen's pioneers arrived, there was no farm or settlement between the Saranac River and the Canadian border.

The site of the settlement, Point au Roche, was on the patent issued to Dr. William Beekman and associates of New York City in 1769, but hitherto unsettled. It was chosen deliberately by Hazen, yet he was squatting on another's land without authorization. His intent initially was to carve a large farm out of the wilderness. Using it as a model, he hoped to attract other settlers and build a town that would become the county seat. Two things kept him from doing a fraction of what he hoped: the Platts made a more successful settlement at the mouth of the Saranac, and his own health collapsed prematurely.

The first season ended at Point au Roche with a visit from Hazen and the sheriff of Albany County, who attached Christie's property farther north. Hazen stopped at Point au Fer, garrisoned by the British, but was denied permission to proceed into Canada. His wife, however, was granted a pass to visit Montreal. Hazen left a letter for General Haldimand and returned to Point au Roche. From there everyone scattered for the winter. British officials in Canada viewed the Hazen settlement with concern—that it would draw other Canadians out of the province and provide easy access into Canada for the "seditious." The only hope of preserving the province, Haldimand thought, was by "bringing back the Canadians to a regular subordination, and by rendering them useful, as a well-disciplined militia."[2]

Meanwhile a dispute arose over the boundary between the

Beekman patent and the Platt lands adjoining it to the south. In 1784 the Platts and other proprietors had obtained from the state the grant of the pre-war patent held by de Fredenburgh, who forfeited his property by remaining a Loyalist. In preparing his lands for settlement Zephaniah Platt, the leading proprietor, subdivided portions of the Beekman lands and contracted for the sale of some of the lots. As a preliminary to settlement of the dispute the Platts, Beekmans, Hazen, and others executed a remarkable document in April 1786 in which they agreed that if Hazen's colony and its "improvements" fell within the township of the Beekmans, they would convey 457 acres to him; if it fell within Platt lands Hazen would receive 1,000 acres.[3]

Hazen seemed satisfied to deal with the Beekmans for he wrote Dr. Beekman in 1787: "You may rely upon it that I shall take all the care I possibly can of your Interest at this place, no one yet has settled upon your land on the western side the Lake—across which I shall make a winter Road some time this summer." Platt meanwhile had obtained a Point au Roche patent adjoining Beekman on the north. The final arrangement allowed Platt to keep a strip in the southern part of Beekmantown in exchange for lands in his Point au Roche patent. Subsequently the Beekmans legitimized Hazen's 457-acre farm at Point au Roche.[4]

For the first several winters Mooers went to his old home in Haverhill and left only caretakers at the farm. Beginning in 1785 livestock were added to the enterprise. Hazen sent an agent to Coos in May to bring four oxen and some cattle to the mouth of the Winooski River and ferry them across the lake. In October Mooers went for more and he had a harrowing experience. He started across Vermont with six mares and two colts, plus harnesses, bridles, saddles and other equipment. Although he employed two men to help him, he had a great deal of trouble crossing the rivers, and he was twice lost in the woods. He waded to Grand Isle at the sand bar, canoed to Point au Roche and returned next day with boats for the horses.[5]

The dominant factor during the last seventeen years of Moses Hazen's life was the stroke he suffered in 1786. It is against the background of permanent invalidism that the frustrations and failures of his many financial ventures need to be viewed. A man used to managing his own affairs, he was now forced to entrust them to others, while his illness seemed to increase his irritability and arouse his suspicions that everyone was plotting against him.

In the winter of 1786 he disappeared from view and his wife and associates feared that he had ventured into Canada and been arrested. However, he had only gone to Coos and he was back in New York in February. In the spring he planned to go to Lake Champlain so as to be present for the arrival of the refugees. But on April 27 he was stricken, as he later wrote President Washington, "with a Violent fit of the Appoplexy, perhaps the Quantity of Blood the Doctors took from him saved his life, and terminated the Disorder into a palsey. The first Year he got a Good deal better but the two latter he seams to be at a stand." [6]

He had actually had a stroke which paralyzed his right side so that if he could sign his own letters, which was not often, it was in a very shaky hand. In June he was unable to stand alone. Four men were required to lift him into his carriage, and two to lead him around. His cousin, Moses White, as well as Udny Hay and others, rallied around to help him temporarily. At first optimistic of recovery and always of an indomitable will, he somehow got to Albany in July to meet Mooers, collect his ration certificates, and take the cure at the mineral springs. He first tried the waters at New Lebanon which, he thought, "have been of little or no service to me." He next went to Saratoga, which also failed to help him although he stayed there for several months. [7]

When he entered Albany in January 1787 he was arrested on six different suits, his creditors apparently eager to collect from him before he died. Five of the suits were instituted by the purchasers of certificates that had been issued to former members of his regiment. The problem was not the certificates, but the interest which Hazen had collected on them and for which he could not produce the receipts on the spot. The sixth suit was a part of Major Olivier's running battle to collect for his military advances in Canada. Hazen had no choice but to obtain bail, which he did by putting up some of his own certificates as security. He set out for New York on February 11. His nephew, John Hazen, accompanied him a mile out of town and tried to go with him the rest of the way, but Moses would not have it. John was "fearfull some very unfair measures will be taken of his situation if some person is not with him," and he urged Mooers to go to his assistance until his affairs were in better order. [8]

Mooers had his own commitments and did not go to New York. Hazen had diffidently suggested an arrangement between them but, he wrote from Saratoga, "I Can not afort to pay for a tenten me." Incredibly, only two months after arriving in New York he set out for Point au Roche on a long visit. There he conferred upon Benjamin Mooers a broad power of attorney to collect and disburse money and to conduct all kinds of business in his name, for which he would receive his expenses. Mooer's rewards were to be a share in the profits of occasional commercial ventures, some uncertain claims to property in Coos, and a portion of Hazen's contested land claims if Mooers could rescue them.[9]

In the late summer Hazen returned to New York, which he now considered his home. With the help of friends and a servant he tried to supervise his complex affairs, sometimes from a sickbed. In 1789 he lived on Great Dock Street and in 1790 he moved to Great George Street, near the hospital. His wife was with him constantly during the rest of his life. Although she could not help with his business affairs, she did offer loyalty and companionship, and she suffered with him during the years of his illness and later poverty.

Between 1786 and 1790, Mooers was Hazen's chief agent in all his affairs. As late as 1790 Mooers still held his uncle's confidence, as revealed by Hazen's plea that he pursue a certain business matter "as you have discover'd a particular genious that is not to be met with in every one." In that year Lieutenant William Torrey of his former regiment was added to the entourage in New York. At the outbreak of the Revolution Torrey had been apprenticed to Joseph Bindon, a merchant in Montreal. Like other Americans in Canada, he joined the American army and left the country at the time of the retreat. His financial arrangements with Hazen are unknown, but his employer left him a small sum of money by a codicil to his will. While he was single he may have lived with the Hazens. Whether he did or not, he handled Hazen's correspondence and made numerous business trips for him. Ultimately he married, started a family and engaged in mercantile business while still serving Hazen. The last known service he performed was the writing of letters in 1796. Beginning in 1793 Hazen's cousin, Moses White, also began to carry out commissions for him and it was he who was named executor of Hazen's will.[10]

Mooers' duties became much more demanding after Hazen's illness. In addition to his involvement at Point au Roche, he made trips for Hazen all over the Northeast, including Philadelphia and Canada. At the same time that he was collecting money, selling certificates, and warding off lawsuits, he was also advancing his own affairs, especially by the purchase of lands. He kept precise records of every penny he spent for Hazen at Point au Roche and on his trips. His accounts appear to have been settled until 1788, and the amounts were surprisingly large. For example, Mooers' expenditures for 1787 were £476 ($1,190), which Hazen met by selling government certificates. Most of Mooers' bill was for labor, equipment, and supplies at Point au Roche.[11]

Subsequently, Mooers kept records as before, but for some reason did not submit them for settlement. He may have realized Hazen's precarious financial condition, or he may have glimpsed the possibility of adding interest to a postponed accounting. As early as 1790 Torrey urged Mooers to come with accounts, otherwise "The Genl will never forgive you." He repeated this request several times as did Moses White, who succeeded him in attending to Hazen's affairs. Mooers privately prepared accounts showing Hazen owing him about £1,460 ($5,475) in 1796, but he never presented them. On the other hand, Hazen died believing that Mooers owed him a large sum resulting from an agreement whereby Mooers was to buy refugee lands with money provided by Hazen and they were to share the proceeds. Unfortunately Hazen was unable to locate the agreement, and he suspected that Mooers had possession of it, for which he threatened a suit of $20,000 against his nephew. In any case, the accounts of the two were never settled during Hazen's lifetime.[12]

The deterioration of relations between the two began gradually but eventually became complete. The trouble seems to have stemmed mainly from two sources: Mooers had his own life to lead on Lake Champlain, where he was elected to county positions of trust and acquired tremendous land holdings; and Hazen's instructions were so voluminous and his affairs so complex that Mooers could not have executed them all even if he had believed they were either possible or practical.

Consequently, Hazen from his sickbed chided Mooers in 1790 that "You cannot conceive what embarrassments you have laid me under by not performing the bussiness I expected and which you agreed to do or giving me some timely and particular account with respect to it." In June 1792 Torrey, writing for Hazen, said that "Genl Hazen is satisfied in general with Mr. Mooers conduct but not in particular." But four months later he was particularly sharp: "Altho you hold a full power of Atty from me yet it can not be presumed by any tortured construction that that power will authorize you to do anything more than the true intent & meaning of it. . . . If you are drawing one way & I another I will leave it to yourself if its not high time for the one or the other to leave my business." The extent of the rupture in their relationship is best seen in Moses White's letter of 1798 in which, after discussing some of Hazen's affairs, he comments: "This is all unbeknown to the Gl—not from any desire of keeping

any secrets from him so much as to prevent any suspicions of in-
treague with you which he might from his present situation with
respect to you, be ready enough to harbour." [13]

At the time of Hazen's death, the estrangement with his
nephew was nearly complete. Yet Mooers at forty-five had become a
first citizen of Clinton County and its largest landholder. He must
have found the voluminous directives from his uncle irksome, and in
1794 he moved to Cumberland Head to start a farm of his own.
Although he married three times and raised a large family, he had
apparently absorbed some of his uncle's swashbuckling proclivities
and, save for the help of his son-in-law, he too would have spent his
old age in relative poverty.

Until he moved away, Mooers' primary occupation was the
development of the farm at Point au Roche. Hazen from his sickbed
showered him with instructions. He laid out in minute detail how
much land to clear and how to do it, what crops to plant and how
many additional cabins to build. As directed, Mooers purchased land
adjoining the farm on the north, which pleased Hazen who called it
the "most proper place upon the Lake for a Town." In 1790 Hazen
made the farm over to his wife, although he continued to oversee its
development. But in the following year he called the operation a
"dead weight" and began to devise ways of making it profitable. He
proposed dairying, and he began to press for the construction of a
lime kiln and a tanning pit. When Mooers remonstrated about any of
the instructions he was chided for letting cows and horses run away
when he should have built fences: "Your being of opinion that 400
acres of cleared land added to about 500 wood is not pasturing
enough for twenty cows is a proof that you know very little about
farming when one acre of cleared land is the allowance to a cow for a
season." To Mooers' complaint that the land produced very little,
Hazen scolded that "you made a bad choice for me when you had that
extensive country to chuse in." [14]

Hazen continued to think up new ventures. He ordered a house
built for him, which he never occupied. He kept demanding a lime
kiln, a tannery, more cows, more houses, and more land. In 1793 he
wanted to buy all the lands he could between the Saranac and Great
Chazy Rivers: "I am determined to lay the foundation of a Town at
Pauroch and to build a Coledge & Convent at that place, as the best
possible means, with occonomy, of settling my Land there, on this
head I have had time enough to consider before my unfortunate illness, I shall not be deverted by any one. I have advanced so far that I

cannot make an honorable retreat—in all your calculations you ought
to bring money to the place & not take it away, which is a maxim I
have ever attended to." [15]

In 1794 he dreamed of establishing an Indian town at the lower
end of Isle la Motte as the best protection for Clinton County, "for
in my opinion you never will have any thing to fear from the Canadians, but much from the Indians at Catnawaga." Not all of his
schemes were impractical. He continually stressed the importance of
engaging in trade. He wanted his cattle sold in Canada if they could
not be wintered on the farm; he urged Mooers to sell potash in
Canada and buy maple sugar and furs there for sale in New York
City, and he made careful calculations of the exchange rate between
the pound and the dollar, as well as comparisons of prices between
St. John and New York. Some moderately profitable trade did take
place, but not often at the time or in the quality that Hazen desired.
Modest profit is illustrated by a shipment in 1792. Three barrels of
potash and thirteen of pearlash were sent to London, where they
were sold to brokers at public auction. They brought £59, but shipping and insurance charges of £15 reduced the net proceeds to about
£43. [16]

The year 1794 almost brought an end to the Point au Roche
venture. James Bell of Chambly won a suit against Hazen and attached
part of his property in Clinton County. This included not only 1,000
acres of land in the Refugee Tract, but also the farm on Point au
Roche with its stock and farming materials. Bell was a merchant living
at Chambly at the time of the Canadian invasion of 1775. He accepted
literally the promise of Congress to liberate Canada. He helped raise
troops in the valley of the Richelieu and he advanced $6,056.34 of his
personal funds for the American cause, of which Hazen guaranteed
$826.

After the war Hazen and Mooers at first enjoyed cordial business relations with Bell. But by 1790 the atmosphere began to change.
Bell appealed to Congress for repayment of his services, but he received no satisfaction in his lifetime. Sensing failure in that direction,
he took Hazen to court to recover his cash advances which Hazen
had guaranteed. Sheriff Daniel Ross auctioned Hazen's property and
Mooers repurchased everything at a cost of £411 ($1,027). Mooers
was compensated for the 1,000 acres by John Tayler of Albany, who
took over the deed. He was also repaid for Point au Roche by Charlotte Hazen, who obtained a loan from Tayler. The financial arrangements had been made in advance when Hazen asked Tayler to hold

Point au Roche in trust for his wife and at her decease to give it to such of Hazen's heirs "as you may think proper." [17]

Hazen had many other irons in the fire. Until 1788 he was involved in providing rations for the refugees on Lake Champlain. He borrowed money, was arrested fourteen times for debt, and instituted at least a dozen suits against others for debt or noncompliance with agreements. He held personal certificates from the government, including the commutation of his half pay for life and advances on his Canadian expenditures in 1776. He gradually was forced to sell them at a discount to escape his more pressing creditors.

Hazen closely followed the market for public securities and certificates of all kinds. For as long as he could get his hands on cash or credit, he speculated in them, as did many others of his contemporaries. During the 1780s, while uncertainty over Confederation finances lasted, state and federal certificates could be bought for seven shillings on the pound, or thirty-five cents on a face value of one dollar. Veterans and other holders were often compelled, for want of cash, to sell them for their depreciated value. Speculators were willing to gamble that some day they would be worth their face value, and they were right. The new government of 1789 was determined to establish the credit of the new nation, and Secretary of the Treasury Hamilton's plan for funding all debts at par sent the price of certificates upward. In 1790 they were worth twelve shillings on the pound (sixty cents on the dollar) and not long afterward they were selling at par.

Hazen's motto had always been to sell high and buy low-priced certificates. But by 1791 he was denouncing the funding operation of the Treasury because it shortchanged the soldiers of his former regiment and because it favored people in New York City over those in the interior. He apparently favored the funding plan that James Madison unsuccessfully advocated—to allow the original holders of certificates to share in the government's redemption plan, even though they had been forced to cash them at a discount.

He extended his holdings of land in Clinton County whenever he could, and he held on to them for as long as possible after his finances began to deteriorate. In 1794 he lost 1,000 acres in Champlain in satisfaction of a debt to James Bell of Canada. In 1800 Charlotte Hazen appealed to Mooers to sell one of Hazen's lots: "We are so much distresst for want of Cash that I know not how we are to get through the winter." By the time of his death three years later, most of his holdings in northern New York had been dissipated.[18]

One of Hazen's major preoccupations was his claims against the government. They fall into five categories, and it was not from lack of trying that he failed to collect. He once estimated that the government owed him about $100,000, including interest, or "I will suffer to be hang'd and drawn in quarters." He repeatedly, passionately and at great length petitioned the Congress under both the Confederation and the new government that followed it, but he did not live long enough to see the conclusion of some of his suits. He died desperately poor with the government owing him thousands of dollars, though not the huge amount he dreamed of.[19]

The first of his claims to be settled was his half pay for life, which Congress voted to all officers in 1783. Hazen accepted a commutation of $4,500 in the form of certificates instead of annual payments. A second claim was the bill for his property losses in Canada. At the time he was commissioned he received $533 as an advance on those losses. A month later he submitted his complete account which, he said, represented lost revenue of more than £500 sterling and an investment of £4,000. By itemizing buildings, livestock, crops, fences and other items, he calculated his property losses at about $11,366. Congress granted him an additional $1,095 in September 1776 for the livestock, hay and other items taken for the use of the American army. To Hazen's remonstrance that the amount was totally inadequate, Congress in October voted another $966 for the tools, anchors, and cables which had also been appropriated for military use.[20]

Instead of the $11,366 he claimed as his losses, he thus received about $2,595. Over a period of years he continued to press the disallowed claims for buildings and their contents as well as ruined crops. He reminded Congress that his estate of houses and buildings, all burned, was worth £5,000 sterling; that he had been deprived of the income for eight years to the value of 4,000 guineas, and that the enemy had cut off much of his valuable timber. Faced with the prospect of an avalanche of petitions from others who could claim similar losses in Canada, Congress in 1784 adopted a principle which for the time being terminated Hazen's claims for further reimbursement. It decided that all inhabitants of Canada who voluntarily accepted the "invitation" to help the American cause had, "by the usage of nations" no further claim for compensation. Efforts to collect this money after Hazen's death are described in the section on his estate later in this chapter.[21]

A third group of petitions dealt with his failure to get the pay and emoluments of a brigadier general after his promotion. Hazen felt very deeply on this issue because he thought the promotion was belated when it came in 1781 (he had been a colonel for five years), and because it was only a brevet (honorary) preferment. He could not see why promotions in his regiment should not be as full and regular as those of other units operating under state quotas. In September 1783 Congress made a start toward defining his status and that of other brevet officers by declaring that brevet promotions did not carry increased pay or emoluments unless they were specifically mandated in the commission. Most brevet commissions were not so worded, and Hazen's was among them. Yet he gave Congress cogent reasons why a promotion at his rank was not covered by the resolution of 1783.

Congress considered each of his petitions and received recommendations from the War Office that his claim be granted, but in 1784 it voted against him. In 1785 Hazen petitioned again but it was not until 1788 that Congress finished considering the matter. Secretary at War Henry Knox recommended against the claim because Hazen "was perfectly informed of the nature of the brevet rank, and yet accepted of the same; That his case was several times fully before Congress during the War when the knowledge of his sufferings and services must have been the greatest; That it is so connected with the cases of a great number of other brevet officers who might perhaps state equal merit, and request similar rewards." Congress concurred with Knox and thus closed the subject.[22]

Hazen's fourth effort to get compensation from the government was grounded on a binding commitment to him, but he did not live long enough to see a settlement. When Hazen joined the American army he was entitled to receive two shillings four pence a day for life (half pay) from the British government as a retired lieutenant of the Forty-fourth Regiment. At his commissioning Congress promised to indemnify him for any loss of British pay he suffered by joining the American cause. It was one of two Congressional commitments that helped persuade Hazen to accept a command in the American army.

By the time he petitioned Congress in 1785 for a settlement of all of his accounts, he knew that he had been stricken from the British pension rolls, effective December 25, 1781. He therefore asked Congress to compensate him beginning with that date. Why the British action was so belated is unknown, but there is no evidence that Hazen continued to receive British pay during the Revolution. His claim met a cold reception in Congress where a committee concluded that his American pay as a colonel was much more than the

British half pay, "wherefore he can have no further Claims to half Pay or Indemnification for the same." Congress referred the question to the Secretary at War for a report.[23]

The next year Hazen was taken ill but he continued his requests for a settlement. In 1789 Secretary of War Henry Knox wrote him reassuringly that his claim was so valid that he could borrow money on it. Secretary of the Treasury Hamilton and his successor, Oliver Wolcott, also acknowledged that the suit was still "founded on principle," the principle being the congressional promise of 1776. The hold-up resulted from the Treasury contention that a special act of Congress was needed, whereas Congress believed that the Treasury had sufficient authority to act on its own in paying legitimate debts. And so the matter rested at the time of Hazen's death in 1803.[24]

Hazen's fifth claim against the government, for his disbursements in Canada in 1776, became even more complicated and protracted. The basis of the claim was the personal funds he advanced to recruit his regiment in Canada, and the notes he signed for the expenditures of Lieutenant Colonel Antill ($800), Captains Olivier ($938) and Liebert ($528), James Bell ($826) and others, with interest. As early as July 1776 he presented his accounts to Congress, but for the time being all he obtained was the $800 that Antill had spent in his name. But he estimated that his total debts amounted to $16,333, of which $7,600 was a private debt to Colonel Christie which was settled unilaterally when Christie seized his Canadian lands.[25]

Repeatedly pressing his claims, he was finally rewarded by a congressional resolution in 1781 which acknowledged a debt of $10,296 in specie which, with interest to May 1 of that year made a total of $13,386 owed to him. It was to continue to bear interest at six percent until paid. Shortly afterward, being pressed for money, he accepted $7,000 in bills of the new emission at the rate of $2.50 in bills to one of specie, or the equivalent in specie of $2,800. In 1785 he petitioned for the payment of the remainder, citing his difficulties with the officers to whom he had pledged his credit, and whom he was unable to pay. He was not exaggerating his embarrassments because in the years just ahead he was jailed at least three times for his debts to Olivier and Liebert, and he lost some of his lands to Bell.

In 1789 he was forced by circumstances to accept a certificate for $6,386, worth on the market at the time from two shillings six pence to three shillings on the pound. His dollar payment converted to pounds at eight shillings to the dollar (New York currency) was £2,554. If the market value of the certificate was three shillings on the pound, he received the equivalent of only about £383, or $957 as of the time he received it. Hazen continued to request a settlement of the entire account, and in 1799 the auditor of the Treasury calculated the balance. Deciding that the first payment was worth $2,800 in specie and the second, $6,386, was the same as specie owing to the new nation's funding of its debt, he figured the balance due Hazen on the $13,386, his credit in 1781, as $4,200 to which he added $4,483.88 in interest from 1781 to 1799. He was therefore owed $8,683.88 as of 1799, although this result was achieved by equating a certificate with specie.

In 1799 Hazen was again arrested for debt, but no money from the government was forthcoming. On the contrary, in 1802 the comptroller looked over the accounts and decided that it was "not reasonable to subject the United States to such an accumulation of interest." Therefore he acknowledged owing only $4,200 by dropping the interest entirely. The resolution of 1781 had clearly pledged *specie and interest,* and at the time of his death he was well on the way to receiving neither.

Another of Hazen's desperate and unsuccessful efforts was to reclaim his lands in Canada. When he left the country in 1776 his financial affairs were in disorder. In his favor was the fact that he held clear although mortgaged title to the three-mile-square seigneury of Bleury-Sud on the Richelieu River opposite St. John and to nine lots (twenty-nine acres along the Richelieu by thirty to sixty acres in depth) in the Barony of Longueuil on the site of St. John. But unfortunately his debts probably equaled the value of his holdings.

All the damage was done between the years 1764 and 1770, during his joint ownership of the properties with General (then Lieutenant Colonel) Gabriel Christie. Owing to Christie's frequent and prolonged absences, Hazen directed the development of the lands. In trying to execute his ambitious schemes he accumulated a considerable debt to Christie and others. In 1766 Christie granted him a mortgage of £800 on his undivided half of the Bleury Seigneury, and in 1770 Christie insisted upon an absolute division of their holdings on both sides of the river. Nevertheless, at the time of the Revolution, Hazen's indebtedness to Christie was about $7,600, as Hazen himself later acknowledged. Meanwhile, for £2,000 he had given his brother William and the latter's partner, Leonard Jarvis, a second mortgage on his part of the Bleury Seigneury and a first mortgage on his part of the Seigneury of Longueuil.

Immediately after the war Christie raised the issue by demanding the payment of his mortgage on Bleury-Sud. Hazen warded off the claim and late in 1783 took the sheriff of Albany County to Lake Champlain for the express purpose of attaching Christie's lands in New York. The action was apparently taken under the state's absconding law and involved property worth up to $100,000.

In 1784 Christie responded with a suit in the Court of Common Pleas in Montreal. He demanded the £800 mortgage with interest and a declaration that all of Hazen's property be considered forfeited in his favor. Hazen fought and lost the suit, for in July 1785 Christie obtained a judgement of £1,900 sterling which covered the mortgage plus some nineteen years of interest. In the same month he caused Hazen to be arrested in New York City in two suits amounting to £4,000. Discrepancies in the monetary figures probably stem from the relative worth of the various currencies then in use. New York currency was valued at eight shillings to the dollar, whereas the more precious British sterling was quoted during this period at about four shillings eightpence to the dollar, requiring almost twice as many dollars as an equivalent.[26]

In conformity with the court's ruling, Sheriff Edward Gray in August seized all of Hazen's lands at the seigneury, St. John, and the Savanne and advertised their sale for the following January. He was forced to postpone the action while Hazen took his case to the Court of Appeal in Canada. This body overturned the ruling of the Court of Common Pleas.

Christie appealed the decision of the Court of Appeal to the Privy Council in London. During the six years consumed by all these proceedings, Hazen became ill and some of his proposals for settling with Christie assumed an unreal quality. He encouraged his brother to settle with Christie for the £800 mortgage, forgetting that that was only part of his indebtedness. In 1787 he was bravely saying: "Their is two methods of Carrying a Point the one by Curtesey the other by boldly ascertaining your rights Never have recourse to the former when you see the Latter fully in Point." But at the same time he offered Christie 500 guineas to settle all matters in dispute by arbitration.[27]

Early in 1790 Hazen was still optimistic about a settlement. He sent his agent and confidant, William Torrey, as well as Benjamin Mooers to Montreal to see Christie, "tho it is the land he is After and not the Money." His long list of instructions included ascertaining

Christie's demands and trying to raise £800, the mortgage money, from various people in Canada. In a memorandum of this period he stated that "No confidence can be had in what Genl Christy says—he formerly resembled a washwoman looking one way and rowing another—what ever he may pretend he wishes to get hold of the land at St. John as cheap as he can."[28]

Hazen was right. Christie was in no mood to compromise on a settlement for as long as he believed that his suit would be favorably acted upon in England. Furthermore, Torrey went to him empty-handed because he was unable to raise money in Canada. Christie was justified by events in postponing a settlement. In the spring of 1790 the King and Council, sitting as a court, ruled in his favor. Hazen's lawyer in England, one Cromwell, called it a clandestine session which provided him no opportunity to appear, or even any warning that a decision would be made before November. The Privy Council restored the ruling of the Court of Common Pleas. Christie, acting under its mandate, again seized all of Hazen's Canadian property. The sheriff put the seigneury up for sale in September 1790 and Christie bought the entire property for £400. Henceforth he was the sole seigneur of a united Bleury.[29]

Hazen, as might be expected, refused to accept the decision as final. He fulminated that the court had not given him the legal time for redeeming his mortgage, and he still thought Mooers could effect a compromise with Christie. In 1791 he began to talk of suits against both Christie and Sheriff Edward Gray, the latter for disposing of his lands. In 1792 he directed Mooers to go to St. John and institute suits against Christie for £15,000 and Gray for £10,000 more. But Mooers, lacking both the financial backing for such an undertaking and the optimism to believe that success was possible, took no further action. The decision of the British courts on Bleury-Sud remained conclusive. Whether Hazen's case received a full hearing in England, or whether he was given the usual period in which to redeem his lands are questions upon which legal authorities can still disagree.

A similar fate overtook Hazen's lands across the river at St. John. They were also seized under a writ of execution from the Court of Common Pleas in 1785. While the writ was being appealed, Hazen was confident that he could win because the lands, unlike those on the east side of the river, were mortgaged not to Christie but to his own brother. After the war several people built houses on the property. Hazen's agent was instructed to collect rents for a year at a time and ultimately to lease or sell lots. But in view of the pending court ruling, none of these things could be done. Hazen later asserted that his tenants had had fourteen rent-free years.

Hazen continued to hope that a compromise could be reached with Christie that would include his holdings on both sides of the river. In 1788 he dreamed of laying out a town at St. John, using the city plan of Philadelphia as a model: "It is a pretty river similar to that of old Haverhill & the land very suitable for a town." But the sheriff had been prepared to auction off Hazen's lots since 1786, and under the new ruling from England he was ready to proceed.[30]

Meanwhile, with the arrival of American Loyalists and their settlement around the old fort at St. John, the Baron of Longueuil, the original owner, woke up to the fact that he was about to lose some valuable property. He consequently repurchased the most desirable lots, which today constitute an important part of the city (between St. George and St. Thomas Streets, ten acres along the river by sixty deep). Christie had to be satisfied with three lesser lots, although they included twelve acres of river frontage. They totaled 450 acres, for which he paid £455 ($1,950).[31]

The only step Hazen could see open to him was to obtain some of Christie's former lands in New York State. In 1792 he initiated a search to discover whether the sheriff, in attaching them in 1783, had acted lawfully or whether there might be grounds for instituting new proceedings of attachment in his favor. He got nowhere in his quest; the sheriff had attached the property *to the state*, which had since granted it all to various people, including the refugees.

One final enterprise which occupied much of Hazen's time and money after the war was the attempt to extend his landholdings. To supplement his property on the Richelieu, which he never expected to lose, he planned to invest heavily in Coos lands on the upper Connecticut River. His near-completion of a road connecting the two locations in 1779 merely whetted his appetite in Coos. Aside from its potential military use, which Hazen yearned for, the road can also be viewed as a big land operation by which Bayley, Bedel, and would-be landholder Hazen obtained free government aid in opening their future lands to settlement. Evidence of this thinking is found in Hazen's letter to Bayley in 1780: "In conjunction with Colonel Bedel I beg you will plant a few potatoes, sew a little turnip seed and grass seed and a few hand fulls of oats on the cleared land at the Blockhouse. You know what I mean by it. A word to the wise, etc., etc." What he obviously had in mind was steps to pave the way for land claims along Hazen's Road.[32]

After the war Hazen's attention did focus upon lands along the famous road, and he petitioned for several large grants of land. But he also acquired substantial properties in at least four Coos towns, plus others elsewhere in Vermont. He purchased thirty-six original proprietary rights in Topsham, Vermont for £5 each when they were sold for C. W. Apthorp's unpaid taxes; twenty rights in Lunenburg, Vermont, and twenty-four across the river in Lancaster, New Hampshire, including the desirable farm lands called the Catbow; 3,400 acres in Moortown (Bradford), Vermont, and some lots in Jericho, in the western part of the state.

There is no intent to follow these transactions in detail. Each of them became complicated, some produced lawsuits, and all were eventually lost to Hazen. At first Hazen's deals seemed to prosper. Until he became ill he took care of his own affairs, attended proprietors' meetings, and kept the taxes paid. Beginning in 1787 Benjamin Mooers, armed with Hazen's power of attorney, attempted to do the same. About 1790 Mooers named Captain Nathaniel White of Bradford to act as his agent. Between the two of them they tried to keep up with the mounting taxes, but more often than not they were in arrears.

Late in 1783 Hazen joined a long list of petitioners in seeking 64 square miles of land along Hazen's Road, two townships in the vicinity of Greensboro and Hardwick. About a year later he petitioned for 216 square miles as a grant for the members of his regiment and the New Hampshire corps of Major Whitcomb. The request embraced approximately six of the future towns of Vermont, and was made in the name of the congressional resolution of 1776 which urged the states to make land grants to veterans. The petition was dated five months after the State of New York voted lands to Hazen's regiment, and it asked for several thousand acres more than New York was about to provide (138,240 compared to 131,500 acres). Hazen told the Vermont authorities that during the construction of the road "a large number of the Officers and Men finding themselves upon ungranted and Unlocated Land; made their Locations of Lands that they conceived themselves Entitled to, by the afore sd Resolution of Congress."[33]

Just to make sure, Hazen joined a long list of Bayleys, Bedels, and others in asking for a tract covering parts of four towns and overlapping previous requests. The legislature took no action on any of these petitions. Concerning the military petition, Vermont had no obligation to reward the wartime services of Hazen's regiment, except possibly for its part in building the road, and its legislature must have known that New York had promised to grant lands to the same outfit.

The first lands that evaded Hazen's grasp were located in Jericho, and they were sold for nonpayment of taxes. Ira Allen was the buyer. A similar fate apparently overtook the property in Lunenburg, although the record is not as clear; he certainly lost them during his lifetime.[34]

The township later known as Moortown had been granted to Hazen and associates by Governor Wentworth of New Hampshire in 1764, and settlers soon began to arrive. However, in the same year the lands on the west side of the Connecticut River were adjudged in London to belong to New York. Subsequently Sir Henry Moore, governor of New York, regranted the town to another group of proprietors. During the war the settlers and original proprietors were concerned about the title to their lands, and Hazen in 1779 promised to get an authentic Vermont charter at his own expense. But the state had some ideas of its own and although in 1781 it granted the lands to Hazen, Barron, and others to a total of sixty-five persons, it decided in the following year to charge each proprietor £9 per share.

The payments were not made before the state's deadline. Instead, the inhabitants petitioned for an extension of time, while Hazen issued a caveat against the granting of any of the land until after a hearing. He needed time to obtain copies of the Wentworth papers in London as proof of the original grant. He and the settlers hoped that Vermont would reconfirm the New Hampshire charter without the payment of any additional fees. In response the legislature in 1785 acknowledged the right of Hazen and the inhabitants to the land and lowered its price to a total of £60. No further action took place at the time except the changing of the town's name to Bradford in 1788.

In 1791 the petitions from Bradford were renewed. The legislature finally ruled that all but 4,000 acres of the town should be granted to trustees for the inhabitants pending their payment of nine pence an acre for their property. Three hundred acres were to be reserved for a school and three hundred acres for the clergy; the remaining 3,400 were Hazen's upon payment of two shillings an acre (a total of about $1,457). All fees were due by April 30, 1792.

Hazen had no such sum of money at his command and he sought and obtained an extension of time, but he was given only until October of the same year, with interest added. Hazen failed to redeem his land in time and it was offered to John Barron at the same price. This was merely one more blow to a sick and increasingly impoverished man who resented Vermont's assessment within a township and still believed that he held valid title under the original New Hampshire grant.[35]

In Topsham, where Hazen thought he had purchased proprietary rights at a tax auction, a dispute arose between him and Apthorp over the title to the lands. The case was complicated by the fact that Hazen bought from the New Hampshire grantees and he admitted his title was not secure because the town, like so many others in Vermont, had been granted twice, by both New Hampshire and New York. He promised Mooers half of the land if he could save it. In 1793 Hazen signed an agreement with Apthorp for settling the dispute, in order to avoid a lawsuit, then quickly disavowed it.

The dispute was not settled in Hazen's or Apthorp's lifetime. It therefore fell to Moses White, executor of Hazen's will, to deal with Apthorp's heirs. He hoped for a settlement by the use of a referee, and he asked Mooers for a precise accounting of the disbursements he had made on the lands. Mooers was unable to comply for he had not at this late date ever settled his accounts with his former agent, Nathaniel White. Moses White was soon disabused of his hopes for a quick and easy settlement. The dispute ended up in Circuit Court in Boston in 1806. Robert Troup, administrator of the Apthorp estate, won the lands but handed over $5,560 to the Hazen estate as an offset payment. This is one of the few instances where Hazen's land speculations ever brought any returns.[36]

The dispute over the Lancaster lands proved even more complex, and it lasted until 1814. Hazen had really made large investments in improving them, and he and his executor exerted particularly strenuous efforts to keep them. Only a brief outline of their history need be presented here.

Much of Hazen's claim at Lancaster was the Catbow, which he had bought with a mortgage from Apthorp. In approximately 1784 he built a house on it and employed several laborers to clear and fence the land. He created a farm on good soil, stocked it, and put two families on it as tenants. In about the year 1787 one Mollineaux ejected the tenants and instituted a rival claim for Hazen's property. In 1790 he was upheld by the Court of Common Pleas but the judgment was reversed by Superior Court. Before the suit was completed, the property was sold for nonpayment of taxes. Mooers hastened to Coos and redeemed the property before the time of redemption expired. He took releases for about twenty-three rights from the purchasers, and receipts for the money paid by purchasers of the remainder.

By 1791, then, the land was apparently safe in Hazen's hands. Nathaniel White was in charge, acting as Mooers' agent. But about 1795 White visited Mooers to report that Apthorp had discovered the possibility of clearing his title to the Lancaster lands he had sold to Hazen. White persuaded Mooers to let him have the releases from the tax sale so that if the need arose he could renegotiate them with the buyers in such a way as to assure Hazen's title. Mooers agreed and received White's receipt for the releases.

From the pressure of other business, or from indifference, Mooers failed to complete an accounting with White before White's death. His widow and heirs knew nothing of these arrangements and presumed that they had inherited the Catbow from Nathaniel, who had inhabited it beginning in 1796. Years later Moses White as executor instituted a suit to recover the Catbow from the heirs, and the case went to the Circuit Court in Portsmouth. White demanded of Mooers all the papers bearing on the property but it was the war year of 1813, during which Mooers was preoccupied as general of militia and could not find the papers. Therefore, Moses White faced the court with a weak case and although the trial was postponed until 1814, the court ultimately decided in favor of the White heirs. At this distance the justice of the ruling is difficult to assess. Mooers may have been hoodwinked by White over the releases; on the other hand he may have misunderstood Nathaniel's purpose in taking them. There is no record that Mooers ever paid taxes on the property after 1795 and if Nathaniel did, he had a large equity in the Catbow. And so the most valuable of the Coos properties was lost to the Hazen estate.

Meanwhile, with the waxing and waning of his strength, Hazen alternated between dreams of exciting new ventures and relapses into deep despair: "I have not determined yet where I shall spend the winter if I should live so long." Secretary of War Knox, with whom he corresponded over his government claims, referred to him as "the unfortunate Hazen—In addition to his disease which is hopeless, nature has marked him with as obstinate a temper as ever afflicted humanity." [37]

By 1792 Torrey was finding his job of business agent for Hazen increasingly difficult. "I know not how to act," he wrote in May, "tis a pity he will not let any one advise him he seems to be more out of temper than he used to be and I think he talks every day more oddly." Hazen's current project was the sending of two families to Point au Roche. When they faltered in their determination, Hazen threatened them with jail "and sometimes so angry I expected he would go into fits." When they finally agreed to go, Hazen paid their passage and provided them with many expensive items. "I hope," said Torrey, "that they are the last that he will buy so dear—I do not love to give his money away with no prospect of profit—The Genl however insists they will give him two dollars a day profit—I wish I could see it, *says the blind man.*" [38]

The next month was an unsettling repetition of what had gone before. Torrey reported that "he seems so full of business—forms so many scheams to get rid of his property—and if I oppose him he get so angry that I know not what to do." His latest project was to invest $400 in liquors to send to Lake Champlain: "He will purchase the Liquors if he send them up the River no further than Tarrytown." In October an associate whom he felt had wronged him arrived in New York, after which Hazen "has neither slumbered or slept." He threatened him with arrest; "indeed," said Torrey, "courts & law suits seem to occupy much of his thoughts   I wish as a friend to him he would care himself less about this World—it seems to me he might be much happier if he chose it." In the same year he lost his trusted servant and Torrey proposed that he get a new one from the poorhouse. Hazen insisted, however, on waiting for immigrants from Europe, or looking even farther afield. He was willing to pay from one to two dollars a month. [39]

In 1788 Hazen was arrested and held in custody in a suit by Major Olivier for £1,000. In 1791 he was arrested three times in suits brought by Captain Liebert, Louis Jennery (Christie's former clerk) and others. And so the "scheams" and frustrations continued year after year. It must have been with some relief that Torrey saw the Hazens move to Troy in 1799. How Charlotte Hazen survived these years is not clear. He owned property and he was the creditor for large sums of money, but he could not collect them. He became so poor that his wife sold her silver spoons to help buy the necessities of life. [40]

His demons continued to pursue him in Troy. He lived in two different houses, for neither of which he ever paid any rent. In 1799 he was in jail, "as Mulish as ever." As he grew older his mind began to desert him. In July 1802 he was again in jail in a suit for $600, with a writ for another debt of $7,000 hanging over his head. On November 15 the sheriff impaneled a jury for a hearing into his affairs, and he was adjudged of unsound mind. On December 16 Moses White and Benjamin Smith were appointed a committee of his person and estate. [41]

Five days later White gave his personal note for $1,000 and the proceeds were used to settle the claims against Hazen which had kept him in jail. He was released on Christmas Day, 1802, and was carried to his home. He was hardly there before he was rearrested in a suit brought by James H. Troup. He was successfully defended and after providing for Hazen and his wife, White left for New York and was gone nearly three months in an effort to collect from Hazen's creditors. In this he was partly successful but before his return, Moses Hazen died on February 4, 1803.

After fourteen arrests on suits by his creditors, a similar number of suits instituted by him, and all the expense and frustrations that accompanied these actions, this troubled man was laid to rest. His body was at first placed in a vault in Troy. The funeral was held in Albany, however, and he was buried there on February 8, 1803.

Moses Hazen thought it was "just & prudent" to make his will on the eve of Yorktown in 1781. Not hitherto a noticeably religious man, he nevertheless gave his soul "to the Lord and soveraing of the Universe in hopes of a joyful Resurection through the Merits of his only son Jesus Christ and hope to die in peace & charity with all Mankind." He modified the original contents by a codicil in the 1780s witnessed, among others, by Alexander Hamilton, and by a final codicil on June 13, 1793.[42]

The will, together with its codicils, named brother William Hazen, cousin Moses White, and wife Charlotte as his executors. After Hazen's death in 1803, William released his executor's duties to the other two, while Charlotte declined to take an active role. So great was her distress that she did not leave her room for three months after the funeral. Consequently, Moses White was left with the sole responsibility for carrying out the provisions of the will which, White admitted, was what Hazen had expected.

Hazen's intention had been to settle legacies or annuities on various friends and members of his family, but most of the terms were never carried out. For example, he left Moses White, Benjamin Mooers, and Zacheus Peaslee, all relatives, his lands in Moortown, Vermont, and St. John, Quebec, but these had been lost to him before his death. His brother William never received the property intended for him in Quebec and New Brunswick, and he inherited only a few lots in northern New York. Charlotte Hazen was promised 100 guineas a year for life (about $262.50), lands already made over to her in Clinton County, and her dowry rights in Canada. She could also share the residue of the estate with William Hazen and Moses White, or she could choose instead to receive $1,000 annually for life.

The execution of the will was off to a slow start because of the difficulty of getting the four original witnesses to certify its authenticity, and it was not until January 1804 that it cleared the Surrogate Court. In May an inventory of the estate was completed. It showed $5,250 in cash, collected by White while Hazen was on his deathbed, and $175 in furniture and equipment. Everything else was hedged with uncertainty. Large claims against the government and individuals totaled $33,337, but they were labeled "doubtful" or "desperate." A total of $8,487 in notes of hand bearing interest were labeled "desperate." Five other claims for or against individuals, including Mooers, were designated "amot unknown." On paper Hazen died a wealthy man but in fact most of his claims were never collected.[43]

Although the farm at Point au Roche was in Charlotte Hazen's name, Moses' will, prepared many years earlier, bequeathed all his real estate in Clinton County to his brother, William. Shortly after Moses' death in 1803, William deeded any claim he had on the farm to Charlotte. Mooers acted as her agent until 1807, when she assigned him a formal power of attorney to act for her. Unfortunately, their first tenant absconded with some of the stock and utensils, and not all of them were recovered. Subsequently, Mooers himself leased the farm and agreed to pay Charlotte $75 a year for the rest of her life, beginning in 1809. Mooers did not move to the farm, but he now had an additional incentive to look for good tenants.[44]

The arrangement should have been a good one for Charlotte, but she had trouble collecting the annual payments. She received nothing until 1814, when the account was balanced, and payments irregularly thereafter. They were usually in the form of cash allocations which she requested when she was particularly hard up, so that at the time of her death in 1827 he had paid $1,057 of a total rental of $1,318. The deed to the Point au Roche farm passed to her lawyer, former Lieutenant Governor John Tayler.

After Charlotte's death in 1827, Mooers presented Tayler with his claim to most of the farm. His reasons were his large unpaid debt from Hazen's estate, his many services to Charlotte, and his role in establishing the farm in the first place. At first Tayler was inclined in his favor until he reread the agreement of 1794, which specifically provided for a division among all of Hazen's heirs, according to Tayler's best judgment. Furthermore, Mooers had not settled his debt to Charlotte's estate and professed inability to do so as late as 1830. Consequently the property was held by Tayler, although Mooers was authorized to sell 250 acres in 1828, the money to go to Albany. The rest was subsequently sold in smaller parcels. Thus was dissipated an area into which had gone much family toil, money, and dreams.[45]

Charlotte Hazen moved to Albany after the death of her husband, where she could be near her trusted friend and adviser, John Tayler. But she lived a precarious existence for the rest of her eighty-seven years. In 1804 she launched a campaign to obtain government compensation for those losses she and her husband had sustained in Canada for which Congress had so far refused consideration. She estimated them at £3,500 Halifax currency and she hoped to receive a grant of bounty lands in Ohio. She obtained attested documents in Canada and the United States to prove the value of their Canadian holdings and to settle without a shadow of a doubt that her husband's property on the Richelieu and her own farm at St. Thérèse had been deliberately burned at the time of the retreat by order of General Sullivan.[46]

By the laws of Canada Charlotte was entitled to her dower rights (her farm worth £231) plus one half the value of her husband's real estate. By this calculation she was owed £1,921, which Secretary of the Treasury Gallatin believed should be compensated with 1,600 acres of bounty lands and to which the Comptroller and Secretary of War Dearborn agreed. Despite this hopeful beginning, Charlotte obtained no Ohio lands at the time, but Congress did approve a pension of $200 a year for life, dating from Hazen's death. Fortunately for her, the deadline for applying for bounty lands was renewed several times, and under the act of 1810 she was finally granted three lots totaling 960 acres in Ohio. This represented a reduction from the 1,600 acres originally intended for her.

The Ohio lands which she received in 1812 were granted to her personally and she was eager to sell them, the more so when the tax bills began to arrive. The taxes on her three lots for 1813 were $10.59, with interest added for late payment. Through her attorney, John Tayler, she made contact with agents in Chillicothe, Ohio, who managed between 1814 and 1816 to dispose of all three lots. For her 960 acres she received $1,472, just over $1.50 per acre, which was probably too little considering that Congress in 1816 mandated the sale of unclaimed lands in the tract for no less than two dollars an acre.[47]

Charlotte owned some lots in New York, including the farm at Point au Roche, and she reasserted her dowry rights to her property at St. Thérèse, but only after an extended lawsuit. However, she never received the 100 guineas annually, bequeathed to her by her husband, because until Hazen's debts had been paid, Executor White said, "it has become a question in my mind how far advances to Madam Hazen, even for her absolute necessities, can be justified." Nor did she share in the residue of the estate because, although she lived until 1827, the settlement of Hazen's large accounts with the government had still not been made.[48]

Charlotte was more distressed than anyone else with the delay in settling her husband's estate, for she was losing a modest annuity in the meantime. In 1818 she made her will. Her small cash bequests were to Roman Catholic organizations or activities. The residue of her real and personal property was left to John Tayler, who was also named her executor. But in 1823 she became the victim of a swindle. She had become acquainted with Father Michael Carroll, a native of Ireland and only two years a naturalized citizen. At the age of eighty-three, she offered him a gift of her property at St. Thérèse, Canada. He prepared a deed for her signature which conveyed the Canadian lands but also included $100 for four lots in the Refugee Tract, one of which she had recently sold to Tayler. A few weeks later Tayler heard of the transaction and instituted an investigation. Charlotte acknowledged that she had been deceived and employed C. D. Cooper of the firm of Bloodgood and Cooper to set matters straight. It was soon discovered that the deeds had been recorded in Clinton County, and Mooers was alerted to prevent their sale. Tayler described the transaction as "too Roguish even for a man of an indifferent Character but for a priest I consider it a villainy in the extreme."[49]

Although several public advertisements were made for him, Father Carroll was not to be found. Cooper instituted proceedings in court which led to a decree that the transaction was illegal. The deed to the property may still be seen, inscribed in red ink as voided on April 2, 1824, by reason of being fraudulent. The most important result of this affair was Mrs. Hazen's decision to place all her affairs in the hands of Tayler. She assigned him $1,300 in cash plus her $200 pension "in consideration of personal esteem, regard & Confidence which the said Charlotte hath beareth unto the said John Tayler." In return, she was guaranteed a $300 annuity for the rest of her life. Her last years were relatively secure and not altogether miserable, as witness the quantities of brandy and wine included among her receipted bills.[50]

Meanwhile Moses White undertook the complicated task of executing Hazen's will with considerable zeal which involved numerous court appearances. Although he lost the remainder of the Coos lands, he managed to salvage $5,560 from the judgment obtained against him over the Topsham property. Curiously, his most irksome chore was his attempt to reach a settlement with Benjamin Mooers. Mooers had a large claim, the amount of which he did not reveal, against the estate dating from the 1780s and early 1790s, presumably with interest. Year after year went by with White trying to get together with Mooers and Charlotte Hazen to arrive at a settlement. Always, the time or the place was not right. Delays were caused by such factors as Mrs. Hazen's temporary absence in Canada, White's pursuit of his cases in court, and the period of the War of 1812, when Mooers was in command of the militia on the northern front and sent all his papers into Vermont for safekeeping.

White finally asked Mooers to send him his accounts so that he could study them at leisure, but Mooers was reluctant to let them out of his hands. Both men seemed eager to reach an agreement but Mrs. Hazen, distressed by a lack of funds, sided with Mooers in feeling that White was not doing his job. White, on the other hand, repeatedly reminded Mooers of the many times the two had met and that each time Mooers had pleaded the unreadiness of his accounts.[51]

As late as 1813 White by his letters was still acknowledging that Mooers had some claim on Hazen's estate. But in 1816 he suggested that the statute of limitations had outlawed the claim and that the other heirs would hold him personally accountable if he disbursed funds at that late date. Mooers took vigorous exception, maintaining that his debt had first claim among the heirs. He obtained from Attorney General of New York Martin Van Buren an affidavit to the effect that under New York law an executor had not only the right but the duty to pay a debt he thought was just, without reference to the statute of limitation. But White protected himself by following a ruling of the Supreme Court of Massachusetts which made it the duty of the executor to reject *all* claims barred by statute or else face personal responsibility for the amount.

Their dispute was brought to a head in a circuitous manner. William Hazen inherited some property in New York State from his

brother. After William's death in 1814, the state seized lot 62, one of
the 80-acre refugee lots in Champlain. The law of the state forbade
an alien from bequeathing property to his heirs if they were also
aliens. Subsequently the federal government bought the lot from the
state, together with five adjoining lots, for the purpose of building a
fort, now known as Fort Montgomery at Rouses Point. The state put
the proceeds from lot 62, about $2,500, in escrow under the jurisdic-
tion of the Court of Chancery in Albany pending a determination of
its disposition.

In July 1818 Mooers petitioned the court for the money as a
settlement of his claim against Hazen's estate. Shortly thereafter he
instituted a suit against White and Charlotte Hazen as executors;
Eddy Thurber, occupant and claimant of the lot; and Samuel Talcott,
Attorney General; and he employed Samuel Foot to represent him.
In August White filed suit for the money as belonging to the estate,
not to any particular heir. The cases lasted four years and were so
intermingled that they produced a single decision from Chancellor
Kent.[52]

White in his suit asserted that he needed the money in the
custody of the court in order to pay Hazen's remaining debts. In 1820
he gave a lengthy deposition in which he rehearsed his repeated efforts
to settle with Mooers and his conviction that the statute of limitations
now outlawed the claim; he made a complete accounting of the funds
he had received and disbursed as executor, and he also reviewed
Hazen's dying conviction that Mooers owed him a large sum of money
based upon an agreement for the joint purchase of lands which Hazen
had lost from his trunk, "and he had nobody to suspect of taking it
but the Complainant [Mooers] who had free access to his Trunk when
there." This phrase was subsequently excised from White's deposition
by Master in Chancery Gideon Hawley as "scandalous or impertinent
matter."[53]

The chancellor's ruling in the case was made on October 10,
1822, accompanied by a lengthy and learned commentary upon its
legal aspects. The decision denied to either party the proceeds of the
sale of the lot. An executor of the day had no control over real estate
left by a deceased person. But he could, within four years, apply for
the court's permission to dispose of landed property if it was needed
to pay the debts of the estate. White had failed to do this, the chancellor lectured him, and it was too late for him to collect for lot 62.
Although Mooers did not get the money either, he won a partial victory by the reminder that White had acknowledged Mooers' claim

against the estate as late as 1813. By this action he had destroyed the effects of the statute of limitations because Mooers' claim, which was already more than six years old at the time of Hazen's death, could have been outlawed immediately. White's later letters kept it alive. Consequently the court gave White and Mooers until the following March to reach a settlement.[54]

No evidence exists that the two reached agreement; White was seriously ill in Lancaster, New Hampshire, and Mooers was in New York State. Instead Mooers, acting in behalf of the heirs, petitioned the court "at a considerable expense on my part" and received and distributed the money that had been held in escrow. There is also no evidence that Mooers' claim against Hazen's estate was ever settled, the court having dismissed the case with the expiration of the deadline.

Moses White's other chores as executor were more productive in the long run. In 1803 he took over the role of petitioner to the government where Hazen left off. Deciding that it was good tactics to attack one of Hazen's claims at a time, he started by asking for his British half pay between 1781 and the time of his death. His petition was favorably acted upon by the House of Representatives in 1804 but reached the Senate too late for consideration. In 1805 a similar bill was lost because of disagreement on details between House and Senate. In 1806 his petition received no action at all because, he was told, of the "low state of the Treasury." In subsequent years of anxiety and expense preceding and during the War of 1812, White refrained from further applications. But in 1819 he renewed the claim, expecting that the appropriate committee would review the papers submitted in 1804. But the committee either overlooked or did not find the documents, and submitted a long, adverse report. Superficially reviewing the various acts by which Congress had dealt with Hazen's affairs, it concluded that he had been amply compensated for all his claims against the government.

At considerable effort and expense, White again collected all the vouchers he could, including another statement from London certifying the termination of Hazen's half pay. He made a new application in 1825 which was approved by the Senate but disapproved by a committee of the House which, pressed for time at the end of the session, dusted off the adverse report of 1820 and adopted it as its own. Persevering to the last, White submitted his claim to the next Congress, having first prepared a fifteen-page pamphlet, *A Statement of Facts,* in which he traced the history of the suit and particularly demolished the arguments in the negative reports of 1820. At last his efforts paid off. On May 26, 1828, twenty-five years after Hazen's death, Congress voted to pay his legal representatives his loss of British half pay in accordance with the agreement of 1776. The amount was $3,998.89, a rendering of two shillings fourpence a day for the period between December 25, 1781 and his death on February 4, 1803, but it specifically excluded interest. A promise was kept, but at a tremendous expenditure of time and effort on all sides.[55]

Concerning compensation for Hazen's disbursements while raising his regiment, White also picked up the pursuit where Hazen left off. In 1802 the comptroller had acknowledged owing only $4,200, and had dropped all interest payments from the account. While Hazen was on his deathbed early in 1803, White accepted the $4,200, all that he could get at the time. In his subsequent petitions to collect the interest, he encountered delays similar to those he experienced in obtaining Hazen's half pay. The two houses of Congress seemed unable to concur during the same session. For example, the Senate in 1826 could see no reason "consistently with good faith or justice" not to pay the interest on a "meritorious debt." But the House failed to take action. Indeed its Committee of Claims in 1828 could "see no good reason why Congress should, at the expiration of twenty-six years and upwards, unravel and unsettle an account, which, after so great a lapse of time, the committee are bound to believe, was settled according to law, upon principles which governed in all similar cases." [56]

But the tide was turning. In 1828 a congressional report dealing with the complicated suit of Captain Dehart of New Jersey enumerated three stages at which he had been shortchanged on interest, for a loss of $2,500. Using this figure as an average, and calculating that 240 officers were still alive, the report totaled their loss at about $608,700.[57]

In 1831 the incredible happened. On March 3 the two houses of Congress at last agreed upon the formula for liquidating Hazen's accounts, even though he was not one of the living officers. They directed the Treasury to pay the interest due on $13,386 2/90, the amount originally determined by Congress in 1781. The accrued interest totaled $12,769.18! This was fifty-five years after the debt was incurred and twenty-eight years after the death of Hazen. Only his heirs, mostly nieces and nephews, benefited from this belated settlement.[58]

Afterword

THE CAREER OF MOSES HAZEN spanned the epic period of two great wars—the struggle with France for control of North America, and the American Revolution. In both he played a creditable and occasionally brilliant role. Most of his service in the French and Indian War was spent as a Ranger which involved the dashing but brutal kind of warfare instigated by the notorious Ranger Commander, Robert Rogers. Indeed, Hazen came to be thought of as Rogers' counterpart in the Canadian theatre of operations. Despite the stain of the massacre at St. Anne, he was promoted and ultimately taken into the prestigious British Forty-fourth Regiment, from which he was retired on half pay for life. If he had been willing to accept the chances of regimental assignments abroad, he probably could have become a career officer in the British army. But he developed a yearning to become a member of the landed gentry, and he went a long way toward attaining that goal by his feverish search for property in Canada.

The American Revolution completely demolished his way of life. His seigneury lay in the path of the American invasion of 1775. For a man of his temperament neutrality was impossible, but the choice of sides occasioned excruciating pains of indecision. On the one hand his fellow countrymen were the invaders; on the other, he owed his military pension and his Canadian estate to British authority. At first his loyalty was British but then, for reasons he never fully explained but which were probably based on his belief in American victory, he tendered his services to the American cause. Once he had made up his mind, he never wavered in his loyalty even though he knew long before the end of the war that Canada was not going to be conquered.

For his choice he paid a high price. Never again would he be a seigneur on the Richelieu, with all the privileges it entailed. Indeed, before he left Canada he saw his buildings and crops utterly destroyed. He received compensation for only those parts of his estate that were confiscated for the use of the American army, and after the war he failed to regain his Canadian property.

The men and their families that he led out of Canada suffered as much as he, although they had fewer material things to lose. Either deluded by the expectation of personal gain, or inspired by the vision of a liberated Canada, they accepted temporary exile until the day they could return as freedom-bearing conquerors. Although several plans were later projected for an "irruption" into Canada, no campaign actually developed. Consequently, Hazen's men never had the opportunity to free Canada from British rule or to return home as warriors at all. And the families who followed them as refugees existed on a meagre public dole for more than a decade.

Most of the difficulties that befell Hazen and his Canadians were beyond their power to correct. The regiment was created and staffed as a special unit subject only to an already overburdened Congress, whereas the rest of the army consisted of units based upon individual states. A few of the states were no more alert to the needs of their men than was Congress, but others, such as Massachusetts, were timely and generous with their assistance. Since Massachusetts tended to be used as a model, Hazen's regiment suffered from a decline in morale whenever comparisons were made. The problem of morale also divided the regiment internally because Hazen, lacking enough Canadians to complete a regiment, was directed to recruit among the states with the result that he led a mixed group, a minority of whom were Canadians. His American officers and men were regularly serviced by their state of origin, but his Canadians had to wait for the dilatory actions of an impoverished Congress. Their sharpest grievance was the congressional system of promotion according to state quotas, which contained no separate quota for the Canadian regiment. Consequently, no Canadian officers received promotions during the seven years many of them served. Only at the end of the war were some of them granted brevet, or honorary, promotions, and those carried no increase in pay or other benefits.

In spite of these drawbacks the regiment gained a reputation for its fighting qualities, although sometimes referred to as the "Infernals." Three years after the war it was rewarded with a large grant of land in northern New York. But the majority of the Canadians preferred to sell out and take their chances back in Canada, where they tried to reestablish their old relationships with homeland and church, from which they had been separated for so long.

Just as during the two wars, when the mercurial Hazen had reflected the spirit of the times, so in the post-Revolutionary world he imbibed the prevailing feeling of freedom from restraint and the vision of a new country waiting to be exploited. In common with many others of his generation he was a speculator in lands, certificates, and other public securities. His ambitions outran both his judgment and his financial resources; his restlessness drove him into ever more impractical projects, and his indebtedness landed him in jail fourteen times. Yet some of his contemporaries—William Duer, Alexander Macomb, and Robert Morris—also spent time in jail after the collapse of even larger speculative enterprises than Hazen seemed to dream of.

Hazen differed from the others in two important respects: he suffered a physical breakdown, and several of his arrests involved money owed him by Congress. He shared with other speculators an insatiable appetite for personal gain. He was, moreover, a victim of circumstance as well as of his own makeup. Through no fault of his own he and his regiment occupied an anomalous position throughout the war; he could not persuade Congress to settle his accounts during his lifetime, and he lacked the influence and resources to battle Christie for control of his Canadian property.

Yet when all this is said in his behalf, he might after the war have lived a life of comfort, dignity, and attention to a few selected projects. But instead of learning to live with his difficulties, he seemed compelled to be doing things, anything, so long as he kept in motion. A psychologist's reflection on Hazen's life leads him to the following conclusion:

The picture is that of an individual driven by uncontrollable personal forces, going from one pointless activity to another, one useless acquisition to another, one inconsistent commitment to another, none of these being at any time integrated into a coherent system of living. It is the picture of a person driven, rather than driving, whose seemingly advantageous activities in fact brought with each of them an ominous increase in his already chronically high physical tensions which, producing in their turn premature physiological fea-

tures of senility, eventually resulted in a stroke, a cerebral catas-
trophe quite unusual in a man of his age, a final explosion of energy
almost typical of the way he lived his life.[1]

Moses Hazen was a man obsessed. Knox saw him marked by
"as obstinate a temper as ever afflicted humanity." His agent, William
Torrey, found him impossible to work for: he could not stand disagreement; he got so angry "I expected he would go into fits," and
"courts & law suits seem to occupy much of his thoughts."

These comments were made after his stroke. Yet throughout
his life he was restless, impatient of restraints and deeply frustrated
when he could not brush them aside, aggressive, combative, and stubborn. He was hypersensitive on the point of his own honor and took
personally any criticisms of his command's performance. In his later
years this took the form of imagined conspiracies against him by
friend and foe alike. He possessed an imperious disposition that
reveled in giving orders, filing complaints, and seeking satisfaction. A
military career was probably best suited to his talents, but even here
he went too far. For example, General Washington thought that his
vendetta with Major Reid was trifling and smacked of persecution. It
is not surprising that Hazen was at the center of several courts-
martial; what is surprising is that he was not involved in any duels.

All of these characteristics were magnified by his illness. His
enforced physical inactivity added to his frustrations. It was galling
to have to rely on others to carry out his instructions, which were
never performed to his satisfaction. His projects became more un-
realistic with the passage of time. Torrey found him erratic, talking
"every day more oddly." During his last months a court found him
of unsound mind.

The career of Moses Hazen is one of the tragedies of the Revolutionary era. A man of marked abilities and great drive was prevented by circumstances and his own temperament from achieving
his aspirations. A buccaneer in an age of buccaneers, he might after
the war have become one of the great colonizers of his generation—
at Detroit, in northern New York, or in the Coos Country. Instead, his
health gave way and his vast dreams came to nothing.

Nevertheless, he made a notable contribution to the American
Revolution by mobilizing and leading its Canadian sympathizers,
fighting for their rights and prerogatives, and heading the drive to get
them onto lands of their own in the United States. These are no small
achievements.

APPENDIX

Locations of the Canadian Regiment During the War

This calendar is as accurate as can be determined for the official assignments of the regiment. It needs to be used with caution, however, because rarely was the entire unit together in one place and under Hazen's immediate command. His companies were constantly being assigned to detached duty under other commanders, so that the career of a given individual might differ markedly from the following chronology. Furthermore, Hazen himself was often absent from his regiment while recruiting, drumming up support for a Canadian campaign, or just pursuing his personal affairs.

1776   Jun.: left Canada for Crown Point
       Jul.: to Ticonderoga
       Sep.: to Albany
       Nov.: to Fishkill, N.Y., for winter quarters
1777   Jun.: to Princeton, N.J.
       Aug.: battle for Staten Island
       Sep.-Oct.: battles of Brandywine and Germantown
       Fall: to Wilmington, Del., for winter quarters
1778   Feb.: to Albany for the abortive Canadian campaign
       Apr.: to West Point
       Jul.: to White Plains to help guard New York City
       Nov.: to Danbury, Conn., for winter quarters
1779   May: to Coos for roadbuilding
       Oct.: to Peekskill, N.Y.
       Nov.: to Morristown, N.J., for winter quarters
1780   Summer: to King's Ferry, N.Y.
       Fall: Garrison, N.Y. Campaign to Morrisania
       Nov.: Fishkill for winter quarters

1781   Jun.: to Albany and Mohawk Valley to guard against ex-
          pected British attack

        Jul.: to West Point

        Aug.: to Dobbs Ferry and northern New Jersey to threaten
          Staten Island

        Sep.: to Williamsburg and Yorktown, Va., for the siege of
          Yorktown

        Dec.: to Lancaster, Pa., to guard prisoners of war

1782   Nov.: to Pompton, N.J., for winter quarters

1783   Jun.: to Newburgh, N.Y. Furloughing begun

        Nov.: regiment disbanded at White Plains

Notes

I: THE START OF A MILITARY CAREER

1. Arthur Mee, *Yorkshire: East Riding and York City* (London: Caxton Publishing Company, n.d.), p. 216; D. H. Hurd, *History of Essex County, Massachusetts*, 2 vols. (Philadelphia, 1888), II, 1128.

2. Tracy Elliott Hazen, *The Hazen Family in America* (Thomaston, Conn.: R. Hazen, 1947), pp. 1ff.

3. *Ibid.*; "The Hazen Family," Miscellaneous Manuscript Collection, New York State Library, Albany.

4. Hurd, *Essex County*, II, 1978.

5. Burt G. Loescher, *The History of Rogers Rangers*, 3 vols. (San Francisco and San Mateo, 1946–69), III, 20; Francis Parkman, *Montcalm and Wolfe* (New York: Collier Books, 1962), p. 183.

6. George Wingate Chase, *The History of Haverhill, Massachusetts* (Haverhill, Mass., 1861), pp. 342–43; Parkman, *Montcalm & Wolfe*, p. 299.

7. Chase, *Haverhill*, pp. 345, 347.

8. Essex Institute, *Historical Collections*, 88 vols. (Salem, Mass., 1859–), 88:6.

9. Loescher, *Rogers Rangers*, I, 280ff.

10. Robert Rogers, *Journals of Major Robert Rogers* (New York: Corinth, 1961), pp. 54ff; Loescher, *Rogers Rangers*, III, 21.

11. Loescher, *Rogers Rangers*, I, 290, 304.

12. Collections of the Nova Scotia Historical Society for the Year 1886–87, V, 98.

13. Captain John Knox, *An Historical Journal of the Campaigns in North-America for the Years 1757, 1758, 1759, and 1760*, 2 vols. (London, England, 1769), I, 230.

14. *The New Brunswick Magazine* I (Jul.–Dec. 1898): 10.

15. Reverend W. O. Raymond, *The River St. John* (St. John, N.B., 1905), p. 124.

16. Loescher, *Rogers Rangers*, II, 263, 78.

17. Parkman, *Montcalm and Wolfe*, p. 524.

18. *The New England Historical & Genealogical Register and Antiquarian Journal* XXVI (1872): 236ff.

19. Knox, *Journal*, II, 279–80.

20. Parkman, *Montcalm and Wolfe*, p. 583.

21. Loescher, *Rogers Rangers*, II, 142.

22. Sir William Johnson, *The Papers of Sir William Johnson*, 13 vols. (Albany: University of the State of New York, 1921–62), 3:409. See also New York Colonial Manuscripts: Land Papers, 16:40–41.

23. Hazen's Summation in "Proceedings of a General Court Martial for the Trial of Col. Moses Hazen, November 1780," Peter Force, Papers, ser. 7E, box 20.

24. Moses White, *A Statement of Facts* (Salem, Mass., 1827), p. 8.

25. John W. Burrows, *The Essex Regiment, 1st Battalion (44th), 1741 to 1919* (London: J. H. Burrows & Sons, 1931), pp. 7–8; Thomas Carter, *Historical Record of the Forty-Fourth of the East Essex Regiment of Foot* (London, 1864), and War Office Records, vol. 12, no. 5637, pp. 38–53, *passim*, in the British Museum, London.

II: Between the Wars

1. A. G. Bradley, *Sir Guy Carleton* (Toronto: Oxford University Press, 1966), pp. 14, 24; Douglas Brymner, *Report on the Public Archives, 1890* (Ottawa, 1891), p. 24.

2. Hilda M. Neatby, *Quebec, the Revolutionary Age, 1760–1791* (Toronto: McClelland and Stewart, 1966), pp. 60–61.

3. *Recherches Historiques*, Jun. 1920, p. 181; Oct. 1896, p. 156.

4. Adela Peltier Reed, *Memoirs of Antoine Paulint* (Los Angeles: San Encino Press, 1940), p. 14.

5. Neatby, *Quebec*, pp. 40–41, 60–61.

6. For the material on the Christie-Hazen relationship I am much indebted to Philippe Demers, *Le Général Hazen, Seigneur de Bleury-Sud* (Montreal: Librarie Beauchemin, 1927). However, the author fails to note the existence of *two* Sabrevois brothers, and believes that Bleury and Sabrevois were brothers. See Manuscript Group 8, ser. F 99-9, vol. 1, docs. 010074 and 009844, Public Archives of Canada, Ottawa.

7. McKay and Hazen to Carleton, Jul. 31, 1767, Record Group 4, A1, vol. 17, Public Archives of Canada, Ottawa.

8. Hazen and McKay, Contract, Mar. 12, 1766, Bailey Collection, State University, Plattsburgh, New York.

9. *The Bulletin of the Fort Ticonderoga Museum* XII (Dec. 1969): 358–64.

10. Philip White, "From Frontier to Farm Community, Beekmantown,

New York, 1769–1849" (Unpublished ms. in the hands of the author, University of Texas, Austin), p. 49.

11. Hazen to Gage, June 25, 1766 and Gage to Hazen, Aug. 3, 1766, Gage Papers, American Series, Clements Library, University of Michigan, Ann Arbor.

12. Manuscript Group 8, ser. F 99-9, vol. 2, doc. 008608ff; vol. 1, doc. 009844.

13. Kent-Delord Collection, vol. 66.7e, no. 8/1/21, State University, Plattsburgh, New York.

14. Manuscript Group 8, ser. F 99-9, vol. 24, doc. 020919-26.

15. New York Colonial Manuscripts: Land Papers, 20:179 and 37:59, New York State Library, Albany.

16. *Quebec Gazette*, Oct. 18, 1770.

17. *Ibid.*, Oct. 27, 1766.

18. *Ibid.*, Apr. 4, 1765; Hazen to Cramahé, Jan. 25, 1773, Record Group 1, L3L, vol. 103, pp. 51055ff and 51058 and vol. 111, p. 54484, Public Archives of Canada, Ottawa.

19. Rev. John Quincy Bittinger, *History of Haverhill, N.H.* (Haverhill, N.H., 1888); William F. Whitcher, *History of the Town of Haverhill, New Hampshire* (Concord, N.H., 1919), p. 19; Frederic P. Wells, *History of Newbury, Vermont* (St. Johnsbury, Vt., 1902), pp. 16ff; Rev. Grant Powers, *Historical Sketches of the . . . Coos Country and Vicinity* (Haverhill, N.H., 1841), pp. 36–37, 52ff, 105ff and 112ff.

20. Hazen to Atkinson, Oct. 11, 1764, Peter Force Historical Manuscripts, ser. IX, box 10, Library of Congress.

21. Hazen Caveat, Jan. 14, 1785, *State Papers of Vermont*, 5:355.

22. *The New Brunswick Magazine*, I, 15ff; Hazen, *Hazen Family*, p. 93.

23. Hazen, *Hazen Family*, pp. 90–91.

24. *The New Brunswick Magazine*, I, 200ff.

25. Nova Scotia Land Grants, Old Book 6, pp. 417ff, Public Archives of Nova Scotia, Halifax.

III: The Coming of the Revoluton

1. Carleton to Hillsborough, Nov. 20, 1768 in Brymner, *Public Archives*, 1888, p. 40.

2. George F. G. Stanley, *Canada Invaded* (Toronto: Hakkert, 1973, pp. 3ff; A. Shortt and A. G. Doughty, *Documents Relating to the Constitutional History of Canada 1759–1791* (Ottawa, 1907), pp. 510–11.

3. *Journals of the Continental Congress*, ed. Worthington C. Ford, 34 vols. (New York: Johnson Reprint Corp., 1968), I: 81ff, 90ff, 105ff.

4. Colonial Office 42, B 32, vol. 34, pp. 128–29, Public Archives of Canada, Ottawa; Justin H. Smith, *Our Struggle for the Fourteenth Colony*, 2 vols. (New York, 1907), I, 103–104.

5. Colonial Office 42, B 32, vol. 34, pp. 179ff; Papers of the Continental Congress, M-247, roll 54, item 42, III, 459, Library of Congress.

6. Allen French, *The First Year of the American Revolution* (Boston: Houghton Mifflin, 1934), Appendix 36.

7. Gustave Lanctot, *Canada & the American Revolution, 1774–1783* (Cambridge: Harvard University Press, 1967), pp. 50ff.

8. Stanley, *Canada Invaded*, pp. 35–36.

9. Manuscript Group 23, B 8, p. 27, Public Archives of Canada, Ottawa.

10. Smith, *Our Struggle*, I, 612, Remarks XIX; Livingston to Schuyler, Sep. 8, 1775 and same to same, n.d., Papers of Congress, M-247, item 153, vol. I, pp. 148–49 and 162.

11. Affidavit of C. Hazen to Cong., Mar. 24, 1804 and Moses White to Sec. of War Dearborn, May 2, 1804, Record Group 217, National Archives, Washington.

12. Demers, *Hazen*, p. 9.

13. Affidavit of C. Hazen to Cong., Mar. 24, 1804, Record Group 217.

14. Antill to Cong., Feb. 13, 1777, *ibid.*

15. Demers, *Hazen*, p. 9; Smith, *Our Struggle*, I, 485ff.

16. Manuscript Group 23, B 8, pp. 5ff.

17. George Washington, *The Writings of George Washington from the Original Manuscript Sources, 1745–1799*, ed. John C. Fitzpatrick, 39 vols. (Washington: USGPO, 1931–44), 4: 64–65.

18. Colonial Office 42, B 33, vol. 34, pp. 265ff; Frederick W. Record and William Nelson, eds., *Documents Relating to the Colonial History of the State of New Jersey* (Newark, 1885), 9:336ff.

19. Colonial Office 42, B 33, vol. 35, p. 16.

20. *Journals of Congress*, 4: 70–71.

21. *Ibid.*, p. 39; Smith, *Our Struggle*, II, 222, 395.

22. "Proceedings of a General Court Martial for the Trial of Col. Moses Hazen," Nov. 1780, Peter Force Papers, ser. 7E, box 20, Library of Congress; Moses White, *A Statement of Facts*, p. 1; *Journals of Congress*, 4: 73, 78.

23. Peter Force, *American Archives*, ser. IV and V (Washington, 1837–53), ser. IV, 4:1655; Hancock to Schuyler, Jan. 24, 1776, Burnett Project of the Library of Congress from the Philip Schuyler Papers, Library of Congress.

24. Papers of Congress, M-247, roll 54, item 42, III, 459.

25. Bayley to Little, Nov. 24, 1775, *ibid.*, roll 166, item 152, I, 391ff.

26. Vermont Historical Society, *Proceedings for the Years 1923, 1924, and 1925* (Bellows Falls, Vt.: P. H. Gobie Press, 1926), pp. 87–140.

27. Vermont Historical Society, *The Bayley-Hazen Road* (Lyndonville, Vt., 1959), pp. 4ff; Ernest L. Bogart, *Peacham, the Story of a Vermont Hill Town* (Montpelier, Vt.: Vermont Historical Society, 1948), pp. 43ff; Bayley to Gates, Aug. 13, 1776, Gates Papers, roll 2, box IV, doc. 40, New York Public Library, New York City.

28. *New Hampshire State Papers,* 14, Jan. 20, 1776.

29. Manuscript Group 21, G 2, B 27, p. 385, Public Archives of Canada, Ottawa; Demers, *Hazen,* p. 9.

30. Hazen to Cong., Feb. 18, 1776, Papers of Congress, M-247, roll 96, item 78, XI, 17ff; *Journals of Congress,* 4: 198–99.

31. Smith, *Our Struggle,* II, 312.

32. Hazen to Antill, Mar. 10 and 26, 1776, Manuscript Group 21, G 2, B 27, pp. 387, 392; Force, *American Archives,* ser. IV, 5: 751; Papers of Congress, M-247, roll 172, item 153, II, 105ff.

33. Benson J. Lossing, *Life and Times of Philip Schuyler* (2 vols., New York, 1872–73), II, 42; Washington, *Writings,* ed. Fitzpatrick, 4: 492ff.

34. Hazen to Antill, Apr. 20, 1776, Manuscript Group 21, G 2, B 27, p. 398; Lossing, *Schuyler,* II, 48.

35. Instructions to Commissioners, Mar. 20, 1776, Papers of Congress, item 12A, no. 2516.

36. John G. Shea, *History of the Catholic Church in the United States,* 2 vols. (New York, 1888), II, 150ff.

37. Vermont Historical Society, *Proceedings,* p. 38.

38. James Wilkinson, *Memoirs of My Own Times,* 3 vols. (Philadelphia, 1816), I, 46.

39. Hazen to Sullivan, June 3, 1776, Force, *American Archives,* ser. IV, 6:1105–106; Hazen to Washington, Feb. 12, 1780, George Washington, Papers, 128: 4, Library of Congress.

40. Wilkinson, *Memoirs,* I, 48; Arnold to Sullivan, 2 letters of June 13, 1776, Papers of Congress, M-247, roll 186, item 169, I, 374–75, 379–80; Malcolm Decker, *Benedict Arnold, Son of the Havens* (New York: Antiquarian Press, 1961), p. 480.

41. Vermont Historical Society, *Proceedings,* p. 49; Antill to Cong., Feb. 13, 1777, Record Group 217.

42. Antill to Cong., Feb. 13, 1777, Record Group 217; Reed, *Paulint,* p. 21.

43. Arnold to Washington, June 25, 1776, Papers of Congress, M-247, roll 186, item 169, I, 377ff; Washington to Gates, July 19, 1776, Gates Papers, reel 3, box V, doc. 3.

44. Force, *American Archives,* ser. IV, 6: 1719; Lossing, *Schuyler,* II, 75–76.

45. Gates to Cong., Sept. 2, 1776, Papers of Congress, M-247, roll 174, item 154, I, pp. 59–60, 73–74, 81–82, 97–98; same to same, Lauran Paine, *Benedict Arnold: Hero and Traitor* (London: Robert Hale, 1965), p. 80.

46. Wilkinson, *Memoirs,* I. 58.

47. John Witherspoon to Gates, Oct. 30, 1776, Edmund C. Burnett, ed., *Letters of Members of the Continental Congress,* 8 vols. (Washington: Carnegie Institute, 1923), 2: 138; Robin McKown, *Horatio Gates & Benedict Arnold, American Military Commanders* (New York: McGraw Hill, 1969), p. 124.

48. Force, *American Archives*, ser. V, 3:1042–43.

49. George Athan Billias, *George Washington's Generals* (New York: Morrow, 1964), p. 175; *Journals of Congress*, 8: 382.

IV: THE AMERICAN REVOLUTION, 1776–1778

1. Examination of Refugees, Aug. 8, 1776, Gates Papers, reel 2, box IV, doc. 22; Reed, *Paulint*, p. 17.

2. The Marquis of Chastellux as quoted in Reed, *Paulint*, p. 23.

3. *Journals of Congress*, 6:900; 7:270.

4. Hazen to Cong., Nov. 25, 1776, Papers of Congress, M-247, roll 96, item 78, XI, 105ff; N.Y. Convention to Washington, n.d., Force, *American Archives*, ser. V, 1: 1263–64; Martin H. Bush, *Revolutionary Enigma, A Re-appraisal of General Philip Schuyler of New York* (Port Washington, N.Y.: Freedman, 1969), pp. 80–81.

5. Antill to Cong., Dec. 30, 1776, Force, *American Archives*, ser. V, 3: 1507–508; John Sullivan, *Letters and Papers of Major-General John Sullivan*, ed. Otis G. Hammond, 2 vols. (Concord, N.H.: New Hampshire Historical Society, 1930), I, 354.

6. Hazen to Cong., Nov. 25, 1776, Papers of Congress, M-247, roll 96, item 78, XI, 105ff.

7. *Journals of Congress*, 5:811–12.

8. *Ibid.*, p. 900; Hazen to Cong., n.d., Papers of Congress, M-247, roll 50, item 41, IV, 3.

9. Bedel to Schuyler, Feb. 16, 1777, *New Hampshire State Papers*, 17: 128ff.

10. Hazen to Cong., Nov. 25, 1776, Papers of Congress, M-247, roll 96, item 78, XI, 105ff; Hazen to Bayley, Jan. 10, 1777, Schoff Collection, Clements Library, University of Michigan, Ann Arbor.

11. Carleton to Germain, Sept. 28 and Nov. 17, 1776, Colonial Office 42, B 33, vol. 35, pp. 171ff, 213–14.

12. General Orders, May 22, 1777, Washington, *Writings*, ed. Fitzpatrick, 8: 99ff; Greene to Sullivan, May 24, 1777, Sullivan, *Letters and Papers*, I, 343.

13. Washington, *Writings*, ed. Fitzpatrick, 8: 179.

14. Sullivan to Washington, July 5, Washington to Sullivan, July 7 and Sullivan to Washington, July 10, 1777, Sullivan, *Letters and Papers*, I, 404–405, 403–404, 413–14.

15. *Journals of Congress*, 8:537.

16. *Ibid.*, 671, 678.

17. General Orders, July 13, 1777, Washington, *Writings*, ed. Fitzpatrick, 8:400ff.

18. Sullivan to Washington, 2 letters of Aug. 24, 1777, Sullivan, *Letters and Papers*, I, 437ff, 442–43; C. Antill to Cong., Nov. 17, 1777, Papers of Congress, M-247, roll 90, item 78, I, 131.

19. Douglas Southall Freeman, *George Washington, A Biography*, 7 vols. (New York: Scribner's, 1948–57), IV, 646, 492.

20. Court of Inquiry, Oct. 10–12, 1777, Sullivan, *Letters and Papers*, I, 482–532.

21. Marquis de Lafayette, *Mémoires, Correspondences et Manuscrits du Général Lafayette*, 3 vols. (Bruxelles, 1837), II, 21–22.

22. Hazen to Mooers, 1793, Bailey Collection.

23. Freeman, *Washington*, IV, 475ff; "The Case with Colonel Hazen's Regiment," p. 5, Peter Force Historical Manuscripts, ser. IX, box 25.

24. Freeman, *Washington*, IV, 502ff; "The Case with Colonel Hazen's Regiment," p. 5, Peter Force Historical Manuscripts, ser. IX, box 25.

25. Sullivan, *Letters and Papers*, I, 592–93.

26. Arnold to Gates, Oct. 1, 1777, Gates Papers, reel 4, box VIII, doc. 3.

27. Hazen to Gates, Oct. 26, 1777, *ibid.*, doc. 141.

28. For details of the unfolding of the "Conway Cabal," see Conway's Statement, Jan. 3, 1778, Sullivan, *Letters and Papers*, II, 14; Washington to Gates, Jan. 4, 1778 and Feb. 9, 1778, Gates Papers, reel 3, box V, docs. 55,56; Stirling to Wilkinson, Jan. 6, and Wilkinson to Stirling, Feb. 4, 1778, *ibid.*, reel 4, box IX, doc. 30.

29. Gates to Bedel, Nov. 15, 1777, *New Hampshire Papers*, 17; 150ff.

30. Lafayette to Washington, Dec. 30, 1777, Lafayette, *Mémoires*, II, 135ff.

31. Gates to Hazen, Jan. 4, 1778, Gates Papers, reel 4, box IX, doc. 24; Washington to Major Taylor, Jan. 28, 1778, Washington, *Writings*, ed. Fitzpatrick, 10: 361.

32. Chittenden to Hazen, Feb. 9, 1778, *State Papers of Vermont*, 17:225–26; Bedel to Hazen, Feb. 7, 1778, Papers of Congress, M-247, roll 183, item 166, pp. 63, 85–86; Clinton to Hazen, Feb. 17, 1778, George Clinton, *Public Papers of George Clinton*, 10 vols. (Albany, 1900–1904), 2:75–76; Smith, *Our Struggle*, II, 497ff.

33. Hazen to Conway, Feb. 17, 1778; Hazen to Lafayette, Feb. 18, 1778; Return of the Troops, Feb. 20, 1778 and Hazen to Gates, s.d., Papers of Congress, M-247, roll 183, item 166, pp. 103, 67ff, 78–79 and 117ff.

34. Lafayette to Gates, Feb. 7, 1778, Gates Papers, reel 4, box IX, doc. 35; Lossing, *Schuyler*, II, 391ff; Lafayette to Hazen and Conway to Hazen, Feb. 18, 1778, Papers of Congress, M-247, roll 183, item 166, pp. 59–60, 65.

35. Troup to Gates, Feb. 19, 1778, Gates Papers, reel 4, box IX, doc. 46; Lafayette to Washington, Feb. 19, 1778, Lafayette, *Mémoires*, II, 154ff; Lafayette to Board of War, Feb. 20, 1778, Manuscript Group 23, ser. B 3, folder 4, pp. 42ff.

36. Albany Committee to Clinton, Mar. 17; Conway to same, Apr. 4, and Parsons to same, Mar. 10, 1778, Clinton, *Papers*, 3:80ff, 123ff, 15.

37. Gates to Stark, May 30, 1778 and Stark to Gates, Jun. 20, 1778, Caleb Stark ed., *Memoir and Official Correspondence of Gen. John Stark* (Concord, N.H., 1860), pp. 155–56, 166.

38. Hazen Memorandum, June 19, 1778, Gates Papers, reel 4, box IX, doc. 257.

39. Bayley to Gates, July 13, 1778, *New Hampshire State Papers*, 17:241; William Kingsford, *The History of Canada*, 10 vols. (Toronto, 1887–98), 6:485; Haldimand Papers, B 129, vol. I, pp. 11–12, 16, Public Archives of Canada, Ottawa.

40. Hazen to Bedel, July 25, 1778 and Bedel to Gates, July 15, 1778, *New Hampshire State Papers*, 17: 248, 241–42.

41. General Orders, White Plains, Aug. 25, 1778, Washington, *Writings*, ed. Fitzpatrick, 12:357–58; General Orders, Fredericksburgh, Nov. 7, 1778, *ibid.*, 13:212–13.

42. "The State of Colonel Hazen's Regiment," Sept. 3, 1778, Peter Force Historical Manuscripts, ser. IX, box 25; "Colonel Hazen's Regiment," 1778, *New Hampshire State Papers*, 17:292ff.

43. Hazen to Cong., Sept., 20, 1778, Manuscript Group 23, B 4; *Journals of Congress*, 12: 1159.

44. Miscellaneous Numbered Records, M-859, roll 64, doc. 29392, National Archives, Washington, D.C.

45. Gates, Bayley, and Hazen to Washington, Sept. 10, and Washington to Cong., Sept. 12, 1778, Papers of Congress, M-247, roll 168, item 152, IV, 359ff, 355ff; Laurens to Washington, Sept. 16, 1778, Washington, *Writings*, ed. Fitzpatrick, 12:436n.

46. Washington to Schuyler, Nov. 20, 1778, Clinton, *Papers*, 4:365–68n.

47. Washington to Cong., Nov. 11, 1778, Papers of Congress, M-247, roll 168, item 152, IV, 451ff.

48. Washington to Gates, Nov. 24, 1778, Gates Papers, reel 3, box V, doc. 116.

49. Captain Gosselin to his wife, Oct. 29, 1778, McLellan Collection, C. W. McLellan, Champlain, N.Y.

50. Christopher Ward, *The War of the Revolution*, 2 vols. (New York: Macmillan, 1952), I, 594; Washington to Measam, Oct. 28, 1778, Washington, *Writings*, ed. Fitzpatrick, 13:173n.

51. Washington to Cong., Nov. 27, 1778, Washington, *Writings*, ed. Fitzpatrick, 13:350ff.

52. William F. Livingston, *Israel Putnam, Pioneer, Ranger, and Major-General* (New York, 1901), pp. 383ff.

V: The American Revolution, 1779–1781

1. Washington to Cong., Dec. 13, 1778, Papers of Congress, M-247, roll 168, item 152, IV, 601ff; Deposition of Andrew Stephenson, Dec. 1778, Clinton, *Papers*, 4: 442ff.

2. Bedel to Gen. Clinton, Jan. 6; to Schuyler, Jan. 11; to Gates, Jan. 12 and to Hazen, Feb. 8, 1779, *New Hampshire State Papers*, 17:310–17.

3. For a full discussion, see Jere R. Daniell, *Experiment in Republicanism, New Hampshire Politics and the American Revolution* (Cambridge: Harvard University Press, 1970), pp. 145ff; Frederic F. Van de Water, *The Reluctant Republic: Vermont, 1724–1791* (New York: John Day, 1941), pp. 221ff.

4. Powers, *Coos Country*, pp. 193–94, 217–18.

5. Bedel to Hazen, Dec. 4, 1780, *New Hampshire State Papers*, 17:384–85.

6. Hazen to Bedel, Mar. 7, June 15 and Oct. 12, 1780, *ibid.*, 358, 365ff, 379.

7. Schuyler to Gen. Clinton, Mar. 2, 1779, Clinton, *Papers*, 4: 602ff; Washington to Schuyler, Mar. 21, 1779, Washington, *Writings*, ed. Fitzpatrick, 14: 268ff.

8. Gates to Washington, Mar. 4, 1779, George Washington, *The Writings of George Washington*, ed. Jared Sparks, 12 vols. (Boston, 1834), 2:256.

9. Washington to Hazen, Mar. 6, 1779, Washington, *Writings*, ed. Fitzpatrick, 14:204–205.

10. Washington to Hazen, Mar. 14, 1779, *ibid.*, 236ff.

11. Benjamin Mooers, "Recollections," Bailey Collection, pp. 2–7; Hazen to Mooers, Mar. 18, 1779, McLellan Collection.

12. Washington to Edward Hinman, Apr. 12, 1779, Washington, *Writings*, ed. Fitzpatrick, 14:371–72; Hazen to Heath, Apr. 12, 1779, Heath Papers, vol. XII, no. 292; Hazen to Bedel, Apr. 12, 1779, *New Hampshire State Papers*, 17:329.

13. Hazen to Maj. Child, Apr. 24, 1779, and same to the Gentlemen Magistrates, Apr. 22, 1779, Schoff Collection.

14. Washington to Hazen, May 5, 1779, Washington, *Writings*, ed. Fitzpatrick, 14:503–504.

15. Hazen to Mooers, Aug. 7, 1777, McLellan Collection; Mooers, "Recollections," pp. 5–6.

16. Washington to Hazen, July 20, 1779, Washington, *Writings*, ed. Fitzpatrick, 15:445.

17. Vermont Historical Society, *The Bayley-Hazen Road*, pp. 6–7; Bogart, *Peacham*, pp. 43ff.

18. Frederic J. Wood, *The Turnpikes of New England* (Boston, 1919), pp. 263ff.

19. Washington to Cong., Nov. 3, 1779, Papers of Congress, M-247, roll 187, item 169, VI, 243ff; Washington to Hazen, Nov. 6, 1779, Washington, *Writings*, ed. Fitzpatrick, 17:83.

20. Brymner, *Public Archives, 1888*, pp. 861ff.

21. Hazen to Bedel, Aug. 24, 1779, *New Hampshire State Papers*, 17:345; Washington to Hazen, Aug. 28 and Sep. 17, 1779, Washington, *Writings*, ed. Fitzpatrick, 16:197, 302–303.

22. Washington to Gates, Oct. 16, 1779, Gates Papers, reel 3, box V, doc. 139.

23. Washington to Cong., Nov. 20, 1779, Washington, *Writings*, ed. Fitzpatrick, 17:150ff.

24. Haldimand to Maj. Carleton, Nov. 1, 1779, and Carleton to Haldimand, Nov. 14, 1779, Haldimand Papers, B 132, pp. 28, 30.

25. Prisoners' Complaint, Mar. 5, 1780, Brymner, *Public Archives, 1888,* pp. 924–25.

26. Burnett, *Letters,* 5:47; Hazen to Washington, Feb. 12, 1780, Washington, Papers, 128:4.

27. General Orders, Oct. 15 and 16, 1780, Washington, *Writings,* ed. Fitzpatrick, 20:186, 199.

28. Allen McLane, "Journal," in Henry Steele Commager and Richard Morris, eds., *The Spirit of 'Seventy-Six, the Story of the American Revolution as Told by Participants* (New York: Harper & Row, 1967), pp. 813–14.

29. Washington to Campbell, Sept. 25, 1779, Washington, *Writings,* ed. Fitzpatrick, 16:337.

30. *Ibid.,* 17: 286–87; 18:222ff; *Journals of Congress,* 13:324ff.

31. Washington to Lord Stirling, Jan. 12, 1780, *ibid.,* 17:379ff; same to same, Jan. 13, 1780, Washington, *Writings,* ed. Sparks, 6:444.

32. James Thacher, *The American Revolution from the Commencement to the Disbanding of the American Army* (Hartford, 1861), p. 188.

33. Washington to Hazen, Jan. 21 and 24, 1780, Washington, *Writings,* ed. Fitzpatrick, 17:418ff, 438–39, and Jan. 25, 1780, Washington, *Writings,* ed. Sparks, 6:451.

34. Hazen to Washington, Jan. 26, 1780, and Washington to St. Clair, Jan. 27, 1780, Washington, *Writings,* ed. Sparks, 6:452ff.

35. Hazen to Washington, Feb. 12, 1780, Washington, Papers, 128:4.

36. Hazen's Orderly Book, Jan. 1 to Apr. 27, 1780, Peter Force Historical Manuscripts, ser. 7E.

37. Steuben to Washington, Mar. 15, 1780, Friedrich Kapp, *The Life of Frederick William von Steuben, Major General in the Revolutionary Army* (New York, 1859), p. 264; Steuben report, May 3, 1780, Revolutionary War Rolls, mic. 246, roll 132, doc. 213-2; General Orders, Jan. 27, 1780, Washington, *Writings,* ed. Fitzpatrick, 19: 75–76.

38. *Journals of Congress,* 18: 896–97, 931, 952–53, 959ff.

39. Hazen to Washington, July 17, 1780, Washington, Papers, 142: 24; Washington to Hazen, July 20, 1780, Washington, *Writings,* ed. Fitzpatrick, 19: 217.

40. Henry Dearborn, *Revolutionary War Journals of Henry Dearborn, 1775–1783,* ed. Lloyd A. Brown and Howard H. Peckham (Freeport, N.Y.: Books for Libraries Press, 1969), p. 200.

41. Hazen to Bedel, Sept. 13, 1780, *New Hampshire State Papers,* 17: 376–77; Nathan Beers, "Journal, 1777–1782," Aug. 23, 1780, Peter Force Papers; "Proceedings of a General Court-Martial on the Trial of Col. Hazen, 1780, Held at Teneck Aug. 29, 1780," Morris-Popham Papers, MS 59-254, box 4, Library of Congress.

42. General Orders, Sep. 17, 1780, Washington, *Writings,* ed. Fitzpatrick, 20: 65–66.

43. Israel Angell, *Diary of Colonel Israel Angell*, ed. Edward Field (Providence, 1899), Sept. 19–22, 1780; Hazen to Bedel, Oct. 15, 1780, *New Hampshire State Papers*, 17:380.

44. Carl Van Doren, *Secret History of the American Revolution* (New York: Viking Press, 1941), pp. 232–33.

45. Mooers, "Recollections," p. 8.

46. Hazen to Col. Chase, June 15, 1780, Schoff Collection.

47. Hazen to Sullivan, Sept. 13, 1780, John Sullivan, *Revolutionary Letters of Gen. John Sullivan*, vol. 5, Massachusetts Historical Society, Boston; same to same, Oct. 15, 1780, Manuscript Group 23, B 4.

48. Hazen to Bedel, Oct. 12, 1780, *New Hampshire State Papers*, 17: 379.

49. Hazen's officers to Washington, Sept. 20, 1780, Washington, Papers, 151: 126.

50. Dearborn, *Journals*, pp. 206–207.

51. William Heath, *Memoirs of Major-General Heath* (Boston, 1798), pp. 239–40; Hazen to Heath, Oct. 22, 1780, and Heath to Hazen, s.d., William Heath, "Heath Papers" in Massachusetts Historical Society, *Collections* (Boston, 1878–1905), 17:192–93.

52. "Proceedings of a General Court Martial for the Trial of Col. Moses Hazen, November 1780," Peter Force Papers, ser. 7E, box 20; Hazen to Washington, Nov. 12, 1780, Washington, Papers, 157: 49–50.

53. General Orders, Jan. 1, 1781, Washington, *Writings*, ed. Fitzpatrick, 21: 45–46; Revolutionary War Rolls, mic. 246, roll 132, doc. 213-4, National Archives, Washington.

54. Reid to Washington, Dec. 7, 1780, Washington, Papers, 159: 43A-44.

55. Washington to Heath, Dec. 10, 1780, Massachusetts Historical Society, *Collections*, 71 vols. (Cambridge, Mass., 1792–), 5th ser., IV, 180; Hazen to Heath, Dec. 14, Heath to Hazen, Dec. 22 and Hazen to Heath, Dec. 24, 1780, Heath, "Papers," 18: 142, 201, 220.

56. "Courtmartial of Moses Hazen" in Peter Force Papers, ser. 7E, box 20; Hazen to Cong., Dec. 10 and 29, 1780, Papers of Congress, M-247, roll 96, item 78, XII, 109, 114.

57. Hazen to Heath, Feb. 8, 1781, Washington, Papers, 165: 53A-B.

58. General Orders, Feb. 18, 1781, Washington, *Writings*, ed. Fitzpatrick, 21: 239ff.

59. Hazen to Heath, Feb. 8, 1781, Washington, Papers, 165: 53A-B.

60. Hazen to Heath, Feb. 20, 1781, Heath, "Papers," 19: 54.

61. Heath, *Memoirs*, pp. 283–84; Revolutionary War Rolls, mic. 246, roll 132, doc. 213-2.

62. Hazen to Heath, Jan. 12, 1781, Washington, Papers, 162:99; Garrison Orders, Dec. 20, 1780, *ibid.*, 160:64.

63. Hazen to Heath, Jan. 12, 1781, *ibid.*, 162: 99; Heath's General Orders, Jan. 13, 1781, *ibid.*, 119.

64. Pickering to Washington, Jan. 14, 1781, Timothy Pickering, Papers, roll 33, no. 302, Massachusetts Historical Society, Boston; Washington to

Heath, Jan. 20 and Feb. 5, 1781, Mass. Historical Society, *Collections*, 5th ser., box IV, pp. 189–90, 193–94.

65. Hazen to Heath, Mar. 12, 1781, Heath, "Papers," 19: 192.

66. Heath, *Memoirs*, pp. 285ff; Benson J. Lossing, *The Pictorial Field-Book of the Revolution*, 2 vols. (New York, 1872–73), II, 624; Mooers, "Recollections," p. 9.

67. Torrey *et al.* to Antill, Mar. 3, 1781, Washington, Papers, 167: 101.

68. Hazen to Washington, Mar. 1, 1781, Papers of Congress, M-247, roll 171, item 152, X, 13ff; Washington to Cong., Mar. 5, 1781, *ibid.*, roll 96, item 78, XII, 293.

69. Washington to Colonel Dayton, June 28, 1781, Washington, *Writings*, ed. Fitzpatrick, 22: 274–75; Hazen to Sullivan, Apr. 4, 1781, Manuscript Group 23, B 4.

70. Hazen to Washington, Mar. 1, 1781 and Hazen to Cong., May 31, 1781, Papers of Congress, M-247, roll 171, item 152, X, 13ff and roll 54, item 42, III, 409ff; regimental return of Aug. 31, 1782, Revolutionary War Rolls, mic. 246, roll 132, doc. 213-2.

71. *Journals of Congress*, 19: 427ff; Papers of Congress, M-247, roll 27, item 19, 91–92; *Journals of Congress*, 20: 668–69.

72. Hazen to Sullivan, Apr. 30, 1781, Manuscript Group 23, B 4.

73. Hazen to Cong., Apr. 2 and May 31, 1781 and Board of Treasury to Cong., Apr. 24, 1781, Papers of Congress, M-247, roll 54, item 42, III, 405ff, 409ff; roll 147, item 136, V, 255–56.

74. George Washington, *The Diaries of George Washington*, ed. John C. Fitzpatrick, 4 vols. (Boston: Houghton Mifflin, 1925), II, 223, 235; Washington to Clinton, June 5, 1781, Washington, *Writings*, ed. Fitzpatrick, 22: 162–63.

75. Heath, *Memoirs*, pp. 311–12; Washington, *Diaries*, II, 255; Burke Davis, *The Campaign That Won America: The Story of Yorktown* (New York: Dial, 1970), p. 20.

76. Washington, *Diaries*, II, 257; Washington to Hazen, Sep. 2, 1781, Washington, *Writings*, ed. Fitzpatrick, 23: 78.

77. Dearborn, *Journals*, p. 217; Thacher, *American Revolution*, p. 280.

78. General Orders, Sept. 24 and 27, 1781, Washington, *Writings*, ed. Fitzpatrick, 23: 134–35; Washington to Scammell, Sep. 26, 1781, *ibid.*, pp. 141–42.

79. Freeman, *Washington*, V, 345ff; Thacher, *American Revolution*, p. 286.

VI: Between War and Peace, 1781–1783

1. Antill to Hazen and Hazen to Washington, Nov. 4, 1781, Washington, Papers, 187: 88.

2. Washington to Sec. at War, June 17, Aug. 6 and Nov. 27, 1782, Washington, *Writings*, ed. Sparks; 8: 309, Washington, *Writings*, ed. Fitzpatrick, 24: 469ff and 25: 376–77.

3. Washington to Hazen, Dec. 6, 1781, Washington, *Writings*, ed. Fitzpatrick, 23: 374; Washington to Heath, Nov. 28, 1781, Mass. Historical Society, *Collections*, 5th ser. IV, 230.

4. "Hazen Trip," Jan. 6 to Mar 24, 1782, Bailey Collection; Hazen to Bedel, Mar. 23, 1782, Charles E. French Papers, 1782–87, Massachusetts Historical Society, Boston.

5. Washington to Hazen, Apr. 10, 1782, Washington, *Writings*, ed. Fitzpatrick, 24: 107ff.

6. Washington to Sec. at War, Apr. 25, 1782, *ibid.*, pp. 164ff.

7. Samuel M. Sener, *The Lancaster Barracks Where the British and Hessian Prisoners Were Detained during the Revolution* (Harrisburg, 1895), pp. 3ff; Frederic Shriver Klein, *Old Lancaster, Historic Pennsylvania from Its Beginnings to 1865* (Lancaster, Pa., n.d.), p. 102.

8. See various ration returns in the Bailey Collection.

9. *Journals of Congress*, 22: 372–73; Sener, *Lancaster Barracks*, p. 8.

10. Washington to Hazen, May 3 and Washington to Lt. Gen. James Robertson, May 4, 1782, Washington, *Writings*, ed. Fitzpatrick, 24: 217–18, 220–21.

11. Mooers, "Recollections," p. 11.

12. Hazen to Washington and Maj. Gordon to Carleton, May 27, 1782, Washington, *Writings*, ed. Sparks, 7:302–303.

13. Washington to Sec. at War. June 5, 1782, Washington, *Writings*, ed. Fitzpatrick, 24: 319ff; Washington to Col. Dayton, June 11, 1782, Washington, *Writings*, ed. Sparks, 7: 305–306.

14. Washington to Cong., Aug. 19, 1782, Washington, *Writings*, ed. Fitzpatrick, 25: 39ff.

15. Vergennes to Washington, July 29, 1782, *ibid.*, 549–50; Washington to Cong., Oct. 25, and same to Asgill, Nov. 13, 1782, Washington, *Writings*, ed. Fitzpatrick, 25: 295–96, 336–37.

16. Washington to Hazen, Nov. 18 and Dec. 4, 1782, *ibid.*, 348–49, 400–401; Hazen to Lt. Stuart, Jan. 15, 1783, Livingston II Papers, box 1, Massachusetts Historical Society, Boston; Washington to Cong., Feb. 25, 1783, Washington, *Writings*, ed. Sparks, 8: 385–86.

17. Livingston to Hazen, June 8, 1783, Papers of Congress, M-247, roll 52, item 41, IX, 231ff.

18. Washington to Hazen, Dec. 25, 1782, Washington, *Writings*, ed. Fitzpatrick, 25: 467; Hazen to Mooers, Jan. 1, 1783, Bailey Collection.

19. Moses White to Eliza Atlee, Dec. 4, 1782, Everett-Peabody Papers, box 1, Massachusetts Historical Society, Boston; Miscellaneous Numbered Records (The Manuscript File) in the War Department Revolutionary War Records, 1775–1790s, M-859, roll 124, doc. 35374, National Archives Washington, D.C.

20. Reid to Washington, May 30, 1782, Washington, Papers, 198: 137; Washington to Reid, June 19, 1782, Washington, *Writings*, ed. Fitzpatrick, 24: 363–64; Hazen to Charles Thomson, Aug. 26, 1782, Papers of Congress, M-247, roll 96, item 78, XII, 241.

21. Hazen to Washington, Jan. 13, 1783, Washington, Papers, 214: 39–40.

22. Washington to Hazen, Jan. 25, 1782, Washington, *Writings*, ed. Fitzpatrick, 26: 65ff; Hazen to Washington, Jan. 29, 1783 (3 letters), Washington, Papers, 215: 16, 21, 22; Hazen to Board of Inquiry, Jan. 1783, *ibid.*, 43; General Orders, Feb. 9, 1783, Washington, *Writings*, ed. Fitzpatrick, 26: 110–11.

23. General Orders, Feb. 20 and 21, 1783, Washington, *Writings*, ed. Fitzpatrick, 26: 148–49, 149ff.

24. General Orders, Apr. 3, 1783 and Washington to Huntington, May 17, 1783, *ibid.*, 283, 440–41.

25. Huntington to Washington, May 27, 1783, Washington, Papers, 221: 45; General Orders, May 28, 1783, Washington, *Writings*, ed. Fitzpatrick, 26: 458.

26. Hazen to Washington, May 29 and June 6, 1783, Washington, Papers, 221: 58, 105; Washington to Hazen, Washington, *Writings*, ed. Fitzpatrick, 26: 460–61.

27. Washington to General Officers, June 23, and same to Hazen, June 24, 1783, *ibid.*, 27: 29–31.

28. Hazen to Lincoln, June 8 and Lincoln to Cong., June 24, 1782, Papers of Congress, M-247, roll 54, item 42, III, 528ff; *Journals of Congress*, 10: 410.

29. Hazen to Comm. of Cong., Mar. 31, 1783, Papers of Congress, M-247, roll 54, item 42, III, 540ff; *Journals of Congress*, 25: 541.

30. Hazen to Cong., Feb. 5 and same to Comm. of Cong., Feb. 10, 1784, Papers of Congress, M-247, roll 96, item 78, XII, 283ff, 289ff.

31. *Journals of Congress*, 26: 242–43; Papers of Congress, M-247, roll 54, item 42, III, 512ff.

32. *Journals of Congress*, 28: 304, 348–49, 434.

33. Hand to Hazen and Hazen to Hand, July 3, 1783, Papers of Congress, M-247, roll 171, item 152, XI, 401ff.

34. Jackson to Cong., July 14, 1783, *ibid.*, roll 163, item 149, III, 73f; Pres. of Cong. to Washington, July 17, 1783, Burnett, *Letters*, 7: 226–27.

35. *Journals of Congress*, 25: 633.

36. *Ibid.*, 24: 291ff.

37. See Merrill Jensen, *The New Nation, A History of the United States during the Confederation, 1781–1789* (New York: Knopf, 1950), pp. 67ff.

38. Hazen to W. A. Atlee, Feb. 23, 1783, Peter Force Historical Manuscripts, ser. IX, box 32. For a good general account of ensuing events, see Louis C. Hatch, *The Administration of the American Revolutionary Army* (New York, 1904), chs. 8–9.

39. *Journals of Congress*, 24: 297–98, 306ff.

40. *Ibid.*, pp. 207–208.

41. Antill to War Office, Apr. 25, 1783, Papers of Congress, M-247, roll 163, item 149, III, 387; Washington to Bland, Apr. 4, 1783, Washington, Papers, 26: 285ff.

42. Washington to Hamilton, Apr. 22, 1783, *ibid.*, 350–51.

43. *Journals of Congress*, 24: 364.

VII: The Canadians after the War

1. *Journals of Congress*, 25: 801; 31: 638, 740.

2. Hazen to Cong., Apr. 8, 1783, Papers of Congress, M-247, roll 54, item 42, III, 451ff.

3. *Journals of Congress*, 5: 763; 18: 726–27.

4. *The Balloting Book, and Other Documents Relating to the Military Bounty Lands, in the State of New-York* (Albany, 1825), p. 6.

5. Hazen to Cong., Apr. 8, 1783, Papers of Congress, M-247, roll 54, item 42, III, 451ff; Hazen to Pickering, Apr. 15, 1783, Pickering Papers, roll 18, no. 157.

6. *Journals of Congress*, 24: 269; Manuscript Group 23, ser. B 3, folder 1, pp. 71–72.

7. Washington, *Writings*, ed. Fitzpatrick, 27: 68ff.

8. Reed, *Paulint*, p. 28.

9. *Journals of Congress*, 5: 646.

10. Washington to Cong., Nov. 1, 1780, Washington, *Writings*, ed. Fitzpatrick, 20: 275–76; *Journals of Congress*, 18: 1042.

11. *Journals of Congress*, 21: 1062; Washington to Lt. Col. George Reid, Aug. 6, 1782, Washington, *Writings*, ed. Fitzpatrick, 24: 277–78.

12. Morris to Cong., Jan. 24, 1784, Papers of Congress, M-247, roll 41, item 35, 75.

13. Comm. to Cong., July 18, 1780, Burnett, *Letters*, 5: 271ff; *Journals of Congress*, 18: 1062.

14. Throop to Clinton, Jan. 10, 1780, Clinton, *Papers*, 5: 452–53.

15. For a full discussion, see Gordon Stewart and George Rawlyk, *A People Highly Favoured of God: The Nova Scotia Yankees and the American Revolution* (Hamden, Conn.: Archon Books, 1972), part I.

16. *Ibid.*, p. 79.

17. Hazen to Cong., April 8, 1783, Papers of Congress, M-247, roll 54, item 42, III, 451–52; *Journals of Congress*, 24: 269; John Blake *et al.* to Cong., Apr. 18, 1783, Papers of Congress, M-247, roll 49, item 41, II, 134ff.

18. Papers of Congress, M-247, roll 30, item 22, pp. 217–18; Hazen to Cong., July 19, 1783, *ibid.*, roll 96, item 78, XII, 267.

19. Clinton to Cong., Jan 20, 1784, Papers of Congress, M-247, roll 41, item 35, p. 79.

20. *Journals of Congress,* 26: 80, 98.

21. Papers of Congress, M-247, roll 41, item 35, pp. 83, 87.

22. *Journals of Congress,* 27: 594; Hazen to Cong., May 18, 1784, Papers of Congress, M-247, roll 96, item 78, XIII, 295; Hazen to Gates, s.d., Emmett Collection, New York Public Library.

23. *Journals of Congress,* 28: 131–32.

24. Hazen to Cong., Sept. 16, 1788, Papers of Congress, M-247, roll 54, item 42, III, 520ff.

25. Ernest L. Monty, "Major Clement Gosselin", *French Canadian and Acadian Genealogical Review,* spring 1968, pp. 27ff.

26. *Ibid.,* pp. 30n, 43; Revolutionary War Rolls, mic. 246, roll 131.

27. Reed, *Paulint.*

28. Olivier to Cong., Jan. 22, 1785, Papers of Congress, M-247, roll 41, item 35, pp. 135ff.

29. Hazen to Cong., Sept. 16, 1788, *ibid.,* roll 54, item 42, III, 520ff; Metcalfe Receipt, Oct. 23, 1789; Hazen to Mooers, July 7, 1790, and Metcalfe to Mooers, Nov. 8, 1790, Bailey Collection.

30. Liebert to Mooers, July 23, 1790 and Hazen to Mooers, Apr. 18, 1791, Bailey Collection.

31. *The Balloting Book,* pp. 7ff.

32. Journals of Congress, 28: 380–81; Carl Wittke, "Canadian Refugees in the American Revolution," *Canadian Historical Review,* Dec. 1922, pp. 324ff.

33. Land Papers, 47: 126–37 *passim.*

34. Land Papers, 37: 60, 77; 38: 127.

35. Nell Sullivan and David K. Martin, *A History of the Town of Chazy, Clinton County, New York* (Burlington, Vt.: George Little Press, 1970), ch. 5.

36. Land Papers, 47: 131ff, 135, 141; *The Balloting Book,* pp. 185ff.

37. Hazen to McPherson, Aug. 21, 1784; Return of Refugees, Sept. 1784; Power of Attorney, Aug. 18, 1784; Hazen Receipt, Nov. 20, 1784; Hazen to McPherson, Nov. 27, 1784 and June 16, 1785; McPherson Certificate, Apr. 19, 1792, Bailey Collection.

38. Carleton to Cong., Dec. 10, 1784, Papers of Congress, M-247, roll 41, item 35, p. 97.

39. Lafayette to Cong., Dec. 12, 1784, *ibid.,* roll 41, item 25, p. 93.

40. Resolutions of the Land Office, June 22, 1786, Bailey Collection.

41. *The Balloting Book,* pp. 185ff.

42. Land Papers, 47: 143.

43. Canadian Refugees to Cong., Aug. 13, 1787, Papers of Congress, M-247, roll 53, item 42, II, 226ff.

44. Refugees to Cong., *ibid.; Journals of Congress,* 34: 591; Platt to Clinton, Sept. 1, 1787, Land Papers, 47: 165.

45. Refugees to Cong., Papers of Congress, M-247, roll 53, item 42, II, 226ff; *Journals of Congress,* 33: 527–28.

46. *Journals of Congress,* 33: 665; H. K. Averill, *Geography and History of Clinton County, New York* (Plattsburgh, N.Y., 1885), p. 22.

47. Census of 1790, McLellan Collection.

48. *Recherches Historiques,* Jan. 1898, pp. 6ff and July 1900, pp. 210ff.

49. Shea, *Catholic Church,* II, 268–69; Reed, *Paulint,* p. 38.

50. Mooers Exploration, Sept. 7–14, 1785, miscellaneous powers of attorney, 1786–1791, and Mooers Travel Journal of 1792, Bailey Collection; Mooers landholdings, Nov. 8, 1808, Misc. Manuscript Collection, doc. 12204.

51. Mooers lands in 1817, Bailey Collection; tax bill, June 10, 1818, Kent-Delord Collection, 66.7e, 3/1/28.

52. Mooers to Astor, Nov. 18, 1828, Bailey Collection.

53. Articles of Agreement, July 3, 1830, amended, May 10, 1834, and Comptroller's Advertisement, Oct. 21, 1833, Kent-Delord Collection, 66.7e, 7/5/11 and 7/3/54; Mooers to Moore, July 21, 1834, Bailey Collection.

54. Hay to Legislature, Feb. 7; Scott to Hay, Aug. 8 and Hay to Scott, Oct. 1, 1789, Bailey Collection; Hay to Mooers, Oct. 3, 1789, Kent-Delord Collection, 66.7e, 7/5/2.

55. Contract of Jan. 17, 1791 and petitions of May 30, 1793 and Jan. 22, 1794, Bailey Collection; Beaumont to Mooers, Sept. 22, 1793, Kent-Delord Collection, 66.7e, 7/2/1; Mooers to Legislature, Feb. 4, 1794 and Refugees to Legislature, n.d., Bailey Collection.

56. Act of Assembly, Mar. 22, 1794; Act of Senate, Feb. 14, 1795, Bailey Collection.

57. Beaumont Report, Dec. 15, 1794, Kent-Delord Collection, 66.7e, 7/2/2; Mooers Deficiencies of Land, Feb. 28, 1804, and De Witt to Mooers, July 12, 1815, Bailey Collection.

58. *American State Papers: Public Lands,* 8 vols. (Washington, 1832–61), 1: 31–32; *Annals of the Congress of the United States,* 42 vols. (Washington, 1834–56), 5th Cong., III, Appendix, p. 3718.

59. *Public Lands,* 1, no. 58, p. 110.

60. *Annals of Congress,* 6th Cong., Appendix, 1549; Clifford N. Smith, "Revolutionary War Refugees from Canada and Nova Scotia," *National Genealogical Society Quarterly,* Dec. 1971, p. 267. Smith lists and comments upon each claimant on pp. 267–73.

61. Wittke, "Canadian Refugees," p. 333.

62. *Ibid.*

63. Smith, "Revolutionary War Refugees," pp. 267–73.

64. Circulars from Ogden, Reed and Bradford, May 31, 1828, Bailey Collection.

65. Averill to Mooers and McNeil, Sept. 22, 1830, *ibid.*

66. Averill to Ingham, Dec. 27, 1830, *ibid.* See the same source for other correspondence during 1830.

67. Ingham to Commissioners, Jan. 29, 1831 and Mooers to Ingham, Feb. 25, 1831, *ibid.*

68. Joseph Martin vs. Nathan Richardson, Sept. 10, 1832, Kent-Delord Collection, 66.7e, 7/6/1/ to 7.

VIII: DREAMS AND NIGHTMARES

1. Mooers, "Memorandum Book," Bailey Collection.

2. John Nairne to Maj. Lernoult, Oct. 11, 1783, Manuscript Group 12, B 50, p. 402, Public Archives of Canada, Ottawa; Haldimand to Lord North, Oct. 24, 1783, Manuscript Group 21, vol. B 57, pp. 574ff.

3. Beekman-Platt Agreement, Apr. 13, 1786, Misc. Manuscript Collection, LP 14821.

4. Hazen to Beekman, July 4, 1787, Collections of the New York Historical Society; White, *Beekmantown*, pp. 25–26.

5. Mooers Travel Journal, 1784–85, Bailey Collection.

6. Hazen to Washington, Apr. 24, 1789, Papers of Congress, M-247, roll 96, item 78, XII, 473.

7. White to Mooers, June 14, 1786 and Hazen to Mooers, Aug. 12, 1786, Bailey Collection.

8. J. Hazen to Mooers, Feb. 12, 1787, *ibid.*

9. Hazen to Mooers, Dec. 28, 1786 and Power of Attorney, Aug. 29, 1787, *ibid.*

10. Hazen to Mooers, Aug. 18, 1790, *ibid.*

11. Hazen-Mooers Account, 1787–88, Kent-Delord Collection, 66.7e, 8/1/3.

12. Torrey to Mooers, Nov. 14, 1790, and Hazen Account with Mooers, 1785 to 1796, Bailey Collection; Deposition of Moses White, Feb. 26, 1820, Misc. Chancery Decrees, box 97, no. 845.

13. Hazen to Mooers, Dec. 2, 1790, June 30, 1792 and Oct. 12, 1792, and White to Mooers, May 16, 1798, *Bailey Collection.*

14. Hazen to Mooers, July 7, 1790, and Apr. 2, 1792, *ibid.*

15. Hazen to Mooers, Sept. 7, 1793, *ibid.*

16. Hazen to Mooers, Sept. 9, 1794, and Potash Sales to Montreal, Jan. 13, 1792, *ibid.*

17. Moses Charlotte Hazen to Tayler, Feb. 1, 1794; Sheriff's sale, Sept. 23, 1794, and C. Hazen to Tayler, Feb. 25, 1795, *ibid.*

18. C. Hazen to Mooers, Dec. 4, 1800, *ibid.*

19. Hazen to Mooers, Apr. 18, 1791, *ibid.*

20. *Journals of Congress*, 5: 811–12; 6: 900.

21. Hazen to Williamson, Feb. 10, 1784, Papers of Congress, M-247, roll 96, item 78, XII, 289ff; *ibid.*, roll 41, item 35, p. 87.

22. *Journals of Congress*, 34: 376ff.

23. Hazen to Cong., Mar. 30, 1785, Papers of Congress, M-247, roll 54, item 42, III, 512ff; *ibid.*, May 11, 1785, roll 27, item 19, pp. 109–10.

24. For this and subsequent chronology, see White, *A Statement of Facts*, pp. 1ff.

25. Papers of Congress, M-247, roll 50, item 41, IV, 3.

26. Demers, *Moses Hazen*, p. 12; M. Hazen to W. Hazen, July 25, 1785, Bailey Collection.

27. Hazen Memo, Oct. 15, 1787, Kent-Delord Collection, 66.7e, 8/1/12.

28. Hazen to Mooers, Apr. 13, 1790 and Hazen Memorandum on Canadian Lands, n.d., Bailey Collection.

29. Hillhouse to Hazen, Jan. 18, 1790, Misc. Manuscript Collection, LP 14821; Demers, *Moses Hazen*, p. 12.

30. Hazen to White, May 8, 1788, Bailey Collection.

31. Demers, *Moses Hazen*, p. 12; Manuscript Group 8, ser. F99-9, vol. 17, docs. 008421-31.

32. Vermont Historical Society, *The Bayley-Hazen Military Road*, p. 8; Hazen to Bedel, June 15, 1780, *New Hampshire State Papers*, 17: 365–66.

33. *State Papers of Vermont*, 5: 342–43, 351ff.

34. Documents relating to these and the following transactions are to be found at intervals in the Bailey Collection, 1784–1813.

35. The Bradford situation is summarized in *State Papers of Vermont*, 5: 271–72, with supporting documents on pp. 355ff, 357, 417, 419ff and 6: 78. See also Hazen to Chittenden, Jan. 14, 1785, *ibid.*, 17: 637–38; and Rev. Silas McKeen, *A History of Bradford, Vermont* (Montpelier, Vt., 1875), pp. 30–31.

36. White to Mooers, May 4, 1803 and Mooers to White, May 26, 1803, *ibid.*; White's "Answers in Chancery," Feb. 26, 1820, Miscellaneous Chancery Decrees, box 97, no. 845, p. 6, Paul Klapper Library, Queen's College, New York City.

37. Hazen to Mooers, Aug. 21, 1790, Bailey Collection; Knox to Gen. Maunsell, May 25, 1790, Henry Knox Papers, roll 26, Massachusetts Historical Society, Boston.

38. Torrey to Mooers, May 3, 1792, Bailey Collection.

39. Torrey to Mooers, June 1, Sept. 1 and Oct. 3, 1792, *ibid.*

40. Hazen to Mooers, Apr. 18, 1791, *ibid.*; Frank W. Thomas, "General Moses Hazen," *Albany Argus*, May 31, 1903.

41. Tayler to Mooers, Aug. 12, 1799 and C. Hazen to same, July 5, 1802, Bailey Collection; Thomas, "General Moses Hazen."

42. Letters Testamentary and Hazen's Will, Jan. 28, 1804, Misc. Chancery Decrees, box 97, no. 845.

43. Inventory of Hazen Estate, May 3, 1804, *ibid.*

44. C. Hazen to Mooers, Mar. 3, 1807, Kent-Delord Collection, 66.7e, 8/1/17; Lease of Farm, Aug. 5, 1809, Bailey Collection.

45. See the Mooers-Tayler-Cooper correspondence between 1827 and 1830, Bailey Collection, and Misc. Manuscript Collection, LP 14821.

46. Affidavit of C. Hazen and accompanying documents, Mar. 24, 1804, Record Group 217.

47. Smith, "Revolutionary War Refugees," p. 270; Misc. Manuscript Collection, LP 14821.

48. White to W. Hazen, Feb. 1, 1804, Hazen Collection.

49. Charlotte Hazen's Will, Dec. 17, 1818, Misc. Manuscript Collection, doc. 14822; Statement of C. D. Cooper, *ibid.*; Tayler to Mooers, June 16, 1823, Bailey Collection.

50. Clinton County Deeds, bk. H, pp. 125, 421ff, County Clerk's Office, Plattsburgh, New York; Albany County, Power of Attorney, bk. 1, p. 241.

51. White to Mooers, Dec. 10, 1816, Bailey Collection. See other letters among the three correspondents in the same source, 1805 to 1818.

52. Foot to Mooers, Feb. 27, 1819, McLellan Collection; Moses White in Chancery, Aug. 17, 1818, Misc. Chancery Decrees, box 97, no. 845.

53. "The Several Answers of Moses White", Feb. 26, 1820, and Master's Report, May 8, 1820, Misc. Chancery Decrees, box 97, no. 845.

54. Chancellor's Decision, Oct. 10, 1822, Bailey Collection; Chancellor's Commentary, n.d., Kent-Delord Collection.

55. *Register of Debates in Congress, 1824–1837* (14 vols., Washington, 1825–37), vol. IV, part II, appendix xlvi; *Resolutions, Laws and Ordinances . . .* (Washington, 1838), pp. 165–66, 216ff; *Account of the Receipts and Expenditures of the U. S., 1828* (Washington, 1829), p. 128.

56. *Resolutions, Laws and Ordinances*, pp. 245, 250.

57. *Abridgement of the Debates of Congress from 1789 to 1856* (16 vols., New York, 1857–61), X: 151–52.

58. *Register of Debates in Congress*, vol. VIII, appendix 71.

AFTERWORD

1. The late Professors Lawrence Scobbie, St. Mary's University, Halifax, Nova Scotia.

Bibliography

Unpublished Sources

Albany County. Power of Attorney, book I. County Clerk's Office, Albany.
Bailey Collection. Feinberg Library, State University of New York, Plattsburgh.
Beers, Nathan. "Journal, 1777–1782." Peter Force Papers, Library of Congress.
Burnett Project of the Library of Congress from the Philip Schuyler Papers, Library of Congress.
Clinton County. Deeds, book H. County Clerk's Office, Plattsburgh.
Collections of the New-York Historical Society, New York City.
Colonial Office 42—Colonial Papers; Canada, Original Correspondence, 1700–1922. Public Archives of Canada, Ottawa.
Emmett Collection. New York Public Library, New York City.
Everett-Peabody Papers. Box 1, 1778–1829. Massachusetts Historical Society, Boston.
Force, Peter. Historical Manuscripts. Library of Congress.
Force, Peter. Papers. Library of Congress.
French, Charles E. Papers, 1782–87. Massachusetts Historical Society, Boston.
Gage Papers. American Series. Clements Library, University of Michigan, Ann Arbor.
Gates Papers. Microfilm copy of originals in New York Public Library, New York City.
Haldimand Papers. B 129 and B 132. Public Archives of Canada, Ottawa.
Hazen Collection. New Brunswick Museum, St. John, New Brunswick.
Kent-Delord Collection. Feinberg Library, State University of New York, Plattsburgh.
Knox, Henry, Papers. Massachusetts Historical Society, Boston.
Livingston II Papers, box 1, 1698–1783. Massachusetts Historical Society, Boston.
McLellan Collection. C. W. McLellan, Champlain, New York.
Manuscript Group 8—Documents Relatifs à la Nouvelle-France et au Québec (xviie–xxe siècles). Public Archives of Canada, Ottawa.

Manuscript Group 12—Admiralty and War Office Records. Public Archives of Canada, Ottawa.

Manuscript Group 21—Transcripts from Papers in the British Museum. Public Archives of Canada, Ottawa.

Manuscript Group 23—Late Eighteenth Century Papers. Public Archives of Canada, Ottawa.

Miscellaneous Chancery Decrees. Paul Klapper Library, Queens College, New York City.

Miscellaneous Manuscript Collection, LP 14821. New York State Library, Albany.

Miscelleanous Numbered Records (The Manuscript File) in the War Department Revolutionary War Records, 1775–1790s. National Archives, Washington, D.C.

Mooers, Benjamin, "Recollections of Benjamin Mooers, Gathered Together and Compiled by Himself." Bailey Collection, Feinberg Library, State University of New York, Plattsburgh.

Morris-Popham Papers. Library of Congress.

New York Colonial Manuscripts: Land Papers. New York State Library, Albany.

Nova Scotia Land Grants. Public Archives of Nova Scotia, Halifax.

Papers of the Continental Congress. Microfilm copy of originals in the Library of Congress.

Pickering, Timothy, Papers. Massachusetts Historical Society, Boston.

Record Group 1—Records of the Executive Council, 1764–1867. Public Archives of Canada, Ottawa.

Record Group 4—Records of the Civil and Provincial Secretaries' Offices, Canada East, 1760–1867. Public Archives of Canada, Ottawa.

Record Group 217—Records Relating to Refugees of Canada and Nova Scotia, 1776–1810, Office of the 1st Comptroller, Records of the U.S. General Accounting Office. National Archives, Washington, D.C.

Revolutionary War Rolls, 1776–1783, microcopy 246. National Archives, Washington. D.C.

Schoff Collection. Clements Library, University of Michigan, Ann Arbor, Michigan.

Sullivan, John, Revolutionary Letters of Gen. John Sullivan. Massachusetts Historical Society, Boston.

War Office Records, vol. 12. British Museum, London.

Washington, George, Papers. Library of Congress.

Published Sources

Abridgement of the Debates of Congress from 1789 to 1856. 16 vols. New York, 1857–61.

Account of the Receipts and Expenditures of the U.S., 1828. Washington, 1829.

American State Papers: Public Lands. 8 vols. Washington, 1832–61.

Annals of the Congress of the United States. 42 vols. Washington, 1834–56.

Angell, Israel. *Diary of Colonel Israel Angell, Commanding the Second Rhode Island Continental Regiment During the American Revolution, 1778–1781*, ed. Edward Field. Providence, 1899.

The Balloting Book, and Other Documents Relating to the Military Bounty Lands, in the State of New-York. Albany, 1825.

Brymner, Douglas, ed. *Report on the Public Archives*, 1888, 1890. Ottawa, 1889, 1891.

Burnett, Edmund C., ed. *Letters of Members of the Continental Congress.* 8 vols. Washington: Carnegie Institute, 1923.

Calendar of Historical Manuscripts Relating to the War of the Revolution in the Office of the Secretary of State. 2 vols. Albany, 1868.

Clinton, George. *Public Papers of George Clinton.* 10 vols. Albany, 1900–1904.

Collections of the Nova Scotia Historical Society for the Year 1886–87. Halifax, 1887.

Commager, Henry Steele and Richard B. Morris, eds. *The Spirit of 'Seventy-Six, the Story of the American Revolution as Told by Participants.* New York: Harper & Row, 1967.

Dearborn, Henry. *Revolutionary War Journals of Henry Dearborn, 1775–1783*, ed. Lloyd A. Brown and Howard H. Peckham. Freeport, N.Y.: Books for Libraries Press, 1969.

Debates and Proceedings in the Congress of the United States, 1789–1824. 42 vols. Washington, 1834–36.

Essex Institute. *Historical Collections.* 88 vols. Salem, Mass., 1859–.

Force, Peter. *American Archives.* Ser. IV and V. Washington, 1837–53.

Hazen, Tracy Elliott. *The Hazen Family in America.* Thomaston, Conn.: R. Hazen, 1947.

Heath, William. *Memoirs of Major-General Heath.* Boston, 1798.

———. "The Heath Papers" in Massachusetts Historical Society, *Collections*, ser. 5, vol. 4; ser. 7, vols. 4–5. Boston, 1878–1905.

Johnson, Sir William. *The Papers of Sir William Johnson.* 13 vols. Albany: University of the State of New York, 1921–62.

Journals of the Continental Congress, 1774–1789, ed. Worthington C. Ford et al. 34 vols. New York: Johnson Reprint Corp., 1968.

Knox, Capt. John. *An Historical Journal of the Campaigns in North-America for the Years 1757, 1758, 1759 and 1760.* 2 vols. London, 1769.

Lafayette, Marquis de. *Mémoires, Correspondences et Manuscrits du Général Lafayette.* 3 vols. Bruxelles, 1837.

Lane, Ranger Daniel. "Diary 1759." *New England Historical & Genealogical Register and Antiquarian Journal*, vol. XXVI (1872).

Massachusetts Historical Society. *Collections.* 71 vols. Cambridge, 1792–.

New Hampshire Provincial and State Papers. 40 vols. Concord, 1867–1943.

O'Callaghan, E. B., ed. *Documents Relative to the Colonial History of the State of New York.* 14 vols. Albany, 1856–61.

Record, Frederick W. and William Nelson, eds. *Documents Relating to the Colonial History of the State of New Jersey.* Vol. IX. Newark, 1885.

Register of Debates in Congress, 1824–1837. 14 vols. Washington, 1825–37.

Resolutions, Laws and Ordinances, Relating to the Pay, Half Pay, Commutation of Half Pay, Bounty Lands and Other Promises Made by

Congress to the Officers and Soldiers of the Revolution. Washington, 1838.

Rogers, Robert. *Journals of Major Robert Rogers.* New York: Corinth Books, 1961.

Shortt, A. and A. G. Doughty, eds. *Documents Relating to the Constitutional History of Canada, 1759–1791.* Ottawa, 1907.

Stark, Caleb, ed. *Memoir and Official Correspondence of Gen. John Stark.* Concord, 1860.

State Papers of Vermont, V: Petitions for Grants of Land, 1778–1811, ed. Mary Greene Nye. Brattleboro, Vt.: Vermont Publishing Co., 1939.

————, *VI: Sequestration, Confiscation and Sale of Estates,* ed. Mary Greene Nye. Montpelier, Vt.: The Secretary of State, 1941.

————, *XVII: Public Papers of Governor Thomas Chittenden,* ed. John A. Williams. Montpelier, Vt.: Richard C. Thomas, 1969.

Sullivan, John. *Letters and Papers of Major-General John Sullivan,* ed. Otis G. Hammond. 2 vols. Concord, N.H.: New Hampshire Historical Society, 1930.

Vermont Historical Society. *Proceedings for the Years 1923, 1924, 1925.* Bellows Falls, Vt.: P. H. Gobie Press, 1926.

Washington, George. *The Diaries of George Washington,* ed. John C. Fitzpatrick. 4 vols. Boston: Houghton Mifflin, 1925.

————. *The Writings of George Washington,* ed. Jared Sparks. 12 vols. Boston, 1834.

————. *The Writings of George Washington From the Original Manuscript Sources, 1745–1799,* ed. John C. Fitzpatrick. 39 vols. Washington: USGPO, 1931–44.

Wilkinson, General James. *Memoirs of My Own Times.* 3 vols. Philadelphia, 1816.

SECONDARY WORKS

Averill, H. K., Jr. *Geography and History of Clinton County, New York.* Plattsburgh, 1885.

Billias, George Athan. *George Washington's Generals.* New York: Morrow, 1964.

Bittinger, Rev. John Quincy. *History of Haverhill, N.H.* Haverhill, 1888.

Bogart, Ernest L. *Peacham, The Story of a Vermont Hill Town.* Montpelier: Vermont Historical Society, 1948.

Bradley, A. G. *Sir Guy Carleton.* Toronto: Oxford University Press, 1966.

Burrows, John W. *The Essex Regiment, 1st Battalion (44th), 1741 to 1919.* London, England: Burrows, 1931.

Bush, Martin H. *Revolutionary Enigma, A Re-Appraisal of General Philip Schuyler of New York.* Port Washington, N.Y.: Ira J. Freedman, 1969.

Carter, Thomas, comp. *Historical Record of the Forty-Fourth or the East Essex Regiment of Foot.* London, 1864.

Chase, George Wingate. *The History of Haverhill, Massachusetts from its First Settlement, in 1640, to the Year 1860.* Haverhill, Mass., 1861.

Daniell, Jere R. *Experiment in Republicanism, New Hampshire Politics and the American Revolution, 1741–1794.* Cambridge: Harvard University Press, 1970.

Davis, Burke. *The Campaign That Won America: The Story of Yorktown.* New York: The Dial Press, 1970.

Decker, Malcolm. *Benedict Arnold, Son of the Havens.* New York: Antiquarian Press, 1961.

Freeman, Douglas Southall. *George Washington, A Biography.* 7 vols. New York: Scribner's, 1948–57.

French, Allen. *The First Year of the American Revolution.* Boston: Houghton Mifflin, 1934.

Gerlach, Don R. *Philip Schuyler and the American Revolution in New York, 1733–1777.* Lincoln, Neb.: University of Nebraska Press, 1964.

Greene, George Washington. *The Life of Nathaniel Greene.* 3 vols. New York, 1871.

Hatch, Louis C. *The Administration of the American Revolutionary Army.* New York, 1904.

Hurd, D. Hamilton, comp. *History of Essex County, Massachusetts.* Philadelphia, 1888.

Jensen, Merrill. *The New Nation, A History of the United States during the Confederation, 1781–1789.* New York: Knopf, 1950.

Jones, Charles Henry. *History of the Campaign for the Conquest of Canada in 1776.* Philadelphia, 1882.

Kapp, Friedrich. *The Life of Frederick William von Steuben, Major General in the Revolutionary Army.* New York, 1859.

Kingsford, William. *The History of Canada.* 10 vols. Toronto, 1887–98.

Klein, Frederic Shriver. *Old Lancaster, Historic Pennsylvania Community From its Beginnings to 1865.* Lancaster, Pa., n.d.

Lanctot, Gustave. *Canada & the American Revolution, 1774–1783.* Cambridge: Harvard University Press, 1967.

Livingston, William F. *Israel Putnam, Pioneer, Ranger, and Major-General.* New York, 1901.

Loescher, Burt Garfield. *The History of Rogers Rangers.* 3 vols. Vol. I, San Francisco: Burt G. Loescher, 1946; vol. II, San Mateo, Calif.: Burt G. Loescher, 1969; vol. III, unpublished.

Lossing, Benson J. *The Life and Times of Philip Schuyler.* 2 vols. New York, 1872–73.

———. *The Pictorial Field-Book of the Revolution.* 2 vols. New York, 1860.

Lower, Arthur R. M. Lumbering in Eastern Canada: A Study in Economic and Social History. Unpublished thesis at Harvard University, 1928.

McKeen, Rev. Silas. *A History of Bradford, Vermont.* Montpelier, 1875.

Maxwell, Lillian M. B. *An Outline of the History of Central New Brunswick to the Time of Confederation.* Sackville, N.B.: Tribune Press, 1937.

McKown, Robin. *Horatio Gates and Benedict Arnold, American Military Commanders.* New York: McGraw-Hill, 1969.

Mee, Arthur, ed. *The King's England: Yorkshire, East Riding and York City.* London: Caxton Publishing Co., n.d.

Neatby, Hilda M. *Quebec, The Revolutionary Age, 1760–91.* Toronto: McClellan & Stewart, 1966.

Paine, Lauran. *Benedict Arnold: Hero and Traitor.* London, England: Robert Hale, 1965.

Parkman, Francis, *Montcalm and Wolfe.* New York: Collier, 1962.

Powers, Rev. Grant. *Historical Sketches of the Discovery, Settlement, and Progress of Events in the Coos Country and Vicinity.* Haverhill, N.H., 1841.

Raymond, Rev. W. O. *History of the River St. John:* St. John, N.B., 1905.

Roberts, Kenneth. *Rabble in Arms.* Garden City, N.Y.: Doubleday, 1948.

Shea, John Gilmary. *History of the Catholic Church in the United States.* 2 vols. New York, 1888.

Smith, Justin H. *Our Struggle for the Fourteenth Colony: Canada and the American Revolution.* 2 vols. New York, 1907.

Stanley, George F. G. *Canada Invaded, 1775–1776.* Toronto: Hakkert, 1973.

Stewart, Gordon, and George Rawlyk. *A People Highly Favored of God: The Nova Scotia Yankees and the American Revolution.* Hamden, Conn.: Archon, 1972.

Sullivan, Nell, and David K. Martin. *A History of the Town of Chazy, Clinton County, New York.* Burlington, Vt.: George Little Press, 1970.

Thacher, James. *The American Revolution from the Commencement to the Disbanding of the American Army.* Hartford, 1861.

Van de Water, Frederic. *The Reluctant Republic: Vermont, 1724–1791.* New York: John Day, 1941.

Van Doren, Carl. *Secret History of the American Revolution.* New York: Viking, 1941.

Ward, Christopher. *The War of the Revolution.* 2 vols. New York: Macmillan, 1952.

Wells, Frederic P. *History of Newbury, Vermont.* St. Johnsbury, Vt., 1902.

Whitcher, William F. *History of the Town of Haverhill, New Hampshire.* Concord, N. H., 1919.

White, Philip. "From Frontier to Farm Community, Beekmantown, New York, 1769–1849." Unpublished ms. in the hands of the author. University of Texas, Austin.

Wood, Frederic J. *The Turnpikes of New England.* Boston, 1919.

PAMPHLETS, JOURNALS, AND NEWSPAPERS

Bulletin of the Fort Ticonderoga Museum, vol. XII (1969).

Demers, Philippe. *Le Général Hazen, Seigneur de Bleury-Sud.* Montreal: Libraire Beauchemin, 1927.

Express & Standard, Newport, Vermont, Aug. 28, 1903.

French Canadian and Acadian Genealogical Review, spring 1968.

New Brunswick Magazine, vol. I.

Quebec Gazette, 1765–1785.

Recherches Historiques: Bulletin d'Archéologie, d'Histoire, de Biographie, de Bibliographie, de Numismatique, etc. Lévis, Quebec.

Reed, Adela Peltier. *Memoirs of Antoine Paulint.* Los Angeles: San Encino Press, 1940.

Sener, Samuel M. *The Lancaster Barracks where the British and Hessian Prisoners were Detained during the Revolution.* Harrisburg, 1895.

Smith, Clifford Neal. "Revolutionary War Refugees from Canada and Nova Scotia," *National Genealogical Society Quarterly,* Dec. 1971.

Thomas, Frank W. "General Moses Hazen," *Albany Argus,* May 31, 1903.

Vermont Historical Society. *The Bayley-Hazen Military Road.* Lyndonville, Vt., 1959.

White, Moses. *A Statement of Facts.* Salem, Mass., 1827.

Wittke, Carl. "Canadian Refugees in the American Revolution," *Canadian Historical Review,* Dec. 1922.

Index

Acadians, 3, 6

Albany, N.Y.: in French and Indian War, 5, 12; as refugee center, 47, 113, 115–16; 127–29; goal of Burgoyne, 55; base for Canadian campaign, 58–60, 69; defense of, 93; burial of Hazen at, 163; 97, 124, 142–43, 145, 149, 165, 168

Albany Committee of Safety, 60

Albany County, sheriff of, 126, 143, 155

Allan, John, 118, 139

Allen, Ethan, 29, 81, 97

Alline, Henry, 118

Alnick, England, 2

Altona, N.Y., 129

Amawalk. See Crompound

Amherst, Gen. Jeffrey, 8, 11–12

Amlane (family name), 133

Amlong. See Amlane

André, Maj. John, 81–82

Angell, Col. Israel, 81

Anglican Church, 1

Antill, Charlotte, 52

Antill, Lt. Col. Edward: settler in Quebec, ix, 34; in Canadian campaign, 34–36; commissioned, 36; recruiting by, 38–39, 47–48; burns Hazen property, 43; accounts of, 51, 153; capture of, 85; Court of Inquiry on, 85–86; and Reid, 90; at Yorktown, 95–96; retirement of, 96; Coos trip by, 97; petition of, 121; land grant to, 138, 140

Apthorp, C. W., 158, 160–61

Arnold, Gen. Benedict: at taking of Fort Ticonderoga, 29; captures Fort St. John, 29; proposes Canadian invasion, 29; and Canadian invasion, 30, 33–36, 39, 59; commands at Montreal, 41–42; quarrels with Hazen, 42–43; and Lake Champlain fleet, 43–45; courts-martial of, 44–45, 76; inquiries on, 45; at Valcour, 50; at Fort Stanwix, 56; at Saratoga, 56; commands at Philadelphia, 76; betrayal by, 81

Arrests, Hazen's, 145, 150, 153–55, 162–63, 173

Articles of Confederation, 110–11

Asgill, Capt. Charles, 100–101

Asgill, Sir Charles, 100

Asgill, Lady, 101

Ashline. See Ausline

Associated Loyalists, 99

A Statement of Facts, 169

Astor, John Jacob, 135

Atkinson, Theodore, 23

Ausline (family name), 133

Averill, C. K., 140–41

Ayotte (family name), 133

Balloting, 130, 132, 136

Balloting Book, 127

Banyer, Goldsbrow, 13

Barron, John, 159

Bartolf, Mr., 103

Bayley, Gen. Jacob; settles Coos, 22–

Bayley, Gen. Jacob (*Continued*)
  23; and Bayley-Hazen Road, 37–38;
  and defense of Coos, 49; and Canadian invasion, 62, 64, 66–68, 71,
  73, 82; court-martial of, 75; and
  land deals, 157–58
Bayley-Hazen Road, 23, 37–38, 68,
  70–74, 157–58
Beaumont, William, 137
Bedel, Col. Timothy: and Canadian
  invasion, 38, 41–42, 57–58, 60–62,
  66–67, 69, 71, 73, 82; court-martial
  of, 44; defense of Coos by, 49;
  host to Hazen, 97–98; land deals
  of, 157–58
Bedford, N.Y., 83
Beekman Patent, 19, 127, 144
Beekmantown, N.Y., 127, 144
Beekman, Dr. William, 127, 143–44
Bell, James, 127, 149–50, 153
Bell Tract, 127
Bennington, Vt., 56, 67, 73
Benzel, Adolphus, 19
Bethel, Conn., 64
Bethlehem, Pa., 58
Biddle, Col. Clement, 97
Bilow. *See* Boileau
Bindon, Joseph, 146
Birmingham Meeting House, 54
Bleury Seigneury, 17, 21, 154, 156
Bleury-Sud Seigneury, 21, 154–56
Bloodgood and Cooper, 166
Boileau, Lt. Pierre, 76
Boileau (family name), 133
Board of Inquiry, 104
Board of Treasury, 91–93
Board of War, 45, 57, 59, 64, 89, 91
Boishébert, Sieur de, 6
Boston: revolutionary fervor of, ix;
  Louisbourg debarkation from, 5;
  route to St. John from, 37; clothing
  from, 58; supports Canadian inva-
  sion, 82; Hazen trips to, 97, 142;
  69, 117, 160
Boston and Maine Turnpike Com-
  pany, 73
Boston Tea Party, 27
Braddock, Gen. Edward, 3
Bradford, Vt. *See* Moortown, Vt.
Brandywine, battle of, 53–54, 56, 61
Brewer, Capt. Jonathan, 5–6, 10, 12
Brewer, Capt. Moses, 5
Briand, Bishop Jean Oliver, 30
Brown, Maj. John, 28, 31, 33, 45
Burgoyne, Gen. John, 48, 55–57, 69

Burk's Island, N.Y., 126
Burton, Gov. Ralph, 17
Butterfield, Maj. Isaac, 41–42
Buylo. *See* Boileau

Cabot, Vt., 38, 71
Cadney, England, 2
Campbell, Capt. Robert, 76
Camp Security, 99
Canada: as British province, 15; settlers in, 16; residence of Hazen in,
  23, 29, 171; property of William
  Hazen in, 24; and Quebec Act, 27,
  115–16; invasion of, 27–32 *passim*,
  36, 40, 42; messages to, 33–34, 120;
  Hazen losses in, 37, 48–49, 151, 154;
  desirability of, 37; retreat from, 38,
  44–46, 49, 172; recruitment in, 38;
  commissioners sent to, 39, 45;
  Hazen's men remain in, 46, 122–23;
  second invasion of, 47, 56–57, 59–
  60, 62–63, 66–68, 70–71, 82–83, 97–
  98; Indians in, 49, 73; Hazen accounts from, 51–52, 153; raids from,
  71, 93; in Hazen's regiment, 91;
  losses of Canadians in, 119–20, 129;
  rations for refugees from, 122; return of refugees to, 123, 173; excom-
  munication in, 133; refugees sought
  by Mooers in, 134; land grants for
  refugees from, 138; American residents of, 140; veterans return from,
  140; Hazen return to, 143–44; trade
  with, 149; Bell's efforts against,
  149; courts of, 155; Hazen *vs.*
  Christie in, 156, 173; claims of
  Charlotte Hazen in, 165; 26, 49, 81,
  93, 116, 125, 150, 167, 172
Canadian and Nova Scotia Refugee
  Tract, 118, 123, 129–30, 134–37, 149,
  166
Canadian invasion: of 1775–76, 29–
  43 *passim*; plans for second, 47,
  56–64 *passim*, 66–74 *passim*, 82–83,
  97–98
Canadian Refugee Tract. *See* Ohio
  Refugee Tract
Canadian Regiment, First: created,
  36; individuals in, 46–47, 123–24;
  merger of, 79; land grants for, 127,
  140; 134
Canadian Regiment, Second: created,
  36; in Canadian invasion, 39, 42–
  43; after Canadian retreat, 43, 46–

48; winter quarters of, 50, 64–65, 76–79, 85, 101–103; under Sullivan, 50–51, 53–55; discipline in, 52; and plans for Canadian campaign, 58–60; assignments of, 60, 80, 83, 115, 175–76; reorganization of, 61–62, 79, 96–97; uniform of, 64; and Bayley-Hazen Road, 69–74; officer complaints in, 75, 83, 90, 117, 119–21; at Staten Island, 77–78; at André hanging, 81; shortages of, 88; size of, 90–91, problems of 91–92, 172; at Yorktown, 93–95; promotions in, 108–109; furlough of, 112; disbanding of, 112; and peace treaty, 113–14; depreciation of pay of, 121; individual officers of, 123–24; land grants for, 125–27, 140, 158; 134

Canadians: new interest in refugees by, x; in French and Indian War, 9; role in government, 16; messages to, 28, 34, 37; recruitment of, 31, 33; warning against 37; changing attitudes of, 39–40, 42; persecution of, 46; and second invasion 61; in Hazen's regiment, 62, 91, 96–97, 113, 115, 172; prisoners of war, 75; land grants for, 114, 125, 127; as refugee families, 116, 128–29; subsidies for, 117; losses in Canada of, 120; rations for, 122; frauds against, 141; recapture of loyalty of, 143; return to Canada of, 173

Canterbury, Archbishop of, 1

Cape Breton, 6

Carleton, Maj. Christopher, 74

Carleton, Sir Guy: as governor of Canada, 15, 18, 26; and Canadian invasion, 29–34 passim, 37, 40; and Indians, 49; at Valcour, 50; in Asgill affair, 100–101

Carleton, Joseph, 128

Carroll, Charles of Carrollton, 41, 45

Carroll, Father John, 41

Carroll, Father Michael, 166

Catbow, 158, 160–61

Cat Tavern, 98

Caughnawaga, 41, 149

Cazeau, Francis, 136

Cedars, The, 41–42, 44

Census, 132–33

Certificates, 92, 113, 121, 145, 150, 153

Chad's Ford, 53–54

Chambers, Captain, 53

Chambly River. See Richelieu River

Chambly, Que., 16, 30–31, 42–43, 73, 133, 149

Champlain, N.Y., 123, 127, 129, 132–33, 135, 137, 150, 168

Champlain Valley, 29, 50, 55, 74

Charles I, 1

Charlestown, N.H., 37, 69–70, 75, 97

Chase, Samuel, 41

Chateau de Ramezay, 39

Chaudière River, Que., 33

Chazy, N.Y., 123, 127, 129, 133, 143

Chazy Landing, N.Y., 132

Chesapeake Bay, 53, 94

Chillicothe, Ohio, 165

Chignecto Isthmus, 118

Chittenden, Gov. Thomas, 58, 97

Christiana Bridge, 93

Christie, Gen. Gabriel: lands shared with Hazen by, 16–18, 20–21; debt of Hazen to, 49, 153; lands in New York of, 126, 143; arrest of Hazen by, 142; claims Hazen lands, 154–57, 173; suit by, 162

Church of England. See Anglican Church

Cincinnati, Ohio, 138

Cincinnati, Society of the, 122–23

Circuit Court: Boston, 160; New Hampshire, 161

Clinton, Gov. George, 58, 97, 116, 119–20, 127, 132

Clinton, Gen. Henry, 55–56, 100–101

Clinton, Gen. James, 74, 81, 93–94, 116

Clinton County, N. Y., 126, 136, 143, 148–50, 164, 166

Cochran, Dr. John, 51

Colden, Alexander, 13

Colden, Cadwallader, 12–13

Colerus, Maj. Chrétien de, 51, 85

Columbus, Ohio, 138

Commissary of Prisoners, 100

Commissioner of Accounts, 124

Commissioners: appointed by Wooster, 39, 48–49; appointed by Congress, 40–42

Committee of Arrangement, 61

Committee of Claims, 170

"Congreganistes," 38

"Congress's Own," 47–48

Connecticut, 69, 91, 125

Connecticut River, 64, 66–67, 82, 122, 157, 159

Continental army, 109–12

Continental Congress, First, 27–28

Continental Congress, Second: message to Canada, 28; and Canadian invasion, 29–30, 35–37, 57–64, 66, 74, 82; and Bayley-Hazen Road, 38; orders hearings after Canadian retreat, 43–44; reorganizes army, 47; and land grants, 47, 114–15, 119, 125; and Hazen's Canadian losses, 48–49; on letters from officers to, 51; and Hazen accounts, 51–52, 92–93, 106–108; and Conway Cabal, 57; and reorganization of regiment, 61–62; and Arnold court-martial, 76; and Reid, 87; on Hazen promotions, 90–91; and certificates, 92, 113, 121; and regimental promotions, 96, 108–109; prisoners of war, 98; and retaliation, 99, 101; debate over powers of, 110–11; and retirement pay, 110–11; custodian of Canadians, 113; and peace treaty, 114; and refugee families, 116–17; and refugee petitions, 119–21; and rations, 119–22, 130, 132; and Canadian officers, 122; and refugee accounts, 124; and Lafayette, 129; and refugee grievances, 172; 81
Conway, Gen. Thomas, 57–60
Conway Cabal, 56–57
Cooper, C. D., 166
Coopersville, N.Y. See Corbeau
Coos: settlement of, 22–23; reactions to Revolution, 37–38; defense of, 49, 60, 74; and Canadian invasion, 60, 62–64, 66–74 passim, 82; road-building at, 84; visit by Hazen, 97–98; land claims in, 146, 167; colonizing of, 174; 142, 144
Corbeau, N.Y., 124, 132–33
Cottingham, England, 1
Cornwallis, Lord Charles, 93–95, 98
Court of Appeal (Que.), 155
Court of Chancery (N.H.), 168–69
Court of Common Pleas: Que., 155–56; N.H., 160
Court of Inquiry: on Hazen, 45; on Sullivan, 53; on Hazen and Livingston, 79; on von Steuben, 80–81; on Antill, 85–86; on Reid, 105
Courts-martial: of Bedel, 44; of Hazen, 44–45, 80, 84–85; of Arnold, 76; of Reid, 87–88, 104–105; of Lippincott, 99–101
Craftsbury, Vt., 71,

Cramahé, Acting Governor Hector, 13, 29, 34
Crompound, N.Y., 83
Cromwell (lawyer), 156
Crown Point: fall of, 29; abandonment of, 43; first stop of refugees at, 43, 115; rebuilding of, 48–49; occupied by Carleton, 50; 3–4, 37
Cumberland County, N.S., 118
Cumberland Head, N.Y., 148
Currency: Halifax, 165; New York, 5, 153, 155

Danbury, Conn., 64, 69
Dannemora, N.Y., 129
Dartmouth, N.S., 6
Dayton, Gen. Elias, 94
Dean, Elkanah, 127
Dean's Patent, 127, 129, 132
Dearborn, Henry, 165
De Bleury (seigneur), 17
Declaration of Independence, 90
De Colerus, Maj. Chrétien. See Colerus, Maj. Chrétien de
De Fredenburgh, Capt. Charles. See Fredenburgh, Capt. Charles de
Dehart, Captain, 170
De Haas, Col. John Philip, 42
De Kalb, Baron Johann, 59
De Lancey, Lt. Col. Oliver, 90
De Lancey, Gen. Oliver, 90
De la Saussaye, Charlotte. See Hazen, Charlotte
Delaware, 92
Delaware River, 50, 53, 93
De Lotbinière, Father François-Louis. See Lotbinière, Father François-Louis de
Depreciation of pay, 92, 121
Desonslavy, Daniel, 20
Detroit, 12, 114–15, 121, 174
Dionne, Germain, 123
Dobbs, Ferry, N.Y., 93, 101
Douglass, Wheeler, 127
Douglass Patent, 132
Duer, William, 127–28, 173
Duer's Patent, 137
Dugan, Capt. John, 36, 39
Duncan, Capt. James, 85, 103

East River, N.Y., 76
Eddy, Jonathan, 118, 139

Edwards, Lt. Thomas, 105
Elizabethtown, N.J., 78, 123
Elk River, Md., 53
Elkton, Md., 93
Engelwood, N.J., 80
England, 1
England, King of, 156
Exeter, N.H., 67

Faesch, Mr., 102–103
Ferriol, Lt. Alexander, 96
Fishkill, N.Y.: winter quarters at, 47,
  50, 85, 88–89; refugee camp at, 47,
  113, 115–16, 119, 127–29; 75, 97
Fishkill Landing, N.Y., 93
Floquet, Father Peter, 40–41
Foot, Samuel, 168
Forts: Beauséjour, N.S., 3; Brewerton,
  N.Y., 12; Carillon. See Ticonderoga;
  Cumberland, N.S., 118, 139; Du-
  quesne, Pa., 3; Edward, N.Y., 4–5,
  55, 143; Frederic, N.S., 6, 8; George,
  N.Y., 143; Montgomery, N.Y., 168;
  Niagara, N.Y., 3, 12, 66, 68, 74;
  St. Frédèric, N.Y., 3; St. John, N.S.
  See Frederic; St. John, Que., 17, 21,
  29–32, 43; Ticonderoga, N.Y., 3–4,
  29, 48, 55, 69; Stanwix, N.Y., 56;
  William Henry, N.Y., 4; "Wilson,"
  76
France, 129
France, King of, 101
France, Queen of, 101
Franklin, Benjamin, 41–42
Franklin, Gov. William, 99, 101
Fredenburgh, Capt. Charles de, 19,
  144
Freeman's Farm, 56
Fredericton, N.B., 8, 118
French and Indian War, 3–14 passim,
  123, 171
Freshwater Cove, 6

Gage, N.B., 24
Gage, Gen. Thomas, 19, 24, 29
Gallatin, Albert, 165
Garrison, N.Y., 83
Garrison Order, 89
Gaspé, 33
Gates, Gen. Horatio: commands at
  Ticonderoga, 43–45; and Saratoga,
  56–57; plans Canadian invasion,
  57–63 passim, 68, 74; 121

General Orders, 52, 61, 76, 79–80,
  86–89
Germantown, battle of, 54–55, 61
Germany, 102
Gill, Chief Joseph Louis, 73
Gilliland, William, 127
Gilmantown, N.H., 3
Gist, Gen. Mordecai, 94
Gordon, Major (British), 100
Gorham, Capt. Joseph, 5–6
Gosselin, Maj. Clement, 64, 109, 119–
  20, 122–23, 134
Gosselin, Lt. Louis, 123, 139
Grand Isle, Vt., 144
Grant, Hannah, 1–2
Grant, Jane, 1–2
Grant, Thomas, 1
Gray, Sheriff Edward, 21, 155–56
Great Britain, 132
Great Chazy River, N.Y., 20, 129, 148
Great Dock Street (New York), 146
Great George Street (New York),
  146
Greaton, Col. John, 91
Greene, Gen. Nathaniel, 50–51, 53
Green Mountains, Vt., 67, 74
Greensboro, Vt., 71, 158
Greenwich, Conn., 65
Grenoble, France, 123
Grimross, N.B., 7
Guilmat, Lt. Francis, 96

Haldimand, Gov. Frederick, 24, 74,
  133, 143
Half pay, 36, 107, 111, 151–53, 169–70
Halifax, 4–6, 118
Halifax currency, 165
Hamilton, Alexander, 94, 110, 150,
  153, 163
Hancock, John, 37
Hand, Gen. Edward, 76, 79–80, 108
Hanover, N.H., 82
Harding, Seth, 139
Hardwick, Vt., 71, 158
Hartford, Conn., 61, 65
Hassen, Edward, 2
Haverhill, Mass., 2, 4, 21, 69, 144, 157
Haverhill, N.H., 22, 71
Haviland, Co. William, 11–12
Hawley, Gideon, 168
Hay, Udny, ix, 130, 133, 136, 145
Hazen, Abigail, 2
Hazen, Anna. See Peaslee, Anna

Hazen, Charlotte: marriage of, 21; arrested, 32; on Gates, 56–57; in winter quarters, 103; Ohio lands for, 139–40, 165–66; attends Hazen, 146, 162; and Point au Roche, 149–50, 164; sale of lands by, 150; as executor, 163; bequest to, 163; death of, 164; and Mooers, 164, 167; business affairs of, 165–67; pension for, 165–66; and Moses White, 166, 168; will of, 166; 41

Hazen, John Jr., 3, 145

Hazen, John Sr., 2–3, 22–23, 73

Hazen, Gen. Moses: Canadian settler, ix–x; ancestry of, 1–3; and French and Indian War, 3–14; passim; Ranger commission of, 5; commands Ranger company, 7–12; and St. Anne massacre, 7–8; at siege of Quebec, 8–10; land deals of, 12–13; half pay of, 14, 107, 152–53; lands in Canada of, 16–22 passim; partnership with Christie of, 16–18, 20–21; lumbering by, 18–19; lands in Coos of, 22–25, 157–61; lands in New Brunswick of, 24–25; lands in Canada of, 24, 30, 154–57, 171; divided loyalties of, 29, 31–32, 171–72; Canadian losses of, 32, 38–39, 43, 48–49, 107, 151; arrests of, 31–33, 124–25, 142, 145, 150, 153–54, 162–63; commissioned, 35–37; recruiting by, 38–39, 47–48; commands at Montreal, 39–41; differs with Arnold, 42–43; courts-martial of, 44–45, 80–81; Court of Inquiry on, 45; and Champlain forts, 48–49; memorials by, 48–49, 90–92, 114–15, 119; and de Colerus, 51; and Dr. Cochran, 51; at Brandywine, 53–54; health of, 55, 122, 134, 144–47, 161–62; on Gates, 56–57; and Canadian invasion, 58–64, 82–83, 97–98; mission to Canada of, 60; sits on court-martial, 61; defends regiment, 61–62; and Bayley-Hazen Road, 68, 70–74; intercepts prisoners, 75; and Arnold court-martial, 76; promotion of, 78, 90–91; dispute over rank, 79; offended by Hand, 79–80; as possible turncoat, 81; troubles with Reid of, 83–88, 90, 103–106; foray into Westchester, 83–84; and inquiry on Antill, 85; commander at Fishkill, 89–90; Morrisania campaign of, 90; accounts of, 92–93, 106–108, 117, 120–21, 124–25; in Yorktown campaign, 93–95; and regimental promotions, 96; Coos trip by, 97, 144–45; guardian of prisoners, 97–99; and Asgill affair, 99–100; pay and emoluments of, 106–08, 151–52; in winter quarters, 109; and retirement grievance, 110; on strong government, 111; ordered to Newburgh, 112; on peace treaty, 114; and Canadian grants, 121, 125–27; attitude toward officers of, 122; suit against, 124–25, 162–63; and refugee lists, 125, 127, 129; and Point au Roche, 127, 142–44, 148–50, 161–62; and refugee rations, 128; estate of, 136; agent of refugees, 136; and Platt-Beekman dispute, 143–44; personality of, 144, 161–62, 173–74; Mooers' power of attorney from, 145–46; Mooers' accounts of, 146–47; sued by Bell, 149; business ventures of, 149–50; suits by, 150; sale of lands by, 150; claims against government by, 151–54, 169–70; Canadian disbursements of, 153–54; dispute with Christie of, 154–57; requests Vermont lands, 158–59; judged insane, 162; death of, 163; will of, 163–64, 167; inventory of estate of, 164; claims against Mooers of, 168; career of, 171–74

Hazen, Moses Sr., 2–3

Hazen, Richard, 2

Hazen, William: business affairs of, 3, 23–24; business of Moses with, 20, 22; and Canadian lands, 154–55; as executor, 163; bequests to, 163–64; and Point au Roche, 164; lands in New York of, 167–68

Hazen, William Sr., 2

Hazenburgh, N.Y., 127

Hazen River. See Rivière des Indes

"Hazen's Infernals," 47, 60, 172–73

Hazen's Notch, 71

Head of Elk, 93–94

Heath, Gen. William: in Hudson command, 69; attack ordered by, 83–84; court-martial ordered by, 84; and Reid, 86–88, 90; and Fishkill supplies, 89–90; and Canadian regiment, 97

Henniker, John, 18
Heron, Capt. James, 52
Hessians, 98
Hillsborough, Lord, 15, 26
Hoboken, N.H., 77
Howe, Adm. Richard, 60–61
Howe, Gen. William, 50, 53–54, 56
Huddy, Capt. Joshua, 99
Hudson Highlands, 60, 64
Hudson River, 56, 76, 94, 101, 143
Hull, Lt. Col. William, 90
Huron River, 114
Hutchinson, Gov. Thomas, 24

Indians: in French and Indian War,
    9; lands of, 13; in Canadian inva-
    sion, 40–44; at Coos, 49, 67, 73;
    and Clinton-Sullivan campaign, 66,
    68, 74; 117, 149
Ingham, Samuel, 140–41
Intolerable Acts, 27
Invalid Regiment, 76, 96
Isle aux Noix, Que., 30, 43
Isle la Motte, Vt., 20, 126, 149
Isle of Orleans, Que., 8–9, 122

Jameson, Lt. Col. John, 83
James River, Va., 94
Jamestown, Va., 94
Jarvis, Leonard, 20, 22–24, 154
Jay, John, 27–28
Jennery, Louis, 162
Jericho, Vt., 158–59
Johnson, Capt. Thomas, 37, 73
Johnson, Sir William, 3, 13, 24

Kelly, Capt. Joseph, 21
Kennebec River, Me., 33
Kennedy, Lt. Samuel, 4
Kent, Chancellor James, 168
Kinney, Lt. Abraham, 102
Knox, Gen. Henry, 51, 132, 152–53,
    161, 174
Knox, Capt. John, 11

Lafayette, Marquis de: on Brandy-
    wine 53; and Canadian invasion,
    57–59, 82; at Yorktown, 94–95; in-
    tercedes for refugees, 116, 128–29
La Bramboise family, 143

La Bramboise, Jean, 127
Lake Champlain: in French and In-
    dian War, 11; lumbering on, 18–
    19; Christie lands on, 20, 155; as
    route to Canada, 37, 57, 63, 68, 97–
    98; battle for, 49; defense of, 60;
    land grants on, 126; goal of
    refugees, 128–30, 143, 145; refugee
    settlements on, 133, 150; Mooers at,
    147; 142, 162
Lake Erie, 114, 125, 138
Lake George, 3, 8, 143
Lake Oneida, 12
Lake Ontario, 11, 68, 126
Lane, Daniel, 9–10
Lancaster, N.H., 158, 160–61, 169
Lancaster, Pa., 97–100, 103
Land Act of 1798, 138
Land commissioners (N.Y.), 126–27,
    129, 136
Land grants: by Congress, 47, 119,
    121, 138–40; by New York, 114–15,
    118, 125–27, 129–30, 136–37; bal-
    loting for, 130, 132, 136
Land Office (N.Y.), 125–27, 136
Land Ordinance of 1785. See Ordin-
    ance of 1785
Lawrence, Gov. Charles, 6, 8
Lévis, Chevalier de, 11
Lewis, Lt. John, 61
Lexington and Concord, 28
Liberty Pole, 80
Liebert, Capt. Philip: resignation of,
    96; petitions Congress, 120; sues
    Hazen, 122, 124–25, 162; no Ohio
    lands for, 139; Hazen debt to, 153
Lincoln, Gen. Benjamin, 59, 97
Lippincott, Capt. Richard, 99–101
Litchfield County, Conn., 69
Little Chazy River, N.Y., 130
Livingston, Brockholst, 126
Livingston, Col. James: Canadian set-
    tler, ix; captures Chambly, 31; com-
    missioned, 33, 36; rank of, 79; ref-
    ugee lists by, 125, 127; Ohio lands
    to, 140
Livingston, Gov. William, 102
Livingston family, 30
Lloyd, Capt. Richard, 104, 113
Loescher, Burt G., 3, 8
London, England, 95, 149, 155, 159
Long Island, 50
Longueuil, Baron of, 17, 157
Longueuil, Seigneury of, 154
Lorimier, François de, 32

Lotbinière, Father François-Louis de, 133
Loudon, Earl of, 5
Louisbourg, 4, 6, 8
Lovell, James, 57
Lowell, Vt., 71
Loyalists (Tory): as American refugees, x, 24, 157; warfare by, 66, 90; in the South, 81; 93, 144
Ludlow, Captain (British), 100
Lunenburg, N.S., 6
Lunenburg, Vt., 158–59
Lyons, Matthew, 75

Macomb, Alexander, 173
McCurdy, Capt. John, 5–8
McDougall, Gen. Alexander, 60
McKay, Francis, 18, 126
McKay, Samuel, 18–19, 126
McMullen, James, 52
McNeil, D. B., 140
McPherson, Murdoch, 123, 128, 134

Madison, James, 110, 150
Maine, 30, 118
Major Rogers & Associates, 12–13
Manhattan, 50
Martin, Joseph, 141
Maryland, 48, 91
Massachusetts: recruiting in, 6, 47; as campaign base, 30; Guy Fawkes Day in, 33; and Canadian invasion, 58; defense of, 74; in Canadian regiment, 91–92, 172; and Nova Scotia, 118; 4, 24
Massachusetts Committee of Correspondence, 28
Maugerville, N.B., 118
Maumee River, 114
Memorials, 48–49, 90–92, 110, 114–15, 117, 119
Miami River, Ohio, 138
Middlebrook, N.J., 50
Mignault, Father Pierre, 133
Mississquoi River, Vt., 57
Mohawk Chiefs, 13
Mohawk River, 56, 68, 93
Mollineaux, Mr., 160
Monckton, Col. Robert, 3, 6
Monroe, Mich., 114
Montcalm, Marquis de, 9, 123
Montgomery, Capt. Alexander, 9

Montgomery, Gen. Richard, 30–31, 33–36, 49, 79
Montmorency River, Que., 9–10
Montreal: in French and Indian War, 11–14; in American invasion, 29–45 passim; and retreat from Canada, 42–43; visited by Mrs. Hazen, 143; Mooers trip to, 155; 60, 146
Monty, Lt. Francis, 123, 127,
Monty, Francis Jr., 127
Monty family, 133, 143
Mooers, Lt. Benjamin: family of, 2; military career of, 69–70, 102; at André hanging, 81–82; on Asgill affair, 100; accounts with Hazen of, 124–25, 146–47; and Point au Roche, 127, 142–44, 148–49; land acquisitions of, 134–36; indebtedness of, 135–36; public career of, 136, 148; surveyors of refugee lands, 136–37; as pension commissioner, 140–41; as agent for Hazen, 145–48, 155–56, 158, 160–61; purchases own farm, 148; bequests to, 163; as agent for Charlotte Hazen, 164–65; claims against Hazen estate by, 164, 167–69; warned on land fraud, 166; dispute with Moses White, 167–69
Mooers, Edmond, 3–4
Mooers, Moses, 2
Mooers, N.Y., 129
Moore, Amasa, 135–36
Moore, Gov. Henry, 20–21, 159
Moore, Pliny, 133
Moortown, Vt., 23–24, 158–60, 163
Morris, Major (British), 8
Morris, Gouverneur, 110
Morris, Robert, 97, 110, 112, 117, 173
Morrisania, N.Y., 90, 92, 123
Morristown, N.J., 50, 76–78, 101–102, 124
Mt. Hope, N.J., 102
Muhlenberg, Gen. Peter, 50, 94–95
Murrary, Gen. James, 8, 10–11, 13, 15–16, 23

Nelson's Point, N.Y., 83
Neuville. See Pointe aux Trembles
Newark, N.J., 78, 102
New Brunswick, 6, 118, 163
Newburgh, N.Y., 109–12
Newbury, Vt., 22–23, 37, 60, 62–63, 70

Newburyport, Mass., 3, 23–24
New England, 1, 5, 47–48, 73, 118
New France, 123
New Hampshire, 38, 67, 74, 82, 92, 158–60
New Lebanon, N.Y., 145
New Jersey: and Antill family, 34; campaigns in, 50, 52–53; hospital in, 69; raids on, 77–78; in Canadian regiment, 92; army of, 99, 106; winter quarters in, 101; civil authority of, 102; 82, 170
New Town, N.B., 24
New Windsor, N.Y., 104
New York Assembly, 136–37
New York Bay, 76
New York City: in French and Indian War, 12; and raids, 50, 81, 83; loss of, 56; British in, 63–64, 73–74, 76, 95; prisoners from, 75; attack on, 83; feint at, 93; siege of, 98; smuggling into, 101–102, 109, as Hazen headquarters, 142, 144–46; 162; 19, 128, 136, 141, 150
New York Convention, 48
New York currency, 5, 153, 155
New York legislature, 136–37
New York Packet, 130
New York Senate, 136–37
New York State: refugee life in, ix; Christie lands in, 21, 126, 155, 157; recruitment in, 48; and Canadian invasion, 58, 63; and Sullivan-Clinton Campaign, 68; as colony, 90; in Canadian regiment, 92; land grants by, 114–15, 118, 125, 138–40, 158, 173; care of refugees by, 119–21, 124; refugee settlement in, 132; refugee names in, 133; Vermont claimed by, 159–60; William Hazen lands in, 163–64, 167–68; Charlotte Hazen lands in, 166; colonization by Hazen, 174; 29–30, 97, 123, 169
Nova Scotia: refugees from, ix, 125–27, 138–39; in French and Indian War, 6, 8; disaffection in, 117–18
Nova Scotians, 113, 117, 126–27, 139

Ogden, Capt. Amos, 12
O'Harra, Captain (American), 52
Ohio, 118, 125, 138–40
Ohio Refugee Tract, 139–40
Ohio River, 27, 138

Old Lorette, Que., 10
Old Northwest, 138
Olivier, Maj. Laurent: promotion of, 96, 109; Congress petitioned by, 120–21; suit by, 122, 124, 145, 162; denied Ohio lands, 139; Hazen indebtedness to, 153
Orderly Book, 78
Ordinance of 1785, 125, 138
Oswego, N.Y., 56, 63, 68

Paulint (family name), 133
Paulint, Amable, 43
Paulint, Capt. Antoine, 43, 70, 96, 115, 123–24
Palmer, John, 135
Parkman, Francis, 3
Parliament, 1, 27–28
Parsons, Gen. S. H., 60
Patriots, 81
Peacham, Vt., 38, 71
Peaslee, Anna, 3, 142
Peaslee, Robert, 3
Peaslee, Lt. Zaccheus, 143, 163
Peekskill, N.Y., 50, 69, 75
Pennsylvania, 48, 50, 53, 88, 91, 95
Pennsylvania Council, 76
Pensions: veteran, 140–41; Charlotte Hazen, 165
Philadelphia: and Howe campaign, 50, 53–56; mob action in, 75–76; Arnold commands at, 76; mutiny at, 88; Hazen trip to, 97, 142; and prisoners of war, 102–103; congressional debate at, 111; Mooers trip to, 146; 93, 110, 157
Pickering, Col. Timothy, 89, 115
Pickering Plan, 115
Pierce, John, 121
Pine's Bridge, N.Y., 83
Pitt, William, 5
Plains of Abraham, 9
Platt, Zephaniah, 127, 132, 144
Platt family, 143–44
Plattsburgh, N.Y., 129, 136
Plattsburgh Bank, 136
Point au Fer, N.Y., 126–27, 132, 143
Point au Roche, N.Y.: lumbering at, 19; settlement of, 127, 134, 142–44; visited by Hazen, 145–46; Mooers bills for, 146–47; attached by Bell, 149–50; Hazen's plans for, 161–62; owned by Charlotte Hazen, 164–66; disposition of, 164–65

Pointe aux Trembles, 33–34
Point Lévis, 9, 33
Poling (family name). *See* Paulint
Pompton, N.J., 101, 111–12
Pontiac, Chief, 12
Poor, Gen. Enoch, 60, 80
Portneuf, Father Robineau de, 9
Portsmouth, N.H., 161
Poughkeepsie, N.Y., 143
Power of attorney: to Hazen, 128; to Mooers, 134, 136, 145–46, 164
Prescott, Gen. Richard, 32–33
Preston, Maj. Charles, 30–32
Price, James, 28, 139–40
Princeton, N.J., 50–51
Prisoners of war, 60, 69, 75, 95, 97–99, 102–103
Privy Council, 155–56
Protestants, 16, 26
Putnam, Gen. Israel, 50, 64–65
Putnam Memorial Park, 64

Quartermaster Department, 130
Quebec (province): refugees from, ix, 113, 125; in French and Indian War, 7; British settlers in, 15; Hazen lands in, 24; and Quebec Act, 27, 62; American message to, 28; in American invasion, 30; refugees from, 113, 125; Hazen claims in, 163; 66
Quebec Act, 26–28, 41, 114
Quebec City: in French and Indian War, 8–11; lumber to, 18; in American invasion, 29, 33–35, 39–41, 122–23; prisoners arrive at, 75; fortifications of, 98; Mooers trip to, 134

Rations, refugee, 116–17, 119–22, 127, 130, 132, 150
Raymond, Rev. W. O., 8
Reading, Pa., 98–99
Redding, Conn., 64
Refugees, Nova Scotia, ix, 125–27, 138–39
Refugees, Quebec: after the retreat, 46–47; land grants for, 114–15, 118, 129–30, 125–27, 132, 138–40; life of, 115–17, 127–29, 132–33, 172; rations for, 116–17, 119–22, 127,

130, 132, 150; grievances of, 119–21; religion of, 133; disposal of lands by, 133–34; land patents of, 136–37; ix
Regiments, American: First New York, 93; Massachusetts Provincial, 3; New Hampshire, 70, 80, 88; Second New Hampshire, 61
Regiments, British: Anstruther's, 10; Fifty-second, 52; Fortieth, 6; forty-eighth, 16; Forty-fourth, 13–14, 152, 171
Reid, Maj. James: accuses Sullivan, 53; challenges Hazen, 83–85; court-martial of, 86–88; challenged by officers, 90; at Yorktown, 94; troubles with Hazen, 103–106, 174
Rhode Island, 63–64, 81, 92
Richeliu River: forts on, 37; in Amer-can invasion, 42; goal of invasion plans, 68, 70; Hazen lands on, 157, 165, 172; 62, 154
Richelieu Valley, 11, 16–17, 20, 29, 123, 149
Rivière des Indes, 18
Rogers, Rev. Ezekiel, 1
Rogers, Capt. James, 5, 8, 10
Rogers, Maj. Robert, 4–5, 9, 12–13, 171
Rogers and Company, 12
Rogers' Island, 5
Rogers' Rangers, 4–12, 171
Rollo, Lord, 12
Roman Catholicism, 27–28, 33–34, 133
Ross, Sheriff Daniel, 149
Ross, Lt. Col. James, 54
Rouse, Jacques, 134
Rowley, England, 1
Rowley, Mass., 1–2
Rush, Dr. Benjamin, 57

Sabrevois, Charles, 17
Sabrevois, Clement, 17
St. Anne, N.B., 7, 171
St. Anne, Que., 41
St. Anne du Sud, Que., 64
Sainte-Anne de la Pocatière, Que., 122–23
St. Clair, Gen. Arthur, 78
St. Denis, Que., 62, 123
Ste. Foy, Que., 10–11
St. Francis, Que., 60, 62
St. George Street (St. John), 157

St. Hyacinthe, Que., 123
St. Joachim, Que., 9
St. John, N.B., 3, 23–24
St. John, Que.: Hazen lands at, 17–18, 20–22, 154–57, 163; road from Coos to, 23, 37–38, 71, 73; in American invasion, 29–32, 41–43; defenses of, 61; invasion route to, 62; attack from, 73
St. John River, N.B., 6–7, 23–24
Saint John River Society, 24
St. Joseph's parish, 133
St. Lawrence River, 60, 62, 68, 74, 122
St. Leger, Col. Barry, 55–56
St. Thérèse, Que., 165–66
St. Thomas Street (St. John), 157
Salem, Mass., 1
Saltonstall, Col. Richard, 3
Saranac, N.Y., 129
Saranac River, N.Y., 19, 143, 148
Saratoga: battle of, 69 81, 98; Hazen at, 145
Satterlee, Capt. William, 96
Saugatuck River, Conn., 64
Savanne de St-Luc, Que., 21, 24, 32, 155
Scammel, Col. Alexander, 94
Schuyler, Gen. Philip: in Canadian invasion, 29–31, 39–40; and Indians, 49; replaced by Gates, 56; and plans for Canadian campaign, 59, 63, 68; potential turncoat, 81; as custodian of refugees, 116
Schuyler Falls, N.Y., 129
Schuylerville, N.Y., 56
Schiefflin, Thomas, 141
Scioto River, Ohio, 138
Scott, Maj. George, 6, 8
Scott, Major (American), 42–43
Secretary at War, 107–109
Secretary of War, 102
Seigneuries: Bleury, 17, 21, 154, 156; Bleury-Sud, 21, 154–56; Lacolle, 16; Léry, 16; Longueuil, 154; Noyan, 16; Sabrevois, 17, 21
Selin, Captain, 102
Shea, John Gilmary, 133
Sherburne, Maj. Henry, 41
Shippen, Dr. William, 51
Shirley, Gov. William, 3
Sidman's Clove, N.Y., 101
Sillery, Que., 10
Simonds, James, 23–24
Six Nations, 68, 74
Skenesborough, N.Y., 43–45

Smith, Benjamin, 162
Smith and Graves Patent, 127
Sorel, Que., 33, 42
Sorel River. See Richelieu River
Spear, Major, 54
Springfield, Mass., 69, 75
Stamford, Conn., 65
State Gore (N.Y.), 137
"State of Colonel Hazen's Regiment," 61
Staten Island: raid on, 52–53, 77–78, 85; Hazen losses at, 61; injury at, 76; feint against, 93
Stark, Gen. John, 60, 80
Stark, Capt. William, 5–6, 10
Stephenson, Andrew, 66
Steuben, Baron Friedrich von, 79–81
Stirling Lord, 77, 80
Strong, Mr. (judge advocate), 86
Stuart, Lt. William, 101–102
Suffern, N.Y., 101, 103
Suits by: Liebert against Hazen, 122, 124–25, 162; Olivier against Hazen, 122, 124, 145, 162; Christie against Hazen, 142, 155; Bell against Hazen, 149; Hazen against Christie and Gray, 156; Troup against Hazen, 163; Charlotte Hazen in Canada, 166; Mooers against executors, 168; Moses White against New York, 168; mentioned against Hazen, 163
Sullivan, Gen. John: and invasion of Canada, 42, 82; Court of Inquiry on, 52–53; at Staten Island, 52–53; at Brandywine, 53–54; at Germantown, 54–55; in Sullivan-Clinton campaign, 74; as potential turncoat, 81; burns Hazen property 165; 50–51
Sullivan-Clinton campaign, 68, 74
Sunbury County, N.B., 118
Superior Court (N.H.), 160
Supreme Court: Mass., 167; N.Y., 124, 126, 141
Surrogate Court (N.H.), 164
Survey of lands: 129–30, 163–37
Susquehanna River, N.Y., 68

Talcott, Samuel, 168
Tappan, N.Y., 80
Tarrytown, N.Y., 162
Tavernier (guide), 60
Tayler, Lt. Gov. John, 149–50, 164–66

Taylor, Maj. John, 51–53
Teaneck, N.J., 142
Three Rivers, Que., 11
Throop, Lt. Col. Josiah, 117–18, 125–
  27, 139
Thurber, Eddy, 168
Tichenor, Isaac, 75, 84
Ticonderoga, Fort, 43–46, 115, 142
Toledo, Ohio, 114
Topsham, Vt., 158, 160, 167
Torrey, Major, 88, 90
Torrey, Lt. William, 134, 139, 146–48,
  155–56, 161–62, 174
Treasury Board, 107
Treaty of Paris: of 1763; 16; of 1783,
  x, 109, 112–14
Trenton, N.J., 50
Troup, James H., 163
Troup, Col. Robert, 59, 160
Troy, N.Y., 162–63

U.S. Congress: and Ohio land grants,
  138–40; pensions enacted by, 140;
  and Hazen claims, 151–53, 173; and
  Charlotte Hazen, 165; and half
  pay, 169–70
U.S. House of Representatives, 169–70
U.S. Senate, 169–70
U.S. Treasury, 150

Valcour Island, battle of, 45, 50
Vallée, Father François, 133
Valley Forge, Pa., 55, 58
Van Buren, Martin, 167
Van Schaick, Col. Goose, 91–93
Varick, Lt. Col. Richard, 84
Vergennes, Count de, 101
Vermont: roadbuilding in, 38; and
  Canadian invasion, 58; troubles
  with New Hampshire, 67; lands re-
  quested of, 158–60; 73, 97, 144 ,167
Versailles, 66
Virginia, 92–93, 106
Von Steuben, Baron Friedrich. See
  Steuben, Baron Friedrich von

Waite, Ranger Capt., 12
Walden, Vt., 71
Walker, Thomas, ix, 16, 28, 33, 139

Walker, Mrs. Thomas, 139–40
War of 1812, 135, 161, 167, 169
War Office, 106, 108–109, 128, 152
Washburn, Bethuel, 128–29
Washington, Gen. George: character
  of, x; and Canadian invasion, 30,
  33, 35–36, 41, 97–98; and Guy
  Fawkes Day, 33–34; and Bayley-
  Hazen Road, 38, 68, 71, 74; on
  Crown Point, 43; loses New York
  City, 50; rebukes Hazen, 51; at
  Brandywine, 53–54; at Germantown, 54–55; and Conway Cabal,
  56–57; plans Canadian campaign,
  57–60, 62–64, 66, 68–74 passim, 82;
  troop dispositions by, 64, 97; supplies requested from, 65; and Sullivan-Clinton campaign, 68, 74; ex-
  onerates Campbell, 76; reprimands
  Arnold, 76; and Staten Island attack, 77–78; trial requested from,
  80; General Orders of, 80–81; and
  Reid, 83, 87, 90; on Antill's trial,
  86; and Fishkill supplies, 89; on
  Hazen's promotion, 90–91; Yorktown campaign of, 93–95; retaliation by, 99–101; inquiry requested
  from, 103; and Canadian promotions, 108–109; on army grievances,
  111–112; on land grants, 115; on
  refugee rations, 116–17; and refugee memorial, 119; Hazen letter
  to, 145; opinion of Hazen, 174; 81,
  102, 124
Watson, Matthew, 127
Wayne, Gen. Anthony, 54, 94
Webster-Ashburton Treaty, 137n
Weedon, Gen. George, 50
Wells River, Vt., 38, 71
Wentworth, Gov. Benning, 18–19, 23,
  159
Westchester County, N.Y., 83, 90
West Indies, 12, 46, 95
West Point: Canadian regiment at,
  60, 93; betrayal of, 81; courts at,
  85, 105; Hazen trip to, 97; refugee
  rations from, 128; Hazen court-
  martial at, 142; 83
Wheelwright, Nathan, 20
White, Abigail, 2
White, James, 23
White, Capt. John, 84
White, Capt. Moses; military career
  of, 100; represents regiment, 104;
  agent of Hazen, 144–48 passim;

pursues Coos claims, 160–61, 167;
guardian of Hazen, 162–63; as ex-
ecutor, 163–64, 167–70; dispute
with Mooers, 167–69; pursues
Hazen's half pay, 169–70; pursues
Hazen's disbursements, 170
White, Capt. Nathaniel, 158, 160–61
Whitcomb, Major, 70, 158
Whitelaw, James, 38
White Plains, N.Y., 50, 60–61, 83, 95,
112, 122–23
Whittier, Joseph, 2
Wilkinson, Col. James, 42, 45, 57
Willett, Lt. Col. Marinus, 78
Williamsburg, Va., 94
Wilmington, Del., 58
Wilson, James, 76

Winooski River, Vt., 144
Wolcott, Oliver, 153
Wolfe, Gen. James, 6, 8–9
Wolfe's Cove, 9
Woodson, Major, 85
Wooster, Gen. David, 33, 35–37, 39,
49, 124

Yankees, 118
York, Pa., 57, 98–99
York Peninsula, Va., 93
Yorktown, Va.: campaign of, 91, 103,
123; siege of, 94–95, 122; capitulation of, 100; Asgill capture at, 101;
war ends at, 109; Hazen's will at,
163; 106

MOSES HAZEN AND THE CANADIAN REFUGEES
IN THE AMERICAN REVOLUTION

was composed in 10-point Linotype Palatino, leaded two points,
with display type handset in Palatino by Dix Typesetting Co.;
printed on Hammermill 55-pound Lock Haven by
Vicks Lithograph and Printing Corp.;
Smyth-sewn and bound over boards in Holliston Roxite
by Vail-Ballou Press, Inc.;
and published by

SYRACUSE UNIVERSITY PRESS

SYRACUSE, NEW YORK